The Energy Crisis and the
American Political Economy

Franklin Tugwell

The Energy Crisis and the American Political Economy

Politics and Markets in the
Management of Natural Resources

1988 Stanford University Press
Stanford, California

Stanford University Press
Stanford, California
© 1988 by the Board of Trustees of the
Leland Stanford Junior University
Printed in the United States of America

CIP data appear at the end of the book

FOR MY WIFE

Preface

During the decade of the energy crisis, roughly between 1973 and 1983, I was fortunate enough to spend several exciting years working on a wide range of energy policy problems in, respectively, the Department of State, the Congressional Office of Technology Assessment, and the United States Agency for International Development. Upon my return to academic life I decided to write a book that would pull together what I had learned as a participant-observer and offer readers a more coherent picture of what we—I use "we" here in the broader sense, to refer to the American people and our institutions—had accomplished over the decade.

I began with a careful examination of the most important policies adopted by the federal government during the years of crisis—what is now Chapter 8—trying to sort out what effect they had, and why. I then worked backward and forward—backward to trace the historical roots of our actions and the governing arrangements that shaped them, and forward to explore implications and possible solutions.

As my work progressed, I grew increasingly uneasy about what I was finding. At the outset, my general impression was that our institutions had, on balance, served us well; that we had passed through a difficult time but suffered little. As I brought the pieces together, however, I was forced to conclude that we had actually done quite poorly. It became evident that, though we did avoid some costly mistakes, our policies on balance actually accomplished little of value. Worse, where they did not cancel one another out, they often increased our economic losses and our strategic vulnerability, and failed to protect the disadvantaged from bearing a disproportionate burden of the costs involved. Nor was the arrangement left after ten years of struggle—"free markets" in energy—likely to work well or endure.

Even more disconcerting, however, was my growing conviction

that these problems could not be written off as simply a matter of bad luck or individual misjudgments, but had deeper causes, ones that had to do with the way our political economy operates and the problems that arise when we try to manage our economic affairs. Successful economic governance in a democracy depends heavily on the framework of legal principles and public institutions that contain and channel the robust competition that we value so much. Unfortunately, insofar as the energy crisis can serve as a guide, the framework we have inherited is simply not working well and seems likely to continue to serve us poorly in the future.

Thus what began as an examination of our energy policies grew into an effort to draw lessons that might be of use in reshaping—as I am now convinced we must—the institutions that regulate and direct our economic affairs. As those readers with the patience to reach Part 4 of this volume will discover, the lessons I have drawn, and the alternative approach for which I argue, are necessarily both tentative and incomplete. I offer them anyway in the hope that the direction in which they point—what I have called "planned markets"—may be of interest to those concerned with the future of our political economy.

I take this opportunity to list the names of a handful of persons who, in my struggle to understand the energy political economy, gave me a chance to learn and contribute, and—most important—who in their own work set personal and professional standards to which I might aspire: Charles R. Blitzer, Thomas E. Bull, Melvin A. Conant, D. Linda Garcia, Alan B. Jacobs, Lionel S. Johns, Richard E. Rowberg, and Robert T. Voelkel. Each will disagree with some of what I have to say here but will, I hope, judge the enterprise to have been worthwhile.

Although this book is not the product of an institutional grant or research program, I am indebted to the Council on Foreign Relations for a fellowship that supported my first work as an energy policy analyst in the Office of Fuels and Energy of the Department of State; to the Congressional Office of Technology Assessment for the opportunity to collaborate with some of the best technical specialists who have worked on energy problems; and to Pomona College for letting me go, and then taking me back, several times, with only a few complaints. Nancy Roessler, Marjorie Rhea, and Michelle Swall helped prepare the final manuscript, their patience, efficiency, and unfailing cheerfulness making this tedious job almost a pleasure.

Finally, there is my wife and best friend Sandy Tugwell, to whom

I dedicate this book. The truth is she does more for human welfare in an average day's work than I have in a quarter century of professional effort. To have lived within the circle of her love has been a privilege and a joy. If there is anything worthwhile in this study, much of the credit goes to her.

F.T.

Contents

Abbreviations

The abbreviations listed below, though defined on their first use in the text, are grouped here in alphabetical order for the reader's convenience. A few very well known ones have been omitted.

AEC	Atomic Energy Commission
API	American Petroleum Institute
BCOA	Bituminous Coal Operators' Association
CAFE	Corporate Average Fuel Efficiency
CEA	Council of Economic Advisers
ECPA	Energy Conservation and Production Act
EPAA	Emergency Petroleum Allocation Act
EPCA	Energy Policy and Conservation Act
FEA	Federal Energy Administration
FERC	Federal Energy Regulatory Commission
FPC	Federal Power Commission
FTC	Federal Trade Commission
ICC	Interstate Commerce Commission
IEA	International Energy Agency
IEP	International Energy Program
IPAA	Independent Petroleum Association of America
JCAE	Joint Committee on Atomic Energy
NGPA	Natural Gas Policy Act
NIRA	National Industrial Recovery Act
NLRA	National Labor Relations Act
NRA	National Recovery Administration
OAPEC	Organization of Arab Petroleum Exporting Countries
OPEC	Organization of Petroleum Exporting Countries
PURPA	Public Utility Regulatory Policies Act
SEC	Securities and Exchange Commission
SFC	Synthetic Fuel Corporation
SPR	Strategic Petroleum Reserve
UMW/UMWA	United Mine Workers (of America)
WPT	Windfall Profits Tax

The Energy Crisis and the
American Political Economy

CHAPTER 1

Introduction

Early in 1984 the federal government decided to shred 4.8 billion gasoline-rationing coupons that were stacked in sealed ammunition bunkers in Pueblo, Colorado.[1] They had cost $12 million to print, and were costing taxpayers $20,000 a year to store. The Reagan Administration had no intention of ever using them, and their existence was troubling at a time of falling prices for petroleum products everywhere in the world. They symbolized in a poignant manner the fears and frustrations engendered by years of anguish over energy. So the best solution was to dispose of them and be done with the matter. The energy crisis was over.

A decade earlier, in the winter of 1973–74, the picture was very different: the United States and other oil-importing countries were in the grip of what we now recognize to be the most damaging and disruptive economic debacle since the Great Depression. To say that we were unprepared for the crisis is an understatement. Neither the general public nor policymakers knew much about the energy economy. Decades of reliable energy supplies at stable prices had left us complacent about the industries producing those products, and neglectful of the country's growing reliance on imports from distant lands. Worse, when problems did begin—first shortages of fuels and then an embargo engineered by the Arab members of OPEC—it quickly became apparent that no easy solutions were available.

The energy crisis was so devastating partly because it forced us to see ourselves anew. The Vietnam War had already made clear the limits to our ability to employ force in behalf of foreign-policy objectives; now a handful of developing countries was using control of resources—resources developed with the aid of American companies—to make us change our foreign policy and, by rigging prices, pay an enormous tax for fuels we used every day. When we began casting about for ways to deny them success, we found ourselves helpless. Our domestic reserves of petroleum, exploited at an accelerating pace for more than a century, were past the peak of the depletion curve, and even at prices ten times those prevailing in 1970 would never again produce at the levels they reached in that year. Natural gas was also reaching its peak; for logistical and environmental reasons, coal was difficult to develop quickly; and other fuels were either too limited or too expensive to come to the rescue. A country whose development was shaped by its rich endowment of land and minerals had now to come to terms with a future of increasing resource scarcity.

For the American political economy, however, it was the OPEC tax—the additional cost of imported crude oil and petroleum products—that created the gravest problems. Not only did it require Americans to send truly enormous sums across the ocean—these reached more than $75 billion dollars a year by the early 1980's—it also forced us to decide, within the country, how these sums would be collected, who would be forced to pay them, and whether domestic owners of energy resources would be allowed to profit from the actions of the OPEC monopolists. By helping precipitate a sharp reduction in economic growth and by altering the value of important assets, it also created a host of new winners and losers in an economy already suffering from problems of adjustment. In short, it created a major crisis of redistribution, fomenting conflicts between individuals, organizations, and whole regions of the country over the allocation of losses and windfall rents.

The American people and their political representatives worried about, dissected, debated, and struggled over energy policies for nearly a decade. The complex and divisive issues that arose with the crisis, many of them the direct results of government actions in response to it, occupied a significant proportion of the time of the nation's Congress and three presidents.

In the light of these extraordinary pressures and responses, it is surprising that there have been so few attempts to assess the overall performance of the American system in its response to this sudden and convulsive crisis. To be sure, there have been many energy-policy studies, attempts to explain and evaluate the consequences of government actions.[2] Several excellent textbooks and primers discuss our energy politics and economics. We also have a detailed administrative history of the crisis years, an analysis of relations between interest groups and the bureaucracy, even a study of energy studies themselves. And the various energy technologies have received careful scrutiny by technical specialists of the highest caliber.[3]

But few observers have tried to stand back and ask what we can learn, in the broadest terms, from the way in which our political economy as a whole responded to the energy challenge. Did we do well, or badly? Does our behavior inspire confidence about the capacity of our distinctive combination of pluralism and corporate capitalism to manage future crises? Or our natural resources in general? Does our behavior appear to confirm or contradict the arguments of the growing cadre of economists and political scientists who detect serious problems in the way we handle our economic affairs?

My objective in this book is to begin exploring this very difficult terrain, using the energy crisis as a window to the political economy, as an opportunity to observe the nation's governing arrangements and come to terms with some of these broader questions. Crises are often especially appropriate for such an exercise. Not only do they test the abilities of people and institutions, they bring long-standing relationships and problem-solving habits into question, and thereby into the open where they can be seen more clearly. The energy crisis that began in the early 1970's serves this purpose well: it reveals a broad landscape of problems that accumulated over many years in the energy industries, as well as the growing inadequacy of the mechanisms we have employed to manage the economy.

In a nutshell, it appears that, insofar as the energy sectors can be taken as a guide, we are in serious jeopardy when it comes to managing our increasingly complex, technologically sophisticated economy. The efforts of our government, though well-intentioned, did precious little to resolve either the equity or the national-security issues raised by the crisis, while exacting a high price in lost efficiency and undermining the legitimacy of the public sector as an actor in the nation's economic life. Although we avoided embracing ill-advised crash solutions and managed to redistribute enormous amounts of wealth with little disruption, the policies we did adopt worked at cross-purposes, often exacerbating the very problems their supporters sought to solve. The policy process itself was dominated by the demands of stakeholders seeking to avoid economic losses, and was therefore unable to define clearly or promote other objectives, among them equity, national security, and efficiency. Our attempts to regulate the energy markets proved especially counterproductive. Indeed, the evidence from the energy sector suggests that such regulation is increasingly prone to degenerate to a process of adversarial conflict that is damaging to the health of the economy and the integrity of our democracy. Unfortunately, our conventional ideological prescriptions do not really speak to these problems, leaving us very much adrift when it comes to identifying viable alternatives.

In this chapter I introduce the key elements of the conceptual approach I use to analyze our response to the oil crisis. I undertake, first, a brief review of the outlook or orientation represented by the term "political economy," and second, an introduction to some of the terms, analytical categories, and theoretical assumptions on which I have relied to bring order to the enormous complexity of the nation's experience with energy matters. In introducing terms, categories, and assumptions, I concentrate on two topics: political participation and regulation. The chapter concludes with a brief summary of the argument of the book, one designed to provide guideposts for readers, especially as they proceed through the historical background in the middle chapters.

Political Economy as an Analytical Perspective

The term "political economy" is used in several different ways today. To many it refers simply to the political aspects of economic policy. To a more specialized subfield of social scientists it signifies the attempt to explain the behavior of groups and organizations by applying one or more of a handful of central concepts concerning the system of incentives—the "logic"—that motivates individuals in their decisions to engage in collective action.[4] This approach, when properly qualified, is one of the most helpful in simplifying the dizzying complexity of human conflict behavior, and I rely on it heavily in the pages that follow.

But political economy also has another, older meaning that is rapidly gaining currency once again: it refers to that ensemble of arrangements, public and private, by which a society defines its material goals and allocates scarce resources and other valued things. It encompasses both politics and markets, on the grounds that they operate together to determine the character of these arrangements and the values they embody. This more holistic perspective, indeed the phrase "political economy" itself, was the one that informed the work of classical scholars such as Adam Smith and John Stuart Mill. They were concerned with the integrity of the means by which society produced and distributed its wealth, and with the proper role of the state therein.[5] It is to this more encompassing conception of the appropriate field of study that I refer when I use the phrase in this study.

Like many other analysts concerned with the future of the American political economy, I have become increasingly convinced that understanding our problems and identifying solutions to them demand a return to the search for principles, or lawlike propositions, that transcend disciplinary boundaries. In analyzing the way we have managed energy resources, accordingly, I bring together subjects that are normally treated in isolation by economists and political scientists. The governance of energy, or the shaping of technical alternatives and the allocation of costs and benefits associated with the exploitation of resources, involves both economic and political processes and institutions. Industrial structures and the technical attributes of markets are as important in this as the political interests that influence the decisions of regulatory authorities.

The attempt to join these areas of analysis in a single study involves significant risks, not the least of which is the criticism of offended specialists from one camp or another. But the rewards can be substantial. Indeed, one of the most interesting—and disturbing—findings of this study is that the political economy of energy is subject increasingly to a kind of degenerative "cycle of failure" that is the result of the joint operation of political and market forces, but that has been missed, largely, by those whose thinking has been constrained by disciplinary walls. Similarly, the kinds of solutions that seem most appropriate have been neglected because they require students of pluralist politics to really understand markets, and advocates of economic efficiency to acknowledge the legitimacy of public authority in economic affairs.

The Energy Regimes

To facilitate this more integrative approach, I have adopted the term "regime" to refer to the amalgam of private and public arrangements that historically has determined how specific energy resources have been exploited and managed, and how the wealth created by these activities has been distributed—in other words, how they have been governed.[6] As a number of analysts have pointed out, energy affairs in the years before the crisis were handled for the most part by sector-specific arrangements of this kind, one each for coal, petroleum, natural gas, electricity, and nuclear power. The term "regime" is convenient because it permits the designation of an analytical target that is broader than usual in policy studies, encompassing private as well as public regulatory systems, and because it suggests the partial independence, in governance terms, of a domain of political economy. The danger in the use of the term is that it can easily

be taken to imply a level of coherence, autonomy, or purposeful-
ness in the creation and operation of regime affairs that may be
inappropriate.

The nature of the energy regimes by the early 1970's reflected, in
each sector, a history of market evolution and political adjustment
that occurred as the interested parties gradually came to terms on
how to govern their piece of the economic world. A central concern
in all cases was the problem of taming market competition. For each
regime this resulted in a different industrial structure and a different
pattern of relationships with public authorities. Though markets for
fuels were interdependent, and there was considerable integration of
ownership in petroleum and natural gas (especially), each fuel type
tended to develop its own political subsystem—often labeled an
"iron triangle"—in which industry representatives dealt with specialized Congressional and bureaucratic counterparts to shape public policies.[7] At no time was the federal government cognizant of, or
administratively involved with, the energy system as a whole; there
was no energy policy as we know it today, no coherent attempt to
manage or influence the energy regimes as a group.

As luck would have it, by the early 1970's each of the regimes was
for different reasons quite vulnerable to the sudden market adjustment that began with the skyrocketing of world oil prices, and the
capacity of the nation to respond to the crisis was heavily influenced
by the patterns of regime governance that obtained.

Changing Patterns of Political Participation

America's efforts to come to grips with the energy crisis also took
place at a time when the nation's political system was experiencing
changes of several kinds, and these also shaped the outcome in important ways. Two trends stand out as particularly important: first,
the rapid proliferation in the number and influence of interest
groups; and second, the parallel and related decline in the strength
and aggregative capacity of the major political parties.[8]

The explosion in the number of interest groups in American society has been widely noted by specialists in American politics. Although there has been little systematic collection of historical data
on the formation and dissolution of groups, recent studies suggest
that the total number participating in politics at the national level
has increased by as much as 40 to 50 percent since the early 1960's.[9]
In addition, the composition of the universe of interest groups has
changed to include a larger percentage of "citizen" groups, those

with no direct occupational basis for membership, and of groups located in Washington with explicitly political purposes.[10]

There are many reasons for these trends. Some have to do with the character of modern civilization itself. As society has grown denser and more complex, its parts more tightly intertwined, the "external" consequences of economic activity have become less tolerated. Increasing affluence and education have changed definitions of personal and community welfare, and have led to rising demands for amenities, for welfare, for security from economic losses.[11] As the government has responded to these demands, it has provoked (and sometimes sponsored) the creation of new groups seeking to benefit from the new circumstances. Crises and periods of economic instability have played an important role in this.[12]

Recent theoretical work on the incentives that lead individuals to join and support group activities has contributed a great deal to our understanding of this process.[13] Mancur Olson more than two decades ago clarified the relationship between the size of a group and the likelihood that the group would successfully organize to achieve its collective goals. He demonstrated, in theoretical terms drawn from an economic model of behavior, why large groups—such as those representing consumers, lovers of wildlife, or opponents of nuclear power—are at a disadvantage compared to smaller groups.[14] According to Olson's logic, only the provision of incentives unrelated to the interests involved—such as retirement plans, health programs, or access to work—can explain the continued existence of many large groups.

The widespread appeal of Olson's argument has drawn attention to the rise of consumer and "citizen" groups in the last two decades, since they seemed to be defying this important principle. Subsequent research by the political scientists Robert Salisbury and Jack Walker, among others, helped explain this trend within the same broad theoretical framework, and in the process added important empirical insights about the universe of group politics.[15] Salisbury, in addition to insisting that noneconomic incentives must be included in any formal theory of groups, also noted that the rise of broad "citizen" coalitions such as those of consumers could be explained as the result of the work of political "entrepreneurs," who paid the costs of organization in return for income and "profits" that they could expend in political activity.[16]

The work of group "entrepreneurs" has been enhanced by technological developments that, even by themselves, have been enormously important in reshaping political behavior in the United

States and elsewhere. Computer-based mailing lists and phone directories, combined with increasingly accurate public opinion research, have permitted political entrepreneurs and candidates for public office to "target" their appeals for funds and support in a manner that has never before been possible. And, of course, television has opened a direct channel between voters and those candidates able to afford the high cost of access to it. This new technology of participation has made it possible for groups as narrow as promoters of Ocean Thermal Energy Conversion (OTEC) and as broad as "energy consumers" to come together, keep informed of each others' work, and support vigorous lobbying activities in Washington.

Finally, there is the growing role of political "patrons" in the process of group politics. In a pathbreaking survey of modern interest groups, Jack Walker demonstrated that a surprising proportion of them depend on individual or organizational patrons to start operations. Groups representing business received such support in 34 percent of the cases in his sample, whereas citizen groups depended on patrons in fully 89 percent of the cases.[17] These findings make sense in terms of Olson's incentives, in that businesses are expected to find it easier to mobilize to protect themselves more frequently without outside assistance. But they also reveal that much of the growth of "citizen" groups is explained by the ability of political entrepreneurs to find capital to invest from many sources—foundations, government, wealthy individuals—in order to set themselves up as representatives of previously unrepresented interests at large.

The quality of representation provided by many of the newer "citizen" groups is a matter of controversy. A 1977 study found that many of these groups were essentially staff organizations, with few real ties to members. As Michael Hayes has noted, 30 percent of the groups surveyed turned out to have no members at all, and those that did often communicated with members only via occasional newsletters.[18] In such instances the degree of actual participation on the part of those represented must be questioned; it is often the patrons, with their own views of the "interests" of citizens, who are gaining political access.

Equally important, the universe of interest groups, with such a significant percentage made up of "entrepreneurs" lacking real ties to members, is likely to be far less stable and more vulnerable to changing elite perceptions about what should and should not be supported. The "issue-attention" cycle, about which Anthony Downs has written so persuasively, may cause greater oscillations in the structure of interest politics than has been the case in the past.[19] The tendency for participation to increase in scope at times of crisis was stressed many years ago by Schattschneider in his thoughtful essay *The Semi-Sovereign People*.[20] The rise of group and policy entrepreneurs and patrons and the new technologies of participation have almost certainly intensified this tendency.

Interestingly enough, the rise of citizen groups and the attraction of many patrons to the support of interests that might not otherwise find political access does not appear to have resulted in a parallel weakening of groups, such as business interests, that might be expected to find it easier to organize for political influence. In many instances, the same technologies of participation and patronage have made it possible for the latter groups to increase the scale and effectiveness of their own activities.[21] In this respect there appears to be clear evidence of the kind of competitive mobilization about which many specialists have written.[22] These interests have, however, been forced more into the open; the old "iron triangles" of private interests, Congressional committees, and bureaucratic agencies have tended to lose their hold, giving way to more adversarial conflicts in what Hugh Heclo has termed "issue-networks," which involve all the parties at stake, including (in the case of energy, for example) representatives of consumers and environmentalists.[23]

The decline of political parties, like the rise of interest groups, has been going on for years. And it, too, appears to have accelerated in the last decade, at least in terms of the capacity of parties to impose unity or coherence on the legislative behavior of their members. The rise of new groups, the new technologies of participation, and changes in the laws governing financial contributions—all have had some part in promoting this change. It is tempting, indeed, to view the growth of group patronage as a direct political alternative to the support of parties—in effect a new outlet for passion and money that might otherwise have gone to party organizations. Opinion analysis and computerized targeting of voting groups, along with the incentives resulting from laws governing the financial activities of political action committees (PACs), have had the effect of freeing candidates for legislative office from party discipline by giving them independent access to financial resources and the ability to key their activities more closely to the particularistic demands of constituents. And the constituents themselves have demonstrated increasing independence, reflecting the loosening bonds of party loyalty.

The patterns of political participation associated with these changes in group and party roles can be summarized as follows. First, we find an increasingly dense and complex politics at the national level, focusing less frequently on broad issues and more often on specific problems and policies placed on the agenda by groups of stakeholders. Second, new opportunities have arisen for groups previously left out to participate in the pluralist process through the exploitation of new technologies of participation, though they have been joined in this by "entrepreneurs" with minimal ties to those whom they claim to represent. Third, there is a continuing tendency, within this generally more complex setting, for smaller, wealthier interests (such as business interests) to predominate, though as the result of continuous political conflict rather than quiet, behind-the-scenes bargaining. Fourth, there is a weakening of the unifying institutions in national politics, including both political parties and the old "iron triangles" that dominated policy in many technically complex areas. And fifth, as a consequence of these changes the national polity shows a greater sensitivity and vulnerability to changes or crises that threaten stakeholders with costly visible redistributions of income or influence.

Government and the Economy: Theories of Regulation

As has been the case with so many other areas of economic activity, the emergence of the energy regimes was accompanied by an increase in the incidence and scope of regulatory intervention in the marketplace. This occurred in most instances after private efforts to tame the market had failed or met with public disapproval. Although the character and degree of formal public-sector involvement have varied greatly, every energy form at one time or another has experienced some kind of direct regulation; indeed, the politics of energy for more than half a century has focused almost exclusively on the desirability and consequences of different regulatory arrangements in different energy sectors.

In recent years both political scientists and economists have turned their attention to the causes and consequences of government regulation of economic activity. They have produced, in the process, an increasingly useful collection of theories about this controversial subject. Indeed, these theories represent some of the most successful work in the new field of political economy (employing the term now in its narrower meaning as the study of collective choice).[24]

Economic regulation, as an institutionally separate and distinct activity, began with the creation of the Interstate Commerce Commission (ICC) in 1887. The ICC was charged with policing the railroad industry to prevent abuses that had become the cause of growing public anger. Behind the Commission lay the idea that problems in the marketplace—or, more accurately, instances of "market failure"—could be managed by the creation of an independent, nonpartisan, technically specialized agency. With its members appointed by the President and approved by Congress, the agency was to have the authority to make rules and oversee their application.

This approach proved an important institutional innovation: as the nation industrialized and political demands for government intervention grew, the formation of regulatory agencies became, along with antitrust legislation, the principal "solution" to the problem of market governance. Congress created new regulatory agencies one after another, until by the 1960's there existed more than 50 major administrative bodies and several hundred minor offices with some authority to regulate private economic activity.[25] The role of the government in the economy, albeit fragmented in many small, uncoordinated pieces, had grown very large.

Note that in this study I am concerned primarily with "old style" or "market" regulation, rather than regulation aimed at protecting the health and safety of consumers or controlling environmental pollution.[26] Market regulation refers to government efforts to control the overall pattern of competition in an industry—the ICC is the original model—usually by managing entry and prices.[27]

As the country came to rely increasingly on state-created market regulation, the evidence mounted that it was not working as intended. The most important charge was that the authority to control competition was being used not to benefit the consumer but to assure profits and security to the private interests that were being regulated. Explanations of why this was the case began to appear in the 1950's, many of them based on careful historical studies of the ICC itself. The research of scholars such as Samuel P. Huntington, Marver Bernstein, and Gabriel Kolko gave rise to what came to be known as the "capture" theory of regulation, which suggested that the conditions under which regulation was conducted led inevitably to domination of the process by private industry.

The work of the political economists Mancur Olson and George Stigler took the first steps toward a technically convincing economic analysis of why this was the case: consumers and voters, as large and diffuse groups in which the stake of each individual is small, will tend to have less influence on decisionmakers than business groups that are more concentrated and wealthier. The latter will have more influence because individual members will more readily pay the costs (to organize and acquire information) to obtain the benefits available from regulation.[28] The most important of these benefits is restriction of entry into a profession or activity, a limitation of supply that grants more security to existing producers and increases the price consumers must pay for products or services. As Stigler put it, "every industry or occupation that has enough political power to utilize the state will seek to control entry. In addition, the regulatory policy will often be so fashioned as to retard the rate of growth of new firms."[29]

These empirical and theoretical insights into the problems stemming from the country's "solution" to the need to manage the economy provided building blocks for a number of much broader critical analyses of the operation of the American political economy. Perhaps the most influential of these was Theodore Lowi's *The End of Liberalism*, which not only criticized the results of regulation but also attacked the ideological underpinnings of the political system that had made "captive" regulation a standard practice. He called this system's ideology "interest-group liberalism," and he traced its development in American thought about the relationship of the government to the economy. Lowi's indictment was especially telling because he was the first widely read critic to emphasize the corrosive effect of misguided ideology and poor policy on the legitimacy and viability of the system itself. Experience with energy in the last decade and a half reveals that this continues to be a serious problem.

Another and still more comprehensive analysis of this genre is Mancur Olson's own attempt to elevate the theory underlying the understanding of regulatory capture to a much more robust explanation of why nations succeed or fail in their efforts to attain and manage economic growth. In a nutshell, Olson has suggested that the power of special-interest groups and collusive associations increases with time at the expense of those who speak for the broad collective interest in efficiency, eventually leading to reduced growth and then gradual economic decline. Collusive associations among other things encourage monopoly, slowing the reallocation of resources and distorting adjustment to economic cycles.[30]

Although these and other studies have been helpful in highlighting problems and in leading the way for further analysis, newer research points to the need for a more complex model of the political economy of regulation than that contained in the "capture" literature. In his attempt to formalize and expand upon Stigler's economic model, Sam Peltzman has outlined a number of theoretical conditions in which, on the one hand, some or all producers might benefit less from regulation and, on the other, consumers might be expected to benefit more.[31] And James Q. Wilson, noting both the large number of instances in which industry complained of regulatory decisions and the growing frequency of successful attempts to dismantle regulatory arrangements (in the fields of transportation, communication, and energy, among others—sometimes over the strong opposition of the industry involved), has suggested that the incidence and outcome of regulation must be analyzed with much closer attention to the complex processes of political negotiation, persuasion, and coalition building that are involved.[32] As we shall see, the experience of the energy industries suggests the wisdom of this broader and more complex perspective.

For the purposes of this analysis I have categorized market regulation into two types: proprietary and compensatory. With proprietary, both the decisionmaking process and the outcome of regulation strongly favor the producers when compared to the conditions that might exist if the market were uncontrolled and competitive. In its extreme forms proprietary regulation approximates the "capture" model described above. As Stigler put it: "regulation is acquired by the industry and is designed and operated primarily for its benefit."[33] Compensatory regulation, in contrast, allows consumers to gain access to the regulatory process and to bargain for benefits that the market might not otherwise accord them.

These categories represent points on a continuum, of course, with producer control on one end and consumer control on the other. Most real-world instances represent some point in between. Indeed, as Peltzman has noted, regulatory arrangements can normally be expected to contain such a mix. In some cases, a fraction of the producers or of the consumers, respectively, receive disproportionate shares of available benefits. In others, the regulatory process involves a continuing adversarial process that fluctuates between the two extremes in response to changing circumstances. The distinction between proprietary and compensatory is nevertheless useful because it signals the broad character of the choice process involved as well as the consequences of government action.

Under the conditions that have prevailed in the United States for much of the twentieth century, proprietary regulation can be considered to have been the "default" outcome, if not at the outset, then by the time the regulatory arrangements matured and became routinized. Generally speaking, this outcome arises because producers are a smaller, more concentrated group with access to resources and technical knowledge, and because they have the incentive to pay the costs involved in influencing the decision process. In contrast, consumers are numerous, are more poorly informed (on average), and have little individual incentive to pay a price to affect decisions. The losses that the process inflicts on them may also be obscure, hidden away as the results of restrictions on entry or supply. In addition, the regulatory machinery is often administratively independent and less "accessible" to consumers. Finally, when consumers as voters seek to influence decisions, they must do so in a single sweeping moment of decision in which a wide range of matters must be decided at once.

Consumer influence in regulatory decisionmaking, and hence compensatory regulation, can be expected to emerge when the conditions that normally disadvantage large, diffuse groups are for some reason nullified or reversed.[34] For this to occur, members of such groups (or subgroups with significant collective resources) must be informed about the process and the costs and benefits involved, and they must be willing to pay a price to influence the outcome. In addition, "political entrepreneurs" (political representatives or interest group leaders) must be able and willing to organize consumers, keep them informed, and act on their behalf. Since this also entails costs, the benefits involved must be both salient and sizable enough to affect the prospects for income, election, or promotion of those in a position to influence the regulatory process.

The Argument in Brief: Politics, Markets, and the Crisis of Economic Governance

The goal of this book is to analyze the American response to the energy crisis in the years between 1973 and 1983, and to draw from that analysis some lessons about the performance of our distinctive combination of democratic politics and corporate capitalism—about how we handled the crisis, and whether we appear well prepared to handle future challenges in energy governance. As the book's subtitle suggests, the intersection of politics and markets—and in particular how the management of competition has been affected by changing patterns of participation—emerges as the central conceptual concern, or "problem," of the study.

The struggle to reconcile markets and politics has been long and frustrating in each of the energy regimes. Indeed, insofar as the energy regimes can be taken as a guide, the fundamental problem of the modern American political economy is our inability to devise formulas for market management that are at the same time compatible with our changing democratic institutions, our ideology, and the technical demands of the modern economy. This is true despite our long history of struggle with the problem and the creation of an enormous body of law, and many powerful institutions, to address it. The result is that we find ourselves adrift when it comes to governing our increasingly complex and politicized economy.

Markets are important to Americans. They symbolize a cluster of freedoms that are among the core public values of the society, and the efficiency they promise in distributing scarce resources is central to the nation's public ideology. But markets, as they operate in practice, are often poorly understood by those who praise them most fervently.[35] As even their admirers will certify, markets left alone foster episodes of economic instability. Moreover, as critical political economists are quick to add, they are associated not just with political liberties, but also with personal insecurity and persistent inequality. They are most effective when they select out and eliminate the most inefficient contenders in the economic system, but they provide no security for those who must then find another livelihood. And they favor those already lucky enough to possess capital, facilitating a process of wealth accumulation rather than distribution.

The attribute of competitive markets that is most poorly understood in the United States is what might best be called their "fragility." Competition may be natural, in the sense that many contenders will seek to take advantage of an opportunity to make money. But just as natural is the desire for order, security, and control. Wherever possible, those forced to live under the withering pressure of competition will seek ways to manage it, if possible by reducing or eliminating the competition itself. Where private measures are available, they will be used to accomplish that goal. Monopolies, holding companies, market-sharing arrangements—the list of inventions is well known and sharply illustrated in the history of energy development. Where private measures are illegal or do not suffice, individuals and groups suffering market discipline will turn to the government for relief. The commitment to market-based free enterprise, in other words, runs strong in academic discourse and public rhetoric, but quickly turns to a search for means of private or public political control by real-world participants when competition breaks out.

Part One of this book traces the evolution of private and public efforts to cope with competition in the energy regimes. Chapters outline the basic attributes of production and market behavior for each, and then detail the career of efforts to tame and regulate the market in the years up to 1970—just before the onset of the energy crisis. These chapters serve several purposes. They present a historical overview of the range of "solutions" that have been devised by Americans seeking to govern competition in the energy regimes, along with an analysis of why these have, for the most part, failed. Among these solutions, of course, has been formal regulation. These experiments, and the problems they encountered, also provide helpful clues to the range of solutions that might fail or succeed in future attempts to manage energy markets.

The background chapters of Part One also provide a picture of the complex mosaic of governing arrangements that characterized the energy system in the years immediately preceding the crisis. As noted earlier, each regime had its own institutionalized mechanisms of market management that had been carefully worked out in a long history of political conflict and compromise. This legacy is of the utmost importance to anyone seeking to understand why the crisis caught us so unprepared and why we found it so difficult to avoid immediate entanglement in a web of regulatory controls that set the terms for a decade of public involvement with energy issues.

Part Two presents a chronology of the energy crisis itself and the American response to it, beginning with the structural changes in the world energy market in 1970–71, proceeding through the Arab oil embargo, and ending with the first Reagan Administration. Although the oil market underwent some dramatic shifts in the years after 1984—marked, in particular, by the continued erosion of OPEC control of international supply and price—none of these shifts involved fundamental changes in the basic political economy of energy in the United States. Indeed, the price fluctuations themselves, and the ripple effects stemming from them, can best be understood with reference to the arrangements (especially price decontrol) in place as the crisis decade came to an end.

Among the conclusions stemming from this history, perhaps the most unexpected, at least to this author, is the degree of continuity in the government's actual handling of energy-policy matters over the administrations of Nixon, Ford, Carter, and Reagan. This occurred despite clear-cut differences in the philosophical orientations of energy-policy elites in different administrations and some vigorous executive and legislative efforts to change the basic thrust of policy. The key legislative decisions that would shape national energy policy were actually designed before the crisis as temporary measures to alleviate problems caused by the Nixon Administration's program of economywide price controls. Once adopted, these measures proved impossible to change. In effect, the basic response of the political economy was "locked in" within months of the actual crisis during the Nixon Administration, and evolved in an incremental fashion thereafter.

The reason for this was the paralysis wrought by an ensemble of powerful interests, most of whom were unhappy with the state of affairs but feared that they would end up still greater losers if anyone's "grand plan" were to be approved. The crisis provoked the formation of two great cleavages: one between producers and consumers, and the regions of the country in which they were concentrated; and the other between the executive and legislative branches, each of which responded differently to claimants and insisted on differing interpretations of the nature of the crisis and the solutions appropriate to it. The resulting stalemate confirms the picture of a pluralist polity well designed to prevent costly, visible redistribution of wealth among important stakeholders, but not to promote other goals, among them equity, national security, or economic efficiency. By the time the nation eventually cast aside the crisis-derived regulatory apparatus in oil and then natural gas, it was, in effect, deregulation by default; no alternative arrangements could achieve enough political support to replace the gradual dismantling of market controls started many years (and presidents) earlier. When the energy crisis finally passed into history, it left behind a strong sense of national frustration and impotence, a feeling that a decade of intense public debate and legislative action had accomplished very little.

Part Three begins with an examination of the changes that actually occurred in the energy political economy during the years of crisis and, more importantly, the role public policies had in shaping them. As it turns out, a lot did change. Imports, after rising dramatically, plummeted suddenly; and the overall energy efficiency of economic activity increased. In most cases, price increases stand out as the single clearest cause of these changes. As noted earlier, the overall contribution of energy policies gives little basis for satisfaction or optimism. Not only did policies prove ineffective, they often worked at cross-purposes: for example, policies seeking to promote conservation reduced the level of import dependence, whereas price controls actually promoted imports. The net effect of policy, in fact, was to increase imports—and payments to OPEC—over the levels they might otherwise have reached. In the meantime, the central political goal of energy policy—that of preventing consumers from paying, and owners of resources from receiving, enormous windfall profits—was accomplished only in small part.

In terms of governance arrangements, the changes wrought by the crisis were of several kinds and varied by regime. The immediate response to the crisis was the creation of an elaborate system of compensatory regulation in oil that affected all the energy regimes. The system worked poorly but could not be replaced by an agreed-upon alternative. It was eventually allowed to wither away because once domestic petroleum prices had reached international levels the problem of wealth distribution became moot. The creation of new institutions to deal with energy issues—notably the Department of Energy—made it more likely that energy concerns would hereafter continue to be treated as a single, interdependent set of problems and issues.

The various regimes emerged from the crisis largely intact—the changes in industry structure that did result represented, for the most part, a continuation of historical trends. However, the regimes were connected to, and influenced by, market and political forces in important new ways. The phased disappearance of much of the regulatory apparatus at the national level left all the regimes vulnerable to market competition to an extent they had not been in many decades. And the years of crisis politics and interest-group mobilization left them less able to control decisions affecting them and less likely to be able to fend off future episodes of compensatory intervention.[36]

The last part of the book returns to the larger problem of economic governance in an effort to draw both practical and theoretical lessons from our experience with energy, and to discover whether other arrangements offer us a better way of doing things. In a political economy such as ours, characterized by chronic party weakness and the growing influence of interest groups able to take advantage of new technologies of participation, this experience suggests the appropriateness, at least for the energy sectors, of a revised model of the evolution of market regulation.

At the heart of this model is the tendency, noted earlier, for markets to give way to some form of control. Historically, the intersection of economic and political changes saw this control evolve in most cases from purely private means to proprietary and then compensatory regulation. This is illustrated in the chapters of Part One for each of the energy regimes. As the political process has changed, and as the energy regimes have grown in technical complexity and importance for the overall economy, the conditions favoring the emergence of compensatory regulation have been strengthened. On purely theoretical grounds, this would appear to be true generally of economic sectors that are unstable—and thus likely to suffer crises of redistribution—and that harbor, or are believed to harbor, significant elements of monopoly. Finally, the same forces and circumstances have increasingly led compensatory regulation to fall victim to a cycle of destructive adversarial conflict that progressively undermines both economic efficiency and confidence in the democratic polity itself.

This model—which I have called, somewhat infelicitously, the "cycle of failure in progressively politicized pluralist market management"—is a logical extension of the work of the regulatory theorists discussed earlier. However, it suggests a "real-world" dynamic that is both more complex and more damaging to the political economy as a whole than the problems of capture or even of corporatist collusion raised by the theorists Stigler, Peltzman, Lowi, and Olson. This is because it predicts, at least for the energy regimes, a greater degree of disorder and chronic adversarial conflict, a kind of directionless pattern of struggle and political and economic decomposition.

The upshot of this analysis is the conclusion that the "solution" contrived during the decade-long energy crisis—in effect, government withdrawal and the return to "free" markets in energy—is not likely to last. This is so despite the growing recognition among specialists of the many difficulties associated with past efforts to manage energy markets. Even worse, because the lessons political leaders have learned are in many respects the wrong ones, any future interventions are likely to consist of still another series of ad hoc measures that work at cross-purposes and affect our lives in costly and unintended ways. Finally, even if the current approach should last, it may exact a toll of both economic and political damage that few of its advocates have characterized responsibly.

The final chapter of the book is devoted to exploring the implications of this disturbing set of conclusions. After briefly examining the difficulties, both theoretical and practical, of the alternative governing arrangements most widely discussed by specialists today, including state ownership and Euro-Japanese corporatism, I suggest the appropriateness of a distinctively American solution, one I call "planned markets." "Planned markets," in brief, is an arrangement whereby the government accepts responsibility for the operation of the economic system, but does not engage in detailed and intensive regulation of economic sectors, relying instead on competitive frameworks wherever possible. It contrasts sharply with the neo-corporatist solutions that many contemporary analysts have prescribed as a response to America's economic woes. The character of this alternative, and the need for it, emerge from the conviction that old solutions, embodied in the ideological slogans of the left and right, have grown obsolete. Unless we are able to develop firm new principles of political economy—guidelines, if you will, to help us reconcile politics and markets—built up by the careful observation of discrete sectors of our economic life, we face the prospect of continuing frustration and failure at a time in the evolution of modern society when it is becoming increasingly urgent that we learn to work together to define and pursue common objectives.

PART ONE   Background

This and the following chapters of Part One detail how each of the energy regimes has responded over the years to the problems posed by the free play of competitive markets. Without exception, this response has included both private arrangements and forms of public intervention designed to contain and tame market forces. The history of these efforts, how they came about and why they failed or succeeded, is central to an understanding of the basic rules of the game governing energy affairs when the Arab oil embargo occurred, and provides important clues to the range of choice available to American policymakers as they confront problems of economic governance. Each chapter contains a brief sketch of the development of the energy form involved and an analysis of the basic attributes of production and market behavior in each.

Coal is distinctive in that its managers have been less successful in controlling the destructive consequences of competition than the managers of the other energy regimes. This made the industry especially vulnerable when cheaper and more convenient substitute fuels—first oil, then natural gas—entered the market after the First World War. The long years of bitter labor conflict and economic decline that followed are familiar to students of American industrial history.

In the two decades before the energy crisis, however, this picture gradually changed: labor peace, technological progress, and improving profits became the order of the day. Coal seemed to have shaken off its chronic troubles and entered an era of stability and prosperity. Accordingly, when oil prices skyrocketed, many observers expected that the industry would experience a welcome boom, especially when it became clear that the nuclear power industry was faltering and domestic oil production was insufficient to displace imports. As Nixon and his successors said repeatedly, coal was America's secure, domestic fossil-fuel alternative.

As it turned out, the industry did benefit: production increased at a rate nearly double that of the pre-crisis years (see Fig. 1 and Table 1). But the hoped-for prosperity was much more modest than many expected. New constraints, several directly related to the governing arrangements inherited from the past, held expansion in check. In order to understand why these constraints emerged and, more broadly, how the coal regime responded to the dramatic changes brought by the energy crisis, it is helpful to begin with a brief review of the development and structure of the industry.

Background

The age of coal coincided with the rapid industrialization of the United States in the years after the Civil War. In 1850 Americans relied on wood to provide more than 90 percent of their energy. By the time of the First World War, the switch to coal was complete, with this new energy source accounting for 73 percent of the nation's energy consumption.

In many ways coal is an appropriate symbol for the kind of civilization toward which our country plunged so enthusiastically in the second half of the nineteenth century. The world of coal was a panorama of grit and steam and steel. Mines that at their peak employed more than 700,000 Americans removed enormous quantities of black fuel from the ground.[1] The work was hard and dangerous, and managerial intransigence and market pressures kept the wages low. Smoke from the stacks of mills and factories combined with the exhaust of locomotives to create urban landscapes of soot and congestion that many now find hard to envision.

By the height of the coal epoch, shortly after the turn of the century, America had become the leading manufacturing nation in the world. Agricultural output had expanded enormously, and the country had become the center of technical and administrative innovation in industrial production. The real wages of American workers had doubled.[2] Much of this progress was powered by coal dug by hand in traditional fashion, since it was not until after the First World War that technical innovation began to transform mining operations.

The era of steady growth in coal consumption ended in 1918. Thereafter the country continued to use large quantities of coal, but the industry began a long period of relative decline as Americans turned increasingly to fuels produced from crude oil and natural gas.[3] This decline included some important shifts in markets: railroad companies, so important as an early source of demand, turned

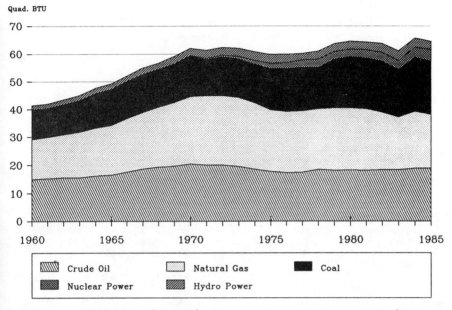

Figure 1. Production of Energy by Source, 1960–1985. Source: United States [23], 1985: 6.

to diesel fuels, as did shipowners. Efficiency improvements curbed the use of coal in the steel industry, and then that industry itself began to wither.[4] Commercial and residential use began to drop off as people replaced their boilers and furnaces with ones designed to use cleaner oil and natural gas. Only the utility companies generating electric power enlarged their use of coal; but the growth of this market came too late, taking place as it did mostly after the Korean War, to restore coal's primacy in a rapidly expanding energy market.[5]

The Political Economy of Coal

The history of the coal industry is a history of market instability, labor turmoil, uncertain profits, and painful and fitful adaptation to changing energy technology and economics. As one analyst has put it: "As a 'sick industry' it spread its malaise as a pestilence. Its economic decline contaminated its politics as if the industry were called upon to act out some tragic destiny. Cruelty, corruption, and violence plagued the politics of coal to a degree unmatched in any other energy arena."[6]

If there is a central theme in the political economy of coal, it is the search for stability, for a means of ending the cycle of boom and

TABLE I

Energy Supply and Disposition in the United States,
Selected Years, 1960–85

(Quadrillion BTU)

	1960	1965	1970	1973	1975	1976	1977	1978
Production								
Crude oil[a]	14.93	16.52	20.40	19.49	17.73	17.26	17.45	18.43
Natural gas[b]	14.12	17.66	24.18	24.76	22.01	21.81	21.90	21.74
Coal	10.82	13.06	14.61	13.99	14.99	15.65	15.76	14.91
Nuclear power	0.01	0.04	0.24	0.91	1.90	2.11	2.70	3.02
Hydroelectric power	1.61	2.06	2.63	2.86	3.15	2.98	2.33	2.94
Other	0	0.01	0.02	0.05	0.07	0.08	0.08	0.07
Total	41.49	49.35	62.08	62.06	59.85	59.89	60.22	61.11
Imports								
Crude oil	2.20	2.65	2.81	6.89	8.72	11.24	14.03	13.46
Petroleum products	1.80	2.75	4.66	6.58	4.23	4.43	4.73	4.36
Natural gas	0.01	0.47	0.85	1.06	0.98	0.99	1.04	0.99
Other	0.07	0.04	0.07	0.21	0.19	0.18	0.30	0.44
Total	4.08	5.91	8.39	14.74	14.12	16.84	20.10	19.25
Exports								
Coal	1.02	1.38	1.94	1.43	1.76	1.60	1.44	1.08
Crude and products	0.43	0.39	0.55	0.49	0.44	0.47	0.51	0.77
Other	0.03	0.09	0.18	0.14	0.16	0.12	0.12	0.09
Total	1.48	1.86	2.67	2.06	2.36	2.19	2.07	1.94
Adjustments[c]	−0.43	−0.72	−1.37	−0.46	−1.07	−0.18	−1.95	−0.34
Consumption								
Petroleum products	19.92	23.25	29.52	34.84	32.73	35.17	37.12	37.97
Natural gas	12.39	15.77	21.79	22.51	19.95	20.35	19.93	20.00
Coal	9.84	11.58	12.26	12.97	12.66	13.58	13.92	13.77
Nuclear power	0.01	0.04	0.24	0.91	1.90	2.11	2.70	3.02
Hydroelectric power	1.66	2.06	2.65	3.01	3.22	3.07	2.51	3.14
Other[d]	0	−0.01	−0.04	0.04	0.09	0.08	0.10	0.19
Total	43.82	52.69	66.42	74.28	70.55	74.36	76.28	78.09

SOURCE: United States [23], 1985:5.
[a]Includes lease condensate.   [b]Includes plant liquids.
[c]This is a balancing item.   [d]Includes net imports of coal coke.

bust that resulted in unemployment, low profits, bankruptcy, abandoned mines, and run-down towns and cities. In contrast to the situation in many energy industries, the coal market remained very competitive for many years, and the market proved a harsh master indeed.

There are many reasons for this. To begin with, coal production is geographically dispersed and for much of its history has been neither vertically integrated nor highly concentrated, at least not at the national level.[7] This made it difficult for operators to use cartels or other private forms of collusion to stabilize the market. The fragmented character of the industry also made it hard for coal producers

TABLE I *(continued)*
Energy Supply and Disposition in the United States,
Selected Years, 1960–85
(Quadrillion BTU)

	1979	1980	1981	1982	1983	1984	1985
Production							
Crude oil[a]	18.10	18.25	18.15	18.31	18.39	18.85	18.88
Natural gas[b]	22.37	22.16	22.01	20.44	18.71	20.20	19.15
Coal	17.54	18.60	18.38	18.64	17.25	19.72	19.39
Nuclear power	2.78	2.74	3.01	3.13	3.20	3.54	4.14
Hydroelectric power	2.93	2.90	2.76	3.26	3.50	3.36	2.95
Other	0.09	0.11	0.13	0.11	0.13	0.17	0.21
Total	63.81	64.76	64.44	63.89	61.18	65.84	64.72
Imports							
Crude oil	13.83	11.19	9.34	7.42	7.08	7.30	6.83
Petroleum products	4.11	3.46	3.30	3.36	3.57	4.13	3.72
Natural gas	1.30	1.01	0.92	0.95	0.94	0.85	0.93
Other	0.38	0.31	0.42	0.36	0.44	0.48	0.52
Total	19.62	15.97	13.98	12.09	12.03	12.76	12.00
Exports							
Coal	1.75	2.42	2.94	2.79	2.04	2.15	2.44
Crude and products	1.00	1.16	1.26	1.73	1.57	1.54	1.66
Other	0.11	0.14	0.12	0.11	0.11	0.11	0.12
Total	2.86	3.72	4.32	4.63	3.72	3.80	4.22
Adjustments[c]	−1.65	−1.05	−0.08	−0.51	1.00	−0.70	1.32
Consumption							
Petroleum products	37.12	34.20	31.93	30.23	30.05	31.05	30.85
Natural gas	20.67	20.39	19.93	18.51	17.36	18.51	17.76
Coal	15.04	15.42	15.91	15.32	15.90	17.07	17.50
Nuclear power	2.78	2.74	3.01	3.13	3.20	3.54	4.14
Hydroelectric power	3.14	3.12	3.11	3.56	3.87	3.77	3.38
Other[d]	0.15	0.08	0.11	0.09	0.12	0.16	0.20
Total	78.90	75.95	74.00	70.84	70.50	74.10	73.83

SOURCE: United States [23], 1985:5.
[a]Includes lease condensate.   [b]Includes plant liquids.
[c]This is a balancing item.   [d]Includes net imports of coal coke.

to employ public institutions to protect themselves from competition—a sharp contrast to the oil and gas industry.

Secondly, underground coal mining, the principal mode of production for much of the industry's history, is highly labor-intensive.[8] Worker pay and benefits typically accounted for more than half the cost of operating an underground mine.[9] Coal mining is also one of the most arduous and dangerous of occupations. The rate of fatalities and serious injuries on the job is one of the highest for any occupation, and coal miners are vulnerable to many debilitating occupational illnesses, among them the crippling Black Lung Disease.

Finally, the cost structure and market relationships of the industry have made adjustments to reductions in demand difficult. This, more than anything else, helps account for the continuing malaise of the industry. Coal production has always responded quickly to demand increases: new mines have been started, old ones reopened, and extra shifts of workers added. But once mines have been opened, the high fixed costs of maintaining them and the personal and community costs associated with unemployment have made operators reluctant to close them down even temporarily. As one student of the industry put it: "Flexibility downward seems to be more 'sticky' than flexibility upward."[10] And these shifts have been very pronounced, especially during wars and periods of recession and depression. Between 1914 and 1920, for example, production increased from 423 million tons to 569 million tons as demand soared for coal during the war. By 1922, however, demand had dropped to 422 million tons. A similar decline took place during the early years of the Depression, and then again after the end of the Second World War.[11] Coal's problems in downward adjustment have also made it difficult for the industry to accommodate the long period of demand reduction associated with the transition to oil and gas.

Finally, coal production and use cause serious environmental damage. To be blunt, coal is a disruptive and dirty fuel; the more of it we use, the more expensive it becomes to assure that mining operations do not scar the land, that the toxic wastes from mines and power plants do not contaminate groundwater, and that the poisons in ash waste and flue gases are reintroduced to the environment safely.

Taken together, these ingredients—market fragmentation, labor intensiveness, inflexibility in response to demand reductions, and environmental disruptiveness—help explain the turbulent political economy of coal. Add to this the relative (and often absolute) decline of the industry in the decades after 1920, and it is easier to understand why the industry has been so chronically "sick" for half a century. Indeed, during two-thirds of the years between 1928 and 1950, at least half of the corporations engaged in bituminous coal mining reported no net income at all.[12] In sum, the harsh discipline of the market has shaped the lives and politics of all associated with the business.

Labor Conflict and Government Intervention

Since workers were forced to pay so heavily for the competitive adjustments made by coal operators, the struggle to unionize and then to achieve improvements in wages, benefits, and job stability figures prominently in coal history. The fragmented character of the industry and the fact that many workers lived in small mining communities that were both politically and socially isolated made the task of unionization particularly difficult. Early attempts, during the first decades of this century, met with little success. Unions had neither legal status nor public legitimacy, and the mine managers considered them a serious economic threat. Workers had to strike to win concessions, and they did so repeatedly, setting a pattern of bitterness and periodic violence in labor relations that has endured in the coal industry.[13]

It was federal legislative action during the New Deal that finally enabled a single union, the United Mine Workers of America (UMW), to consolidate its hold on the industry. The plight of workers during the Depression created a public mood much more favorable to union action. First the National Industrial Recovery Act (NIRA) in 1933, and then, when the NIRA was declared unconstitutional, the National Labor Relations Act (NLRA) in 1935, established the right of unions to organize and bargain collectively.[14] Under the vigorous leadership of John L. Lewis the UMW thereafter took advantage of every opportunity to improve the pay and benefits of miners, and the union became the acknowledged representative of workers in national collective bargaining.

Labor unity, however, did not lead to labor peace. Workers still had to wrest concessions from mine operators, who were often desperately trying to cut costs in response to the pressures of competition. Again and again the UMW struck, often choosing moments of national vulnerability to increase its power. National dependence on coal, though decreasing, was still extensive enough during and immediately after the Second World War that the President was forced to seize the coal mines on several occasions to keep production going while the federal government intervened in the bargaining process to assure a settlement.[15] During most of these years the UMW made impressive gains, winning higher wages and better benefits for miners. After the mid-1930's, these outstripped the gains of other workers, a result that several careful studies have attributed directly to aggressive union activity.[16]

The triumph of the United Mine Workers and the federal decision to legitimize union activity and intervene more actively to promote labor peace helped to stabilize the coal industry somewhat. The Taft-Hartley Act of 1946 contributed to this end by providing for a mandatory cooling-off period and mediation when private efforts failed to resolve labor disputes. And the union leadership, most notably Lewis himself, accepted the need to adjust to the declining fortunes of coal. Indeed, union policies often sought to accommodate rather than resist change, facilitating the introduction of new technology while seeking to cushion the impact of labor-force reductions by restricting the entry of new workers, enforcing seniority rules, and fighting for generous unemployment compensation for those who were displaced.[17]

The Politics of Private and Public Regulation

Though the union movement helped workers, it did not solve the deeper problems caused by demand instability, chronic overcapacity, and the long-term shift in national patterns of energy consumption away from coal. Indeed, the strikes and labor conflicts associated with the union struggle—itself made more difficult by the stagnation of the industry—led to increasing public and government concern about the plight of this critical industry.

The first peacetime effort to address this problem was the creation in 1931 of a private cartel among a group of producers in the Appalachian region.[18] This followed a period of intense competition and price wars between 1924 and 1930, when the industry was forced to abandon the production capacity that was developed during the First World War. Appalachian Coals, Inc., was an attempt to set up a regional marketing cartel in order to maintain a minimum price among the operator-members and to support that price with a pro-rationing system that would control production by allocating available orders within the group.[19] Not surprisingly, the Appalachian Coals arrangement was immediately challenged as a violation of the Sherman Antitrust Act. The Supreme Court, however, allowed the arrangement to continue, finding that the Provisions of the Sherman Act did not prevent "the adoption of reasonable measures to protect [commerce] from injurious and destructive practices and to promote competition upon a sound basis."[20] Shortly after Appalachian Coals was finally legalized, however, more comprehensive federal measures to control the nation's coal market were passed by Congress.

The 1930's was a critical period in the evolution of American attitudes toward the overall economic system. Instability resulting from the operation of the market, and the damage caused by boom and bust cycles in the capitalist economy generally, were a widespread concern. As the ranks of those Americans who remember the Great Depression thin, it is easy to forget how great a disaster it was. It shook the nation to its roots and led to a brief but intense period of institutional experimentation. Widespread structural changes were introduced, revised, and (in many cases) abandoned as the President and Congress groped for solutions and found themselves checked repeatedly by the Supreme Court.

The 1930's was also a period of ideological turmoil. Free enterprise doctrine stood in partial disrepute, and many Americans reexamined their basic beliefs about the economy. Leaders suggested a variety of alternatives, from outright nationalization of industry to variations of European syndicalism, and many found lifetime converts among those disillusioned with laissez-faire, American style. But none of these new doctrines took hold, and the country went forward to economic recovery, the Second World War, and the national security preoccupations of the Cold War without resolving many of the issues raised during the Depression. This legacy would prove an increasingly severe handicap as patchwork solutions accumulated in a climate of gradually worsening ideological schizophrenia about the respective roles of the market, government, and private corporations.

To many, the coal industry in the 1930's represented an extreme in the failure of the market, and as an industry it was deeply involved in the institutional experimentation that began with the New Deal. Congressional hearings and special commissions repeatedly scrutinized the turbulent industry, and many experts came forward with proposals for government intervention to bring stability and end the "destructive competition" that was plaguing mine operators. But none of these solutions was tried. Instead, Congress established as a part of the New Deal the National Recovery Administration (NRA), a corporatist mechanism designed to govern the market by means of negotiations among producers and between producers and workers. The NRA set up "codes of fair practice" to prevent cutthroat conflict and to stabilize production, distribution, and labor relations, all within a framework set out by the government itself. The code for the bituminous coal industry went into effect in 1933, administered by a system of national and divisional boards, known as authorities, composed of representatives of the industry itself along with one member appointed by the President. Marketing agencies, voluntary associations of producers, set "fair market prices" for each area.[21]

The NRA attempt to manage the coal industry was an ambitious undertaking to say the least, one that can only be understood as the program of a government determined to make sweeping changes and at the same time ignorant of the problems involved in market regulation. And it failed. For administrative, technical, and political reasons, the system was simply too unwieldy and vulnerable to abuse. As one study noted: "The administration of minimum prices was a task rendered difficult at the outset by the vagueness of the code provisions regarding them, and aggravated by the necessity of coordinating the work of largely autonomous Divisional Code Authorities. At the close of 1934, violations of the minimum price structure were occurring widely and frequently, and by the early months of 1935 the structure had all but collapsed."[22] The NRA died when the Supreme Court ruled its authorizing legislation, the National Industrial Recovery Act, unconstitutional in 1935. According to the Court, the NIRA was too broad, and it was unconstitutional for the Congress to hand over so much of its authority to administrative agencies.

For all of the problems of the NRA—an experiment today dismissed by many as an historical aberration—the coal operators and the United Mine Workers remained strongly committed to some form of market-management arrangement, and within six months of the Supreme Court decision the Congress had passed, and the President had signed, a replacement bill to achieve that goal. This was the Bituminous Coal Act of 1935, which established a special commission within the Department of the Interior, advised by a board composed of representatives of the industry, empowered to regulate both prices and production. The new law also guaranteed collective bargaining to the coal miners.[23] But the Court intervened once again, this time striking down the law on the grounds that the labor provisions were unconstitutional.[24]

Undaunted, and under considerable pressure from both mine operators and the unions, Congress passed still another bill, the Bituminous Coal Act of 1937. This time the law stood, and the federal government went about the tedious business of setting up one of the most ambitious price-regulatory systems in U.S. history, a system that remained in force until 1943. It was designed to do more than protect the profits of the coal operators—although this was one objective. The goal was much broader: to restore health to an industry that was of enormous importance to American economic life and whose chronic problems affected owners, miners, mining communities, and consumers of coal and coal products.

Because of its prominence as an early example of price regulation, the Coal Act of 1937—also known as the Guffey Act—has been studied carefully.[25] Three conclusions stand out in this body of research. First, those responsible for administering the minimum prices did a commendable job despite truly enormous obstacles—it has been estimated, for example, that they had to set as many as 400,000 prices for coal of different qualities moving over different forms of transportation to different destinations.[26] Second, in the short term the program benefited greatly from the demand escalation that began with the outbreak of the Second World War. Because of the complexities in the administration of the system, the first full schedule of prices was not issued until 1940, and prices by then had already begun to increase. Indeed, during the War itself the Office of Price Administration ended up having to establish a price ceiling for coal. And third, there is broad consensus that in the long run the system simply would not have worked; indeed, the effort to sustain minimum prices might well have driven the administration to extend control over other aspects of the coal industry (such as production) and to consider controls on the prices of related fuels such as oil and gas.

In the end, Congress abandoned the price-control experiment. The Coal Act lapsed in 1943 when legislators, after several brief extensions, refused to renew it on the grounds that it "(a) established a system of regulation inimical to free competition; (b) was no longer necessary because conditions in the industry had improved, and (c) had failed to prevent strikes in the industry."[27] In theoretical terms, the problem with regulated minimum prices in an industry of this kind are clear enough: over the long run they worsen the problem of excess capacity and make adjustments to reduce demand even more troublesome. Because of opportunities for fuel switching in energy, a price floor also tends to enhance the competitiveness of alternatives, thus creating an even more rapid drop in demand than would otherwise occur.[28] These economic problems would inevitably have led, it seems clear, to political conflicts that in turn would have undermined the tenuous consensus upon which the regulatory system in coal rested.

Cooperation and Stabilization

Although coal continued its relative decline as an energy source after the Second World War, the industry as a whole was able to stabilize and then gradually improve its overall economic position. Prices held and profits increased. Wages rose as mechanization and an increase in strip mining brought improvements in worker productivity.[29] The market for coal continued to shift to electric power utilities and away from residential, commercial, and other industrial uses. By 1969 electric utilities were purchasing nearly two-thirds of the coal produced, and the proportion was still growing. The steel industry maintained its demand for coal-derived coke, and demand from that sector held steady.

The key to the improved prospects was the emergence of a powerful but informal alliance between the UMW leadership and the operators of the very large mines that took shape in the years after 1950. Changes in mining technology and in the market for coal posed serious challenges to both labor and management. John L. Lewis had long favored mechanization of the industry; he saw this as the only way to improve the wages and status of mine workers, even if it meant a decline in overall employment. He also favored control of competition in the industry, even if this meant supporting greater concentration and eliminating the smaller, independent mining operations.[30]

Under the leadership of George Love, head of the largest company (Consolidated Coal), the big operators coordinated their activities by establishing the Bituminous Coal Operators' Association (BCOA) in 1950. However, they chose not to request federal assistance in managing competition. The Department of the Interior, which had become a bureaucratic ally for the industry over the years, did maintain a national Bituminous Coal Advisory Council to advise the government, copying the more successful advisory council in the petroleum industry. And representatives of the industry complained bitterly that their economic problems resulted from government policies favoring the oil and gas industries—notably the different depletion allowances (5 percent for coal, 27.5 percent for oil and gas). They also complained about monopolistic practices (artificially low prices for residual oil) and unfair rates set for the railroads.[31] But they did not seek direct regulation. As one historian points out, there is considerable irony here: "It is especially noteworthy that by 1951 the coal industry, unlike oil and gas, did not appeal for government assistance through lessened competition, nor did it follow the lead of agriculture and seek either price supports or supply restraints. Instead it called for fair competition in the markets in which it operated; ironically this was perhaps the hardest bounty of all for government to bestow."[32]

Instead Love and the BCOA turned to Lewis and the United Mine Workers for assistance. The catalyst for the creation of a tacit alliance between large operators and the union was a drop in demand for coal that took place in the years immediately following the war. As a recent analysis of the UMW/BCOA cooperation has characterized it, Lewis and Love both realized that a return to the old pattern of oversupply and price competition, accompanied by wage reductions and unemployment, would be disastrous. Accordingly, "Labor relations were turned upside down after 1950. Between 1950 and 1972, Lewis and his successor, W. A. (Tony) Boyle, fashioned a strike-free partnership with the major coal operators. All earlier coal stabilization mechanisms—federal intervention, self-regulation, and union regulation of supply—had failed. But a fourth—labor-management alliance—did not."[33]

Stability of supply was especially important if the industry was to compete with inexpensive oil and gas and consolidate its position as a preferred fuel in the electric utility industry.[34] Stable and low prices for coal were also essential, and they could best be achieved through rapid mechanization. In return for UMW cooperation in controlling labor, the BCOA agreed to support a special welfare and retirement fund for miners and their families.[35] The new allies also sought to further strengthen the very large companies in the industry and eliminate, where possible, the small coal companies that were so important in spurring competition. And the means they used were often direct and brutal:

Lewis used UMWA resources to further the competition-limiting ends of his partnership with BCOA. His organizing drives in the 1950's focused on the small companies exclusively. It appears that the real purpose of the union's campaign of dynamite and sabotage was less to organize the companies than to eliminate them. While battling the non-BCOA operators, Lewis signed "sweetheart" contracts with a number of BCOA members. These secret agreements allowed the favored operator to pay less than Union-scale wages or suspend royalty payments to the UMWA's Welfare and Retirement Fund. Coal companies often had difficulties finding money to finance mechanization. Lewis solved this problem for certain BCOA companies by lending them $17 million from UMWA-owned National Bank of Washington and the Fund.[36]

Large producers and consumers of coal also sought to regulate the market by other means. As the sale of coal to utilities expanded, so did the proportion of long-term contracts. Utilities and steel companies began to acquire "captive" mines, in order to prevent interruptions in supply and reduce the likelihood of wildcat strikes. Operators and their customers also built reserve stocks, so that when strikes did take place there was almost no real interruption in production of energy or steel.[37] Finally, and in the long run more importantly, the larger operators engaged in a series of intra-industry and, later, conglomerate mergers that transformed the structure of the coal business.[38]

The actions and policies of the UMW and the large coal operators, working independently and in alliance, significantly altered the coal industry in the years between 1950 and 1970. Although it is difficult to quantify precisely the contribution of individual measures, there can be no question that the competitive process itself was significantly altered in favor of order and stability, assured profits, and overall productive continuity in the industry. Labor "peace" reigned: there were no strikes by the UMW against members of the BCOA; and wildcat strikes occurred much less frequently.[39] Labor-controlled production limitations reduced competition, as did long-term contracts, the elimination of many smaller independent operators, the establishment of captive mines, and the merger movement that in the end involved nearly every major producer of coal in the country. Excess capacity declined. And technological innovation proceeded rapidly as underground mines became mechanized and strip mines rapidly increased their share of the business. Enormous mining machines, conveyer belts, and dragline shovels became the order of the day. Labor productivity tripled as the amount of coal loaded by hand declined dramatically.[40] Because of these changes, the larger companies were able to register an increase in profits despite periods of demand fluctuation (notably in 1950–54), very little long-term growth in coal output, and virtually no price increases.

From the perspective of the economy as a whole, many of these changes were constructive and beneficial. Because of them a major American industry shook off chronic instability and uncertainty; energy supply became more predictable; and the many people and communities dependent upon the industry lived more securely. Insofar as these market-control arrangements increased the price of coal and discouraged investments in cheaper energy sources, of course, they imposed costs on the rest of society.

But trouble was brewing beneath the surface, trouble that would, in the early 1970's, undermine the capacity of the UMW to contribute to the industry's stabilization arrangements. In brief, union leaders, in their efforts to stabilize the industry, had left the workers out. Wages, although higher (for workers who did not lose their jobs), were no longer increasing at the speed they were for comparable jobs in other industries.[41] Mine safety no longer improved after 1950. Mechanization added new hazards, especially in the form of coal dust kicked up by machinery, and Black Lung Disease became a major concern in a labor force that, because of limits on entry, was growing older.[42] Most important, perhaps, union leaders lost touch with the rank-and-file workers, who no longer had the right to ratify contracts or influence the disposition of union funds.[43] In sum, from

the perspective of the workers, the BCOA/UMW alliance, and stabilization of the industry, proved to be seriously flawed. In their
efforts to transform the industry, union bosses had made concessions and compromises that would not stand up to worker scrutiny
when the energy crisis brought a new era to the American political
economy.

The coal industry also proved vulnerable to growing demands for
control of the environmental damage associated with coal production and use. These focused on damage to the land caused by strip
mining, and to the air caused by mining operations and power plant
emissions. As luck would have it, these demands, and the groups
promoting them, became politically irresistible at the same time
that the complaints of miners began to undermine the stabilizing
union-management alliance. And all of this coincided with the
weakening of the international petroleum cartel that ushered in the
era of OPEC ascendancy and energy crisis.

Conclusions

The turbulent history of the coal industry provides an interesting
laboratory for the student of political economy. Of all the energy
forms it provides the clearest illustration of the social and political
costs associated with unrestrained competition where technical and
structural attributes of the industry assure chronic instability and
oversupply. The incentive to relieve the insecurity created by competition was strong for owners as well as miners, as was the public
interest in a stable supply of coal and an end to the suffering of miners and coal-dependent communities.

The industry also illustrates why market management can be especially difficult to achieve and sustain under certain conditions.
Some of these have to do with the technology and economics of coal
development, including the ease of entry to the industry, the large
number of producers, and the regional fragmentation of production.
More interesting, however, are the political and organizational difficulties that have constrained efforts to tame the market.

The most notable feature of the troubled history of the coal regime is the absence of more decisive and enduring federal intervention, especially at those times when the industry was in its worst
slumps and when labor conflicts were most politically disruptive.
Certainly this contrasts sharply with the experience of the other
energy regimes. When the government did take a hand in coal—
through wartime price controls, the NRA, the Coal Act, and presi-

dential strike-busting—no one was very happy with the results. The federal government worried about the coal industry, but remained indecisive when it came to doing anything about it.

There are many reasons for this. Perhaps the clearest is the government's unwillingness to consider solutions that departed from the free market ideal, except during the first days of the New Deal. There was also a widespread belief that the decline of the coal industry, though painful, was inevitable; that it would be a mistake to intervene and prop up a dying concern. Certainly there seemed little understanding that price control alone was simply not feasible on technical grounds, and that the key to any market-stabilization system was control of supply and entry. But most important was the fact that the industry itself was unable to agree on acceptable terms for government protection and intervention, especially after the widespread dissatisfaction with the NRA and the Coal Act. As an industry, coal was politically weak and deeply divided. Bitter conflicts between labor and management, and between operators of different sizes and from different regions, absorbed much of its energy and prevented it from taking advantage of the responsiveness of the American polity to demands for proprietary regulation.

When cooperation to constrain competition finally became possible, largely because of the centralization of power in the UMW and BCOA, private arrangements appeared attractive to an industry grown desperate, even if those arrangements were achieved by corrupt and violent means. In the end, however, this private corporatist solution failed as well—just as the earlier ones, under the NRA and the Coal Act, had. The reasons for this failure are worth noting. To be sure, an elite made up of owners and union leaders reshaped the industry in order to promote market stability, encourage technical innovation, and initially provide greater benefits to a much reduced work force. But, in addition to using unacceptable means—the instruments of private collusion and coercion—union leaders proved such poor representatives of worker interests and concerns that the governing structure had begun to crumble even before the energy crisis struck.

CHAPTER 3

Oil

This chapter, like the preceding one, focuses on the intersection of politics and markets. The objective is to analyze the structure and operation of the petroleum industry and to relate these to the evolution of private and public efforts to manage competition and create governing mechanisms for the oil regime in the years before the energy crisis. A grasp of this legacy is essential to an understanding of why the American government reacted the way it did after the OPEC embargo and what the alternatives available to us are in future attempts to fashion workable energy policies.

The energy crisis was first and foremost an oil crisis. Not only did an oil embargo trigger it, but what made it a crisis was the profound dependence of the United States and other industrial economies on petroleum fuels of all kinds. There were no substitutes for them, and rather than do without we were willing to pay an enormous tax to monopolists across the ocean. The really hard part was deciding who would pay this tax, how it was to be collected, and whether those in a position to benefit from domestic energy price increases would be allowed to do so.

In an unregulated market these costs and benefits would have been allocated automatically, roughly in accordance with consumption of oil products and ownership of natural resources. But the market was not unregulated—and even if it had been, the political rules of the game would not have permitted it to remain so when it became clear that so great and so visible a redistribution of wealth was at hand. At the time of the crisis, petroleum affairs were governed by elaborate regulatory arrangements put in place by the federal government and the states, mostly in compliance with industry requests. Although costly to the country, these served industry interests well for decades, assuring stability and profits to participants in the petroleum regime. But they provided little help in the aftermath of the embargo. The crisis, in fact, made these arrangements obsolete overnight, forcing the government and the industry to address the issue of regime governance at the same time that they were struggling with problems of wealth redistribution.

Background

The oil industry was born a century ago in rural Pennsylvania at a time when coal was just beginning its own ascendancy. The date of Drake's successful well in 1859 is one of the few that stick in the minds of students of American economic history. In its early years, the oil industry supplied light, not energy. It was the principal new source of inexpensive "illuminating oil" as the cost of whale oil and other substitutes for it increased. Not until after the turn of the century did Americans in large numbers begin to use oil for heat and power. But the rise of oil was rapid once it began. Petroleum fuels first displaced coal in railroad engines and then captured the market for transport fuel in ships, automobiles, and finally airplanes. Especially after the discovery of large new fields in Texas, Oklahoma, and California in the 1920's and 1930's, petroleum fuels had a clear cost advantage over coal. They were also cleaner, easier to handle and store, and produced fewer waste products.

The speed with which the nation shifted to petroleum fuels is also explained by the character of the industry itself. As one historian has put it: "In comparison to the companies that sold bituminous coal, the major oil companies were paragons of efficiency, dependability and innovation. They grew quickly by competing aggressively . . . and for the consumer this generally meant good service at decreasing prices. This was in sharp contrast to the conditions in the 'sick' bituminous coal industry, which Herbert Hoover properly labeled 'the worst functioning industry in the country' in the 1920's."[1]

As most Americans are aware, the oil industry went on to become the country's largest, wealthiest, and most powerful industry. Of the 50 largest industrial companies in the United States in 1986, twelve were oil companies. Among the top 25, ranked by sales, oil companies accounted for nine and took in fully 30 percent of the net earnings. Exxon, the industry leader and the second-largest industrial corporation in the United States, had revenues in 1986 of more than $69 billion.[2]

In its century of growth and expansion, the oil industry demonstrated an unusual degree of flexibility and inventiveness in addressing the problem of market stabilization. The mechanisms employed ranged from outright monopoly and cartelization to laboriously constructed regulatory arrangements operating at every level of government. Although some of these, such as the Standard Oil Trust, are familiar to students of economic history, others such as the Red Line Agreement, the Texas Railroad Commission, and the Interstate Compact to Conserve Oil and Gas are less so. But they operated effectively for a surprisingly long time.

These arrangements were possible because of the remarkable political adroitness of oil industry leaders—perhaps the most distinctive feature of the petroleum regime. I refer here to two kinds of skills. The first, which has been the more widely recognized, was skill in dealing with governments. The power of oil lobbies in state and national legislatures has long been renowned, and justifiably so. But there was a second kind as well: skill in managing conflicts and disagreements among the diverse interests within the industry itself. The world of oil is so diverse and complex, and touches the lives of so many different people, that the degree of order and stability that has been maintained over so many years can only inspire awe in the serious student of politics. But for these skills, the history of oil might have been much like that of coal.

The Political Economy of Oil

Oil, like coal, is prone to market instability under free market conditions. The physical and economic characteristics of both production and consumption make the industry vulnerable to large fluctuations in both supply and price that can be devastating. The same attributes give rise to a pattern of production that results in a physical waste of the resource itself.

Deposits of petroleum, like coal, come in all sizes and are geographically dispersed. Since access to drilling technology and the necessary capital has always been relatively easy, entry into the production business has also been easy, at least to onshore production within the United States. Once a field has been discovered, however, the incentive to produce oil is very strong, for this is the only way to recover the venture capital spent in exploration and drilling. This is true even if prices are forced down by the new supply placed on the market, since even a small return is better than none at all. This means that supply in the short run tends to be very inelastic with respect to price. A new find can, and often does, flood the market, driving prices well below the cost of production and keeping them there for an extended period of time. The result can be financial disaster for any producer unable to absorb losses on invested capital.

This problem has been made even worse where landowners with

access to the same pool of oil have found themselves competing to see who could produce the most from the deposit. Most of the larger oil fields in the United States are big enough so that the land surface above them was owned by many individuals when they were discovered. Because there is no way to determine precisely what portion of an oil pool is beneath the land of a particular owner, the legal principle applied has been the ancient "rule of capture," which emerged originally to determine the legal right to wild game that freely crossed land boundaries. The application of this legal rule, of course, simply adds another incentive to produce oil from a new field regardless of the impact on price, since the portion of the total income to be garnered by the individual landowner depends on his ability to bring crude to the surface. The incentive to pump as much oil as quickly as possible has often resulted in production techniques that are wasteful, in the sense that loss of pressure, caused by too many wells and a production rate that is too rapid, reduce the total amount of oil recovered from the deposit.

The other side of the equation, of course, is consumption. Here the problem is also one of slow adjustment to changes in market conditions. Once a consumer has purchased equipment that uses a particular fuel, whether it be a car or furnace, he tends to stay with that source, and will be inclined to pay more rather than incur the much greater expense of buying new equipment. Again, in technical terms, this means that demand is also inelastic with respect to price. The adjustment mechanisms that might otherwise tend to dampen demand, or even increase it, in the short run operate very slowly. This tends to exacerbate short-term price fluctuations.

The history of oil is punctuated by episodes of instability and resource waste brought on by these technical and economic attributes of production and consumption. In one form or another, the threat of oversupply, of "distressed oil" on the market, has been the single greatest challenge to the industry and, as we shall see, the object of constant attention and vigilance.

Another characteristic of the oil industry, one that has been the source of both frustration and fascination to outside observers, is its enormous complexity. This stems partly from the technical sophistication of the operations involved in finding, handling, and transforming petroleum, and partly from the very great number of firms involved in the process, all interconnected and interdependent in one way or another. To trace a barrel of oil as it moves from an underground deposit and is transformed into several hundreds of products—ranging from house paint and plastics to fuel oil and gasoline—is to follow a path of awesome technical and organizational intricacy. For analytical purposes, it is convenient to view the oil business as an amalgam of four distinct industries, each with its own attributes. These are crude oil production, refining, transportation, and marketing. Each is different in important respects and has followed a somewhat independent pattern of transformation in the century of petroleum industry development.

Consider production first. There are many hundreds of firms engaged in the business of discovering and producing oil, and they range in size from tiny "wildcat" outfits that specialize in high-risk exploratory drilling to companies such as Exxon, which controls more than 10 percent of the annual 8–9 million barrels per day of crude oil production in the United States.[3] Although small firms have found entry easy in the past, this has been changing as more remote areas, such as Alaska and deep-water offshore leases (where very expensive equipment is essential), have become more important in overall production.

Refining companies specialize in chemically transforming crude oil into a variety of more useful products. In the early days of the industry, it was common for customers simply to burn raw crude oil for energy. As the science and art of separating and reforming the complex hydrocarbon structures of petroleum has advanced, the refining industry has grown in importance and complexity. Today there are over a hundred refining companies in the United States, operating 223 separate refineries.[4] Again, these range in size from very small firms with a single plant to very large ones with many installations. The refineries themselves range in capacity from Oriental Refining's 150 barrels a day to Amarada Hess's giant Virgin Islands complex, which handles more than 600,000 barrels per day.[5]

In the transportation industry, pipeline companies are the most important component within the United States. A network of more than 200,000 miles of lines collects crude from wells, delivers it to the refineries, and transports products to retail jobbers. It also provides a critically important link in the structure of control over the industry as a whole.[6]

Finally, the petroleum products themselves are sold to many thousands of other businesses and retail outlets. Large amounts go as a feedstock to the petrochemical industry. The most important retail outlets, of course, are gasoline stations, and, more than any other group, station owners and operators today bear the brunt of market discipline in the oil business.

Sorting out the interdependent workings of these phases of the business is difficult enough, but it is further complicated by the fact that the American industry has critically important structural connections with an even more complex international industry. These connections add an important element of political as well as technical diversity to industry affairs, vastly complicating the task of the analyst because decisions that affect American operations and activities are often heavily influenced by international considerations.

If complexity is the most notable structural feature of the petroleum business, the most striking fact about the decisionmaking process is the degree to which this diverse multisector set of operations has been orchestrated by a small number of large integrated companies. "Integrated" refers to the fact that these companies are active in all phases of the petroleum business, from production through marketing. The best known of these giants, also known as "majors," are the famous "seven sisters" that played such an important role in the history of international oil—Standard Oil of New Jersey (Exxon), Texaco, Gulf, Standard Oil of California (Socal), Standard Oil of New York (Mobil), British Petroleum, and Royal Dutch Shell. In recent years the industry has become more diverse as the classic seven sisters—reduced now to six by the merger of Gulf and Standard of California—have been pushed offshore by the birth of some very large state-owned companies in the producer countries, and as a number of middle-sized corporations in the United States have expanded to the point where they clearly also qualify as important integrated companies.

The precise role of the integrated majors in the petroleum industry is a matter of enormous contention. It is probable that more time and energy have been spent arguing about this than any similar problem of economic organization in the history of the nation. Critics charge conspiracy and monopoly, point to the enormous size of the majors and the historical evidence of cartelization, and charge that the industry giants have exerted an improper influence on public policy. The industry defends itself by claiming that competition is real, that integration is efficient, and that its history of service to the country, in the form of continuity of supplies and relatively low prices, is justification enough for the current pattern of organization.

The issues raised in these arguments are important. They touch upon values and concerns that remain central to any evaluation of the organization of economic life and of the relationship of the state to private power in our society—themes to which we will return in Part Four. For our present purposes, however, it is useful to begin with some basic terms of reference, points upon which there is wide-spread agreement among those who have studied the matter.

First, there is a very significant degree of concentration of owner-ship and control in the petroleum business. Second, this control is exercised by a small number of companies whose operations span most or all of the phases of the industry—this, of course, is why they are called integrated companies. Third, this very integration, along with a wide range of technically helpful forms of association and cooperation, have given the large companies the means of main-taining their advantaged position vis-à-vis the firms that operate in only one area of the business. Fourth, although the objective condi-tions exist in the United States for effective competition among these large companies (and this has not always been the case), a no-table feature of the history of oil is the success with which they have worked together and harnessed public institutions to restrict uncon-trolled supply to the market in order to stabilize prices. There is no reason to believe that they have entirely lost the ability to do this; indeed, most would agree that the degree of competition in this in-dustry has always been less than might be expected by a simple reci-tation of the concentration ratios themselves.[7] The reasons lie in a complex pattern of joint ventures and structural interdependencies that bind the companies together and strengthen their relative posi-tion while creating very strong incentives for them to cooperate with each other.

Finally—and this is an important point—nearly everyone who has studied this industry carefully would agree that the cooperation involved does not normally take the form of simple collusion or con-spiracy of the old-fashioned kind, partly because that would be very difficult in view of the enormous diversity of companies and person-alities involved, but mainly because it has not been required most of the time—at least not within the United States and not in recent years.[8] It is simply not necessary for the executives of the major companies to sit down together in a back room and make deals. Joint planning at lower levels and extensive signaling of intentions by other means, both of which appear to contribute to rational resource allocation, make such behavior unnecessary. The fact that such col-lusion may be technically illegal is a different, albeit still troubling, issue.[9]

To understand how the largest integrated companies are able to dominate the business, it is necessary to dig a bit more deeply into the way things actually work. At the level of production, for ex-

ample, large companies control very large proportions of the reserves: according to a recent estimate, the top 20 companies control
as much as 85 percent of domestic proved reserves.[10] They are able
to do this because of their greater financial resources. To develop
these reserves, however, it is common for them to "farm out" the
right to drill and produce to smaller independents while retaining
the right to purchase the crude produced.[11] More importantly, the
same companies dominate the transport system in such a way that
independent producers, even those with their own leases, usually
must sell their product to a collection and distribution network controlled at one point or another by an integrated major. As analyst
Walter Measday has put it:

The crude producer does not sell his oil on an open market. Almost always he sells it to a major-owned pipeline company at the price posted for
his field by the major buyer; his alternative in most fields is to have his
oil trucked out at considerably greater cost than the pipeline gathering
charge. . . . Thus the crude pipeline operations of the majors give them control over most of the oil produced by independents, in addition to their own
70-plus percent of total production.[12]

As it turns out, this, plus their predominant role as marketers of
imported oil, also gives integrated majors a substantial degree of
control over entry into the refining business, since the decision to
construct a new refinery typically depends on a guaranteed access to
large amounts of crude oil for a decade or more.[13]

The fact that they span every stage of the business also gives the
large companies a degree of financial flexibility that the smaller
companies do not enjoy. Thus, for example, they can adjust their
prices in a such a way as to maximize their profits across a range of
activities, taking profits where it is most advantageous, in tax terms,
and their losses where they are most helpful. For many years, this
meant that the integrated companies took their profits mainly at the
level of crude production, taking advantage of the percentage depletion allowance, a tax subsidy that allowed producers to deduct 27.5
percent of the value of their production from the calculation of net
profits. It made sense to set a higher price for crude, and to run refineries at very little profit, since no deduction was available for earnings at that stage of the business. To the independent refiner with
no crude production, of course, this meant very tight margins.

If control of the transport bottleneck has been critical in helping
the majors maintain their position, it is the interconnections among
them that have made more detailed cooperation both necessary and
desirable. Again, this does not mean an old-style, smoky-room con-

spiracy, but rather efficiency-related joint planning necessitated by structural relationships. These relationships take many forms. The most visible are outright joint ventures in which the participating companies must, perforce, make decisions about their activities in common. Every major is bound together with others in joint ventures of this kind. These were central to the control of foreign oil production in both Iran and Saudi Arabia, as they continue to be important in offshore production and pipelines in the United States.[14] To take advantage of joint-venture opportunities, the companies involved must be in constant contact, exchanging information about future plans and about new technologies.

The majors are also interconnected as a result of elaborate swapping and exchange arrangements for crude and products. These are essential in controlling costs—they allow companies, for example, to supply customers far from refineries more cheaply—but they are carried on outside the price system and involve extensive exchanges of information.[15] Again, the evidence suggests that many of these forms of cooperation and interdependence contribute to the efficient operation of the industry; economic rationality and structural collusion thus appear to complement each other in important ways—a difficult problem for theorists and practitioners alike.

The Politics of Regulation

The relationship between the petroleum industry and government in the United States has evolved through several distinct phases, each leading to more extensive collaboration and greater interdependence. In its early years the industry was quite competitive, as oil fields were discovered and firms formed to take advantage of the new market, and the state did little more than provide a legal framework for private enterprise. But the industry soon came under the control of a powerful monopoly, and this fact, along with the growing economic influence of oil in national affairs, eventually forced the government to take a more active role.

The rise of Standard Oil and the ruthless and secretive ways of its founder, John D. Rockefeller, is one of the best-known stories in the history of American business. Although Standard Oil was but one of many economic empires that arose in the United States in the last half of the nineteenth century, it was the most successful and the most notorious. From it sprang the largest family fortune in the world.[16] And the methods of aggrandizement perfected by Rockefeller gave rise to the antitrust movement as well as a literary tradition of critical attacks that finds a new champion in every generation.[17]

Rockefeller entered the oil business by investing in a Cleveland oil refinery in 1865. He consolidated his position in refining by making elaborate and secret rebate arrangements with the railroad companies. He later extended his control to pipelines. Quietly but ruthlessly, he used his earnings to buy out his competitors.[18] By the 1880's the Standard Oil Company, transformed into a trust to allow it to reach across state boundaries, controlled fully 90 percent of the refining capacity in the country.[19] Standard Oil then moved "upstream" into production, becoming a completely integrated operation. The production business was chronically unstable, afflicted by periods of glut and fluctuating prices as landowners in new fields feverishly drilled wells to "capture" oil. This made many producing companies vulnerable to the "octopus" Standard Oil, and Rockefeller's company grew apace.

The rise of monopoly in oil is a striking contrast to the experience of coal, where early efforts to concentrate economic control failed (except in the anthracite fields) despite a similar problem with unstable markets. The key to this difference lay in the availability of bottlenecks or control points in the oil transport and refining sectors. Leadership was also important; it was Rockefeller's strengths in this regard that enabled him to bring the industry under control despite the continuing ease of entry into production.

The Standard Oil monopoly began to weaken at the turn of the century when a combination of large new discoveries in Texas and growing political hostility made it possible for new entrepreneurs to enter the production business and gradually build themselves into integrated companies. The practices of the Standard Oil Trust had already led many state governments, including that of Texas, to pass antitrust laws, and these made it difficult for Standard to control the new fields. Texas legislation made it illegal for Standard Oil even to operate within the state, and though the company did establish secret ties with Texas operators, the barrier was firm enough to permit new companies to survive and grow.[20] Two of these, Gulf Oil and Texaco, subsequently became majors.

In the meantime, the antitrust movement was gathering momentum at the national level. In 1911, in a historic decision, the Supreme Court upheld the massive divestiture suit brought against a weakened Standard Oil under the Sherman Act, forcing the trust to break up into its constituent companies in the various states. Of the more than 30 such units, the larger then proceeded to integrate by merger and expansion. Three of these, Exxon (formerly Standard of New Jersey), Mobil (formerly Standard of New York), and Socal

(Standard of California) eventually became majors that were larger and wealthier in every way than their parent. Others became independents, integrated to various degrees but still important entities in the industry. Because ownership of the new companies was transferred to the same stockholders—notably the Rockefeller interests—and because officials of these companies had long experience working together, the restructured industry began with a degree of mutual cooperation and interdependence that has characterized the relationships of the majors ever since.[21]

If the first episode of industry-government interaction was purely adversarial in character, the second was far less so. By the time of the First World War, the industrial economies had become increasingly dependent on oil. The navies of all the great powers also relied on petroleum fuels. Because of this, Woodrow Wilson chose to bring the industry under the wartime control of the federal government to assure stability of supply. To manage the industry, he created a special National Petroleum War Service Committee made up of industry representatives. Formed by renaming an existing industry advisory group, the Committee operated very much like a legal cartel under the authority of the Executive Branch. This arrangement was widely criticized by those who felt that businessmen gained undue influence in the setting of government policy, but it was defended as an emergency measure.[22]

The experience of government-industry cooperation during the war had a lasting impact. Although the Committee was formally disbanded after the war, industry representatives subsequently replaced it with the private American Petroleum Institute (API), which has since functioned as the principal lobby and center of analytical studies for the industry as a whole. More broadly, the experience also made clear the possible advantages of federally sponsored market stabilization. A decade later, when oil again found itself threatened by oversupply, the experience of wartime controls clearly influenced industry leaders as they sought new solutions.[23]

Market Control Through Proration

The setting for the third major "round" of industry dealings with the federal government was still another episode of uncontrolled production which, coinciding with the reduced demand caused by the Great Depression, brought turmoil and financial distress such as the industry had not experienced for many years.[24] Drillers discovered two giant oil fields in 1929 and 1930, one lying under Oklahoma City and the other in East Texas. Overnight a forest of oil rigs sprang up, covering the land in the producing areas. In some cases the rigs were so densely packed that their bases actually touched. Production flooded the market and prices dropped in a few short months from nearly a dollar a barrel to less than ten cents. The glut threw the industry into a panic, and both Oklahoma and Texas were forced to declare martial law and take control of the oil fields to keep the peace and enforce production controls.[25]

Faced with an industry in collapse—and, incidentally, with a serious loss of revenues—the governments of the afflicted states eventually accepted the need to control production permanently. The political, legal, and ideological struggles associated with the design of state production-control systems capture in microcosm all of the important issues and problems that arise when a society committed to market allocation of resources comes face to face with the need to depart from that ideal. It had been clear for years that enormous physical waste could result from the mad scramble to exploit new fields. Regulation was thus always justified on the grounds of conservation. With the collapse of prices, a further argument was added: production controls were needed to prevent "economic" waste, or the losses to society caused by the lost profits and bankruptcy of businesses that were otherwise quite efficient. But how to define economic waste and protect threatened producers without assuring excess profits? And how to allocate production quotas?[26]

Conflicts over these matters came to a head in Texas in 1932. Like Oklahoma and other states, Texas had charged a regulatory body, the Texas Railroad Commission, with controlling oil production to prevent wasteful overproduction in the oil fields. But at the same time it had explicitly prohibited the Commission from using its power to prop up prices. As was the case in the days of the Rockefeller monopoly, the Texas legislature was reluctant to bow to the demands of oil companies if those demands meant significant alterations in the operation of the free market.[27] But the demands for action mounted.

The majors were among the strongest supporters of production control. Their concern stemmed from the impact of Texas on the world market. Several of the majors had agreed at a 1928 meeting at Achnacarry Castle in Scotland to create a cartel to govern the world oil market. To be effective, this necessitated the formation of local cartels to control production in the various regions of the world. Standard Oil of New York, Standard Oil of New Jersey, Gulf, and Texaco were all party to this agreement, and therefore had a strong interest in stemming the runaway production in East Texas.[28] Although antitrust laws prohibited the formal inclusion of U.S. production in the cartel, some arrangements were clearly needed.

The Texas legislature eventually capitulated and passed a regulatory act granting the Texas Railroad Commission authority to prorate supply to prevent "waste" and keep prices at "acceptably" high levels.[29] The pattern of state-based production control, for which the Texas decision was crucially important, subsequently formed the basis for a system of nationwide prorationing that took shape in the United States between 1932 and 1935. With the exceptions of California and Illinois, all the producing states adopted similar prorationing systems governed by state agencies.

State commitments to control production, however, could not be effective without three additional elements: some way to prevent producers from circumventing state quotas by selling their oil in other states; some means of setting national quotas or targets; and some mechanism by which states could allocate these quotas among themselves.[30] Out-of-state oil sales were addressed in the NIRA, which contained a provision prohibiting the crossing of state boundaries by "hot" oil. Although the industry was nervous about enlarging the role of the federal government, no other solution seemed available. With the demise of the NIRA, therefore, the industry pushed for, and got, a replacement: the Connolly "Hot Oil Act" of 1935.[31]

The problem of national quotas was more difficult, and in the end only a partial solution to it was possible. At the request of the API, the Bureau of Mines of the Department of the Interior agreed to make monthly forecasts of the demand for oil, dividing these among the producing states. The basis for Interior's estimates was information provided by the industry itself. The forecasts were carefully designed so that they did not take into account any possible influence of price changes on demand; this meant that they were, in effect, forecasts of demand at existing (but not lower) prices. These then became the basis for state decisions in allocating quotas.

To address the problem of coordinating state decisions, the API and the governor of Texas suggested the creation of an interstate agency that could make binding decisions. But Congressional support for legally enforced allocation was weak, and some in the industry feared the creation of too assertive a federal authority in the oil business. The industry thus had to settle for a nonbinding mechanism to promote "conservation." In 1935 this was formalized when Congress passed legislation approving the Interstate Compact to

Conserve Oil and Gas. In practice, the principal function of the agency thus established was coordination of production controls to support prices.[32]

Thus by 1935 the oil industry had pieced together an effective system of market management. It was capable of keeping prices high and stable, and lasted for more than four decades. It relied on state regulation backed by federal laws and continuous interstate cooperation. It is still in place today, although it is neither needed nor used. The most important challenge to the system during the first years came from the state of Illinois, which refused to control its output in accordance with the goals of the Interstate Compact Commission. Between 1938 and 1940 output from Illinois rose dramatically—by nearly 100 million barrels per year—and forced significant adjustments on the part of other members of the system. As it turned out, in this and subsequent cases it was the regulatory agencies of Texas and Oklahoma, which together accounted for nearly four-fifths of the national output, that saved the day by making the adjustments needed to balance the actions of the "free riders." Although prices fluctuated slightly and some "shading" occurred at the field level, the regime held together remarkably well through the 1960's.[33]

Although the regulation of oil was justified primarily as a means of preventing waste, its accomplishments in this area were actually very modest. The system made conservation possible but not necessary. Production limits curtailed the more blatant examples of all-out exploitation, but regulators generally avoided mandating such really effective means of preventing waste as well spacing and unitized management of petroleum deposits.[34]

Import Management

The market-management system pieced together in the 1930's ran into trouble again in the late 1950's when the breakdown of the international petroleum cartel led to price erosion and a growing threat of cheap crude oil and products in the American market. Once again the industry rose to the occasion, overcoming political divisions and ideological uncertainty and securing public assistance to protect itself. The result, however, was still another alteration in the relationship between the industry and the federal government.[35]

The market challenge posed by low-cost imports materialized over a number of years. The problem can be traced to the "outbreak" of competition in the world market during the 1950's as the majors lost the ability to control the entry of new companies into new, low-cost producing areas overseas. Soaring world demand (which grew at more than 10 percent per year after the Second World War), the willingness of foreign host governments to grant concessions to independents who outbid majors by offering beneficial terms, and the subsequent need of those independents to market their oil to recover costs—all contributed to the change.[36] The protected American market became increasingly attractive to companies with access to cheap foreign oil. Domestic prices were held high by state authorities in order to assure profits to the owners of the most marginal wells.[37] At the same time, many of the new overseas fields were proving astonishingly productive, allowing developers to pump oil at a fraction of the cost of American operations.

The need to control imports had been acknowledged in the 1930's when the system of oil market management was created. At that time the main importing companies entered into a voluntary agreement with the Department of the Interior to stabilize imports at approximately 5 percent of domestic demand, and Congress levied a small excise tax on imported oil. This arrangement held until the late 1940's when imports began to grow. By the mid-1950's imports had reached the level of about 12 percent of domestic production, and seemed likely to increase still further.[38]

This set off a long and complex political struggle. The first to react were domestic independent producers with no foreign production, especially those in Texas and Oklahoma whose output levels were reduced by state agencies to accommodate imports without price increases.[39] Represented by the Independent Petroleum Association of America (IPAA), they launched a vigorous campaign to secure government protection. They were joined by coal interests, who feared that their product would suffer a further loss to cheap foreign substitutes. On the other side were representatives of New England consumers of fuel oil as well as those larger independents who had investments in foreign oil fields and were counting on marketing crude in the lucrative U.S. market. The international majors were, with some exceptions, more ambivalent; they were domestic producers, but they were also in a position to make handsome profits by importing cheap oil and products.

The government responded first by pressing importers informally to enact limitations on their own. Neither the President nor his advisers were comfortable with the idea of restricting trade, and they hoped that noncoercive mechanisms would suffice. When informal pressure proved ineffective, therefore, Eisenhower set up a formal program of voluntary quotas in 1957.

In pressing their case, the domestic independents relied heavily on the argument that imports threatened the nation's security. The Trade Agreements Extension Act of 1955 gave the President the authority to restrict imports upon a finding that they were of such a volume as to constitute a threat to the national security. Those seeking restrictions found this a more politically attractive path than seeking separate legislation. In what way the national security was threatened, and how this should be remedied, were never clearly analyzed in the debates that led to control decisions. Eisenhower himself at several points expressed doubts about the idea that restricting imports, and thereby depleting American reserves more quickly, was the best way to seek energy security.[40]

As it became clear that the voluntary program was not working, demands for restriction became more and more strident. To make matters worse, a recession had begun to cut into overall demand, forcing state authorities to reduce production quotas further. By 1958, even the majors began to acknowledge the need for control. The symptoms of the outbreak of competition were growing clearer; price "wars" were erupting as prices of gasoline and other products began to erode, along with profits.[41] Eisenhower finally acceded and, by proclamation, made the import-control system mandatory in 1959, citing the threat to the national security posed by cheap foreign oil. Thereafter—and the system thus established lasted for the next fourteen years—those seeking to import crude oil or petroleum products would require a license from the Department of the Interior. Interior, for its part, would grant licenses to "historic" importers and to other refiners in such amounts as to limit the total to 9 percent of forecast demand.[42]

The administration of this addition to the petroleum market-control system proved technically complex and politically sensitive. Because foreign oil was entering a protected market, an import license was valuable. And since many of the inland refiners receiving them had no use for them, a barter system quickly arose in which those operators were able, by selling them, to capture a part of the rents available to importers. In political terms, this was an essential compromise, assuring a redistribution within the industry of benefits that would otherwise have gone primarily to coastal refineries. The arrangements thus set up also set the pattern for an even more elaborate redistributional system that crisis managers invented in the first years of the oil crisis.

As the import-control program got under way, other adjustments also proved necessary. Regulators exempted "overland" imports as nonthreatening to the national security, a means of letting Canadian imports continue and then grow. And they allowed imports of fuel oil from the Caribbean and Venezuela to increase in response to demands for special treatment by interests representing those sources of oil.[43] They also favored petrochemical feedstocks in response to pressures from the American chemical industry.[44] Overall, however, the system worked quite well. It controlled imports of cheap foreign oil and made it possible for the prorationing system to continue managing the domestic market to assure continuity and high prices. And it did so without seriously altering the basic distribution of influence and benefits within the industry itself. In this respect, it demonstrated once more the impressive political sophistication and capacity for compromise that has characterized the oil regime.

Although the import-control system provided many benefits to the oil industry and a few to the American public—the latter chiefly in the form of stable prices and rapidly expanding supply—it also imposed some very large economic costs on energy consumers. One analyst put these costs, for the years between 1959 and 1969, at over $50 billion, "probably the largest subsidy to any single industry in U.S. history."[45] This estimate does not, of course, include the costs associated with the many distortions in the domestic and international economy caused by high prices for energy and the other raw materials derived from petroleum.

From the perspective of the oil regime the arrangement was not without its costs as well. The most serious was that it forced the industry to fashion an entirely new relationship with the federal government, one that involved the government as an arbitrator in industry affairs. To be sure, it was clear to everyone involved that the goal was to prop up the established regime. But the market-control mechanism was no longer seated exclusively at the level of the more pliable state regulatory commissions. This meant greater vulnerability to federal action, which required more detailed attention to the political process at the national level.

Political Engagement

As most Americans are aware, the wealth and economic importance of the oil industry have brought it enormous political leverage, leverage that has been the more effective because of the coordination made possible by the interdependence of the large companies. In this respect the experience of the petroleum regime has been a striking contrast with that of coal. In the early years, state governments were the principal targets of the petroleum companies. It was here, after all, that the important decisions were made. Except at those times when the threat of uncontrolled supply forced the industry to seek federal regulatory support, its political goals have been largely defensive in character as far as the federal government has been concerned.

In the first decades of the century, however, the industry won a number of lucrative subsidies from Congress, and these had to be defended against periodic attack. The most important of these took the form of special tax treatment of its costs and profits. Since 1918, oil companies have been able to deduct a variety of "intangible" drilling and development costs. And between 1926 and 1975 they were able to deduct a significant percentage of the value of crude oil—27.5 percent until 1969 and 22 percent until 1975—as a compensation for the "depletion" of their resource base. According to one study, these two deductions alone have been worth some $50 billion to the industry.[46] And there have been other subsidies, ranging from the collection of geological data to the provision of direct, industry-related research and development.

The oil industry has also found it necessary to defend itself against periodic attacks by reformers seeking more competition in the name of consumers. Since the original antitrust victory of 1911, consumer and free-market advocates have mounted several major attacks. The most serious, the "Mother Hubbard" case and the International Petroleum Cartel investigation, were eventually terminated in ineffectual consent decrees. The most recent was abandoned by the Reagan Administration on the grounds that essential data, in the hands of Saudi Arabia, were uncollectable. As economist John Blair put it: "An antitrust action against this industry, once launched, has invariably generated political opposition sufficient to insure its demise."[47] But the threat that these suits would succeed was always there. The same was true of repeated legislative attacks on the structural integrity of the petroleum regime, ranging from extended investigative hearings to proposals to break the industry up once again.[48]

It is quixotic, but not surprising, that the U.S. government should at the same time provide the means of market regulation to an organized oligopoly and harbor bureaucratic centers, such as the Department of Justice and the Federal Trade Commission, that invest enormous amounts of time seeking to undo the work of the regulatory system. Structural contradictions thus parallel the ideological contradictions that are such an important part of our political economy.

The petroleum industry protects itself by means familiar to all students of American politics, but greatly fortified by the enormous financial resources of one of the country's wealthiest industries. Indeed, there is an important symbiosis between political influence and successful market management; the latter makes available additional income that can then be "spent" to assure continued stability and profits. Regulated oligopolies may or may not be economically less efficient, but they are surely politically more efficient than their market-constrained counterparts like the coal industry.

For decades oil interests have been able to dominate, in matters of concern to them, the governments of oil states such as Texas, Oklahoma, Louisiana, Alaska, Kansas, and Arkansas; and they exert great influence in the many other states with significant production. At the national level oil-state congressmen and senators have provided a nucleus of support for the industry.[49] The names of the "friends of oil" have always been familiar ones in the nation's legislature. They include, among others, Sam Rayburn, Lyndon Johnson, Everett Dirksen, John Tower, and Russell Long.

The industry has also carefully cultivated its links to the Executive Branch. Close working ties with the Department of the Interior and smaller agencies like the Geologic Survey have, over the years, created a widespread understanding of, and sympathy for, the problems of the industry. The National Petroleum Council, an advisory group to the Department of the Interior with representatives of every sector of the industry, has helped communicate industry concerns to the government. And the API has provided high-level analytical support for industry positions.

To back up its representational and analytical work, the industry has relied heavily on its financial resources. Indeed, its contributions (legal and illegal) have been so extensive that in some instances they have proved a liability—as when it was revealed, in the aftermath of the Watergate scandal, that oil companies provided, directly and indirectly, fully 10 percent of Nixon's reelection funds.[50] Testimony associated with that scandal revealed, again and again, a degree of penetration of the democratic political process that was startling to many observers.[51]

In the course of the 1950's and 1960's, industry representatives were increasingly forced to turn their eyes to Washington. This was partly because they had chosen to involve the federal government more extensively in industry affairs through import regulation, but also because of the growing influence of environmental, consumer, and "public interest" groups hostile to the industry and its goals. In the new political climate, the old defensive posture, even when backed by generous contributions, was less effective than it had been. At the same time, the hold of the industry on Congress weakened as that institution redesigned its rules, changed seniority regulations, and diversified its committee structure. Oil-state congressmen and senators found that safe districts and long careers in Washington no longer brought legislative power. Oil interests remained influential, but they were forced to operate in a more complex and politically "open" environment.

By the late 1960's the oil regime appeared to have adjusted to the challenges of the times. It had fended off the threat of low-cost imported oil and had begun to adapt to the new, more participatory political environment. It had done so by institutionalizing a more intimate regulatory relationship with the federal government, by helping set up a redistributive mechanism within the oil industry, and by bolstering its political resources to fend off the attacks of its critics and to compensate for its weakened legislative base. In short, things still seemed under control, despite the fact that affairs had become very much more complicated. As we shall see, however, the industry was more vulnerable than anyone suspected. Indeed, the energy crisis turned the world upside down for the petroleum regime, converting its carefully erected system of proprietary regulation into a dangerous liability.

Conclusions

From the history of the oil regime we can obtain a number of insights about the emergence of highly sophisticated market-management arrangements in a society as deeply committed to free competition as any in the world. The incentives for control of competition in the petroleum industry were the same as for coal: profits, stability, security, and gains in efficiency for producers and investors; political and economic stability and generous financial contributions for politicians; good working relationships and an orderly management of resources for public administrators. But, in contrast to coal, the petroleum industry had several features that facilitated the taming of the market.

The first of these—and beginnings are important in the emergence of industrial regimes—were the structural opportunities and incentives, in particular the existence of key "bottlenecks" in transport and refining, that made it possible for Rockefeller to build a private monopoly quickly. The cooperative relationships that subsequently emerged in the international oil cartel, and the collaborative personal ties that continued in the leadership of successor companies to Standard Oil, all helped the industry avoid the bitter regional and personal conflicts that so damaged the coal industry. Those running the oil industry learned from the outset that supply control was the key, and they never lost sight of this goal, systematically plugging the leaks in their complex system one after another. They also learned to use ideas—"conservation," "national security"—to balance the obvious contradiction between their determination to impose privately dominated public planning on a competitive market and their strident free-enterprise ideology. And success built upon itself. The funds and political control available from the early era of monopoly and from generous public subsidies made it easier for the industry to use the public sector when private arrangements proved insufficient to stabilize the market.

Finally, we must note an experience that petroleum did share with coal: producers dealt with a public sector that consistently lacked a coherent or "principled" orientation toward the industry and its affairs. Those in the oil regime made a virtue of this: government reactions to industry requests for subsidy, protection, or authority to control supply were always pragmatic, incremental, ad hoc responses to particular situations, allowing the industry great influence in defining the problems and the regulatory solutions proposed for them.

These "achievements," of course, were expensive from the perspective of the American consumer and taxpayer. Though stabilization agreements did assure a steady and ample supply of petroleum fuels to the American economy, and did prevent the losses and inefficiency associated with wide swings in price, they required public subsidies in enormous and unprecedented amounts. By the middle and late 1960's, as changes in the political system made old-style proprietary regulation increasingly vulnerable, the costs of stabilization arrangements became more and more visible and the industry was forced to invest more and more time and funds defending them. As we shall see, when the energy crisis brought a host of new participants into decisionmaking affecting oil, these arrangements became a real liability.

CHAPTER 4 Natural Gas

If the history of coal is marked by the predominance of the market, and that of oil by the influence of producer-designed regulatory mechanisms, the distinctive character of the natural gas and electricity industries stems from the persistent efforts of consumers to regulate these energy forms by controlling prices. Both of these industries are "natural" monopolies in the sense that capital costs, especially for transport and distribution facilities, have been so large that competition has been judged too wasteful. Accordingly, both industries have experienced heavy and continuous compensatory regulation.

When John D. Rockefeller was consolidating his petroleum empire, natural gas was regarded as a nuisance in most oil fields. It was simply flared or vented into the atmosphere. A few cities piped gas from nearby fields for lighting and domestic use, but most preferred gas manufactured from coal or crude oil. It was not until the 1920's that advances in pipeline technology, including the development of new metal alloys and welding techniques, made it possible to transport gas over long distances. Then demand for gas grew swiftly. It was cleaner and more manageable than petroleum or coal and, more importantly, it was much cheaper per unit of delivered energy. It reached customers over nearly half a million miles of pipeline. In the late 1950's gas overtook coal; by 1970 it had become the most important domestically produced source of energy in the United States, even surpassing petroleum. In 1984 it accounted for fully 26 percent of the energy produced in the country, supplying more than 20 of the 74 quads produced.[1]

Of the energy industries, natural gas is perhaps the most difficult to penetrate. In a purely technical sense it is the least complex, since the fuel itself requires very little processing between wellhead and final consumption. But in political, economic, and administrative terms, it presents formidable problems. If there is a key to untangling these, it lies in understanding the structural transformations that have taken place in the industry since the late 1930's, and in grasping the critical role that the government has played in these changes.

Regulation of natural gas began as the industry was just emerging in the 1930's, and it was imposed with the acquiescence of the private interests involved. The reasons were familiar: opportunities for the exercise of monopoly power had to be removed, or that power had to be contained and controlled, and the market had to be tamed to assure security and profits and to prevent a waste of resources.

As the gas regime became institutionalized, the industry began to change. This created new interests, which in turn undermined the original regulatory consensus. To make matters worse, the responsible federal agency, the Federal Power Commission (FPC), was increasingly unable to handle its expanding administrative responsibilities, especially when these came to include the setting of prices for gas sold to pipelines by independent producers. Consequently, the government was forced to experiment with different pricing formulas, each of which proved unsatisfactory to producers and led to long and expensive court challenges.

This complex process of political conflict and administrative adjustment exhausted and frustrated both the industry and the regulatory authorities, eventually resulting in a steady decline of gas reserves and then in shortages of this popular fuel. By the late 1960's the failure of the regulatory system was manifest and there had emerged a widespread agreement on the need for new rules of the game. It was at this point that the industry became entangled in the larger energy crisis that beset the country.

The Structure and Evolution of the Gas Industry

As with coal and oil, a grasp of the distinctive structural attributes of the gas industry is critical to understanding the way the resource has been allocated and the role the government has played in industry affairs. The first of these attributes is the association of the gas industry with the petroleum industry, beginning with the close physical relationship of the fuels themselves in the ground. A second is the absence of vertical integration in the industry. A third is the political and economic regionalization of the stakeholders in matters affecting natural gas. All of these are related, and all have gradually emerged over time, greatly complicating the task of governance.

The Link to Oil   Consider first the connection with oil. Most oil fields contain large amounts of natural gas; indeed, in the early days most natural gas sold was discovered in the search for oil.[2] Gas also exists in deposits that contain no petroleum, and as the fuel acquired market value over the years, exploration for fields containing only gas became increasingly common. But the exploration and drilling techniques have been similar for both.

Under these circumstances, it is not surprising that the petroleum industry came to dominate the production of natural gas. Gas and oil, for the most part, were joint products of the same activities. This, in turn, meant that "associated" natural gas was affected by the market conditions and regulatory controls that affected petroleum.

Like oil, gas suffered a propensity to dramatic price fluctuations owing to oversupply when new fields were discovered—actually the problem was even more severe at first because much gas could find no market at all unless a pipeline had been built to collect it. As one author has put it, when new oil fields were being opened up in the Southwest "gas production was plagued by hypercompetition, overproduction, and falling prices."[3]

When state-based prorationing to protect the petroleum industry went into effect in the 1930's, gas was regulated as well. The impact on the gas market, of course, was of secondary concern to the oil industry because gas was worth so little, but the control of supply was nevertheless real. The justification was the same: to prevent physical and "economic" waste of the resource.[4]

As might be expected, gas from the outset has tended to receive a much lower price, when measured by its energy content, than has petroleum. Where there was no pipeline, gas had little or no value; where there was, the pipeline was often in a position to exercise monopsony power with respect to those offering gas reserves for sale.

The fact that oil and gas are frequently joint products has greatly complicated regulatory efforts because it has made estimates of the "true" cost of gas development entirely artificial in the many instances where exploration, drilling, and production have involved, or even might have involved, both fuels. Under these conditions, prices set by regulators on the basis of information from one set of private investors in one field might have little applicability or pertinence to those exploring or developing another field close by.

One of the key changes that took place in the gas industry as it expanded is that the proportion of natural gas produced in direct association with petroleum steadily declined. As gas became more valuable, the search for it alone made more and more economic sense. In a geophysical sense, the industry became increasingly separate. Although oil interests, small and large, continued to dominate the production of gas, the fuel itself became increasingly independent, with a market of its own. In 1984, only 30 percent of the natural gas withdrawn was produced from oil wells, down from more than 50 percent in 1952. The rest came from wells that were producing only natural gas—though in some cases they may have been discovered as a result of exploration and drilling aimed at oil or oil and gas together.[5]

This meant that gas production was increasingly freed from the restrictions imposed by the petroleum prorationing system; it also meant that gas production was forced to stand on its own as an economic enterprise. Gas discovered and produced by itself could not rely on the artificially high price received for its co-product. As it happened, in the postwar years the demand for gas grew very rapidly, and therefore the liberation of the fuel from oil-derived supply restraint did not result in a widespread return to the staggering price fluctuations so often associated with fossil fuels. Where this did occur, as it did at times in both Kansas and Oklahoma, state regulatory agencies stepped in and set up price floors to govern sales to interstate pipelines.[6]

The Lack of Integration   A second key attribute of the natural gas industry is its lack of vertical integration. The gas industry is composed of three distinct activities: production, transport via pipeline, and distribution to individual end-users. Each of these is conducted by different groups of companies operating under different financial and market conditions and subject to different regulatory constraints. In this respect the industry differs markedly from the petroleum industry.

It was not always so. As with oil, the gas industry very early came under monopoly control. By the mid-1930's, a handful of financially powerful holding companies had consolidated their grip on the regime. Transportation was the key here too. Pipelines were expensive to build—indeed the cost of transportation and delivery has always been the larger part of the cost of gas paid by the consumer—and were in most respects "natural monopolies" in the sense that economic losses to society resulting from competition would have been very large.

As the industry grew, vertically integrated utility systems quickly arose as local distribution systems joined in financing pipelines, and these in turn sought control of gas resources to assure security of supply. By the mid-1930's four great utility holding companies controlled nearly 60 percent of the interstate pipelines, and had acquired vast tracts of producing lands.[7] These companies exercised their monopoly power at will, dividing up markets, controlling the distribution of natural gas to protect investments in more expensive municipal synthetic gas plants, and paying very low prices to independent producers who relied on them to market their gas.[8]

Widespread complaints against the holding companies led to hearings by the Federal Trade Commission (FTC) and then to Congressional action to curb their growing power. The resulting legislation, the Public Utility Holding Company Act of 1935, was one of the most far-reaching attempts by the U.S. government to restructure an industry to promote economic freedom and diversity, exceeding, in scope and consequences, the oil divestiture decision of 1911 by the Supreme Court.

Empowered by the Holding Company Act, the Securities and Exchange Commission (SEC) systematically dismantled the integrated gas industry. As one specialist put it: "Fifteen years after the Act, holding company control of interstate pipeline mileage was reduced from 80 percent to 18 percent. . . . After the mid-1940's, there was also a sharply declining trend in pipeline ownership of producing properties."[9] As a result of this process, the modern gas industry has little structural resemblance to the industry controlled by the utility giants of the 1920's and 1930's. The local distribution of gas is managed by a large number of public utilities of varying sizes. As "natural" monopolies, these are regulated by public commissions and agencies whose jurisdictions are limited to the states or localities within which the gas is distributed and consumed. The interstate transmission of natural gas is still the stronghold of a handful of very large companies, and is characterized by a relatively high degree of concentration. In 1980 the top four companies still delivered 22 percent of the gas sold in the interstate system, and the top 20 companies delivered 70 percent of the total natural gas consumed in the country.[10] However, because of the potential for monopoly in this market—most of the pipelines are the exclusive suppliers for their market areas—the interstate transmission business is closely regulated by federal authorities.

Finally, the actual production of gas is handled by a larger and much more diverse group of firms. A number of very large outfits, most of them oil companies, control significant shares of production. The largest, Exxon, in 1980 accounted for 6.3 percent of the gas produced, and sixteen of the top twenty integrated oil companies accounted for some 44 percent of the nation's total.[11] Although this proportion has been increasing in recent years, many thousands of smaller independent firms also produce gas, and entry into the business remains quite easy.

Because of the decision (described below) to extend federal regulation to field prices for natural gas destined for interstate sale, the question of the degree of competitiveness of the producing industry has been a subject of heated debate and controversy. A number of careful studies by economists demonstrated in the 1950's that there was, in fact, more competition in this industry than many critics believed. And available evidence suggests that this conclusion still applies. Indeed, it would appear that the gas-producing industry can be categorized as having "effective" or "workable" competition within the definition that specialists in the field apply to industrial and commercial activity more generally. This said, it should be added that this does not necessarily mean that this competition is, by itself, sufficient to protect the interests of consumers and the general public in this critical fuel.[12]

Vertical fragmentation led to political disunity within the industry as subsectors acquired their own perspectives and interests. Producers remained closely tied to the oil industry (via ownership) even though gas gradually emerged as a distinct and separable sector. Pipelines and distributors clustered together in the American Gas Association, the single most influential interest group in the industry. And city-owned utilities founded the American Public Gas Association to represent their views. Reflecting their different perspectives, representatives of these groups often found themselves on opposing sides in conflicts over gas policy.

Regionalization   The third key attribute of the natural gas system is its economic and political regionalization. By this I mean that major producers and consumers are found in different areas of the country and hence form different constituencies. The principal producing states are clustered in the Southwest; their customers are found in the Midwest and Northeast. Pipelines connect the two. Politically, these divisions are critically important.

Again, this was not always the case. Before the introduction of interstate pipelines, gas consumers, chiefly municipal utility districts and some large industrial customers, were able to draw fuels only from nearby fields. Appalachian gas went to some Eastern cities, and Ohio fields supplied some important centers in the Midwest. But cities far from fields had to manufacture their own gas or do without. Pipelines changed this: cities could now receive supplies from distant sources. As the oil industry moved west and south, long-distance shipment became more and more common. At the same time, the breakup of the holding companies fragmented the industry so that distributors and producers were no longer under the same management. The process was gradual, but profound in its consequences. As regulation extended to include more and more of the industry, decisions about markets and prices became increasingly politicized because consumers suspected the abuse of monopoly by distant "oil and gas" interests. Fearing that producers and unregulated transport companies were making large and unjustified profits, consumers turned to the courts and to Congress for protection.[13]

To recapitulate, several broad characteristics are especially important for understanding the character of the gas regime and how it has evolved. The first is its connection to petroleum and to the petroleum industry; the second is its lack of vertical integration, with closely regulated monopolies dominating transport and distribution and a more diverse and competitive group of companies prevailing in production; and the third is its political and economic regionalization. Finally, there is the fact that each of these has, in a sense, evolved from its opposite at an earlier time. Thus as Congress and regulators struggled to discover equitable and politically acceptable ways to manage the industry, the industry itself was changing in ways that would frustrate those efforts. From a minor by-product of oil production controlled by a handful of integrated companies, gas grew into a major separate industry controlled by regionally divided and managerially fragmented clusters of corporations. While responsible authorities sought to define workable rules of the game, the game itself and the players changed.

The Politics of Regulation

The federal government did not begin regulating the natural gas industry until 1938 with the passage of the Natural Gas Act. By this time, however, local and state authorities had already stepped in to control the activities of both distributors and producers. As a natural monopoly, the distribution of gas was from the very outset treated as a public utility, like water and sewage, and was regulated by public service commissions in most areas. The production of gas, as already mentioned, had come under the jurisdiction of state conservation and prorationing boards like the Texas Railroad Commission.

But these agencies could exert no jurisdiction over the interstate transportation of gas. It was to remedy this that Congress, in the aftermath of the FTC revelations about the abuses of gas holding companies, in 1938 brought interstate pipelines under the authority of the Federal Power Commission (FPC), which was already charged with supervising the interstate transmission of electricity.

The Natural Gas Act was carefully crafted, and it passed with little controversy.[14] The appropriateness of regulation as a remedy for monopoly was widely acknowledged at the time, and the Act itself contained the compromises necessary to avoid threatening the interests affected. The pipelines, the principal targets of the Act, avoided common carrier status, a key threat. And the producing companies won a guarantee that regulation would not extend to the prices paid for natural gas in the field—at least so they thought.[15]

In conferring authority to regulate the sale of gas for interstate commerce, the Act exempted "the production and gathering" of gas. Since the objective of the legislation was widely understood to be that of "closing the gap" in regulation, those involved assumed that the prices charged by producers would remain a concern of state authorities only.[16] But the wording of the Act was vague enough that the phrase "production and gathering" could be construed to mean only the physical activity of bringing the gas up and setting up means of delivering it to pipelines—not the pricing of the gas for interstate sale. This imprecision in drafting the law later provided the basis for an extension of the regulatory regime to encompass far more than was originally intended.[17]

At the time, the arrangement seemed ideal. Without challenging the federal-state separation of powers, the activities of a potential monopoly had been brought under comprehensive, if unintegrated, regulation to prevent waste and protect the public interest. States would control production and assure conservation of resources, the federal government would prevent price gouging by transport companies, and the cities and regional authorities would take care of local distribution and use. Private investors also accepted the arrangement, expecting federal regulators to grant a reasonable return on the large capital investments needed to build pipelines, and to be able to continue to operate under the protective supervision of state oil and gas commissions.

For many years the gas regime, thus arranged, worked in the expected way. The industry prospered, thanks in part to a stream of beneficial regulatory decisions. To be sure, disputes arose, and some of them led to court challenges. The FPC interpreted its mandate broadly, and vigorously asserted its control over the activities of the pipelines. Pipeline companies began to compete for the right to expand to new market areas, embroiling FTC commissioners in a number of difficult conflicts. And parties disagreed about the accounting methods used to determine a fair return to pipeline investments.[18] But the broad picture was one of a regulatory process that, by and large, was working.

Within a decade, however, the regime began to run into trouble. Structural changes in the industry created new stakes and interests, and the original consensus upon which the Act was founded began to erode. Regional conflicts emerged. It was now the consumers of the Midwest and Northeast against the producers of the South and Southwest. As gas became popular and demand increased, prices also increased. Soon these conflicts began to permeate the political process. Congress split into broad factions reflecting the interests of constituents. Commissioners, dependent on the President for appointment and Congress for confirmation, became targets in the political struggle.[19]

Conflicts between consuming and producing regions focused increasingly on whether the FPC should regulate the prices of natural gas sold to interstate pipelines by producers. The Natural Gas Act, of course, appeared to prohibit this. But the FPC, charged with regulating monopoly, had successfully extended its jurisdiction to include the price of gas produced by integrated companies for their own interstate trade, and consumers began to press for control of all prices for gas sold for interstate commerce.[20] As Sanders put it: "Where a Louisiana Congressman saw thousands of farmers and small businessmen drilling for gas on modest leaseholds, a Michigan senator saw giant monopolies sanctioned by the producer states themselves, and determined to charge their distant customers all that the traffic would bear."[21]

By the early 1950's the lines were drawn. Gas regulation was the subject of a continuing stream of legislative proposals, and the FPC was caught in the middle. After regulators asserted control over integrated companies, producer interests realized that the protection afforded by the "production and gathering" clause in the original Act was insufficient and made repeated efforts to pass legislation limiting the powers of the Commission. One of these, a bill introduced by Senator Kerr of Oklahoma in 1949, actually passed both houses but was vetoed by President Truman because he suspected monopolistic practices in the industry.

Under heavy political pressure, the FPC practiced greater self-restraint after the Republican electoral victory in 1952. As early as 1951, though, a majority of the FPC agreed on a restrictive interpretation of its authority to control the prices of gas sold by independent producers. This interpretation, however, was quickly challenged by the state of Wisconsin on behalf of its consumers, and the case went to the Supreme Court.

The judgment of the Court in *Phillips Petroleum Company* v. *The State of Wisconsin*, handed down in 1954, represents a turning point in the governance of natural gas as important as the Natural Gas Act itself. In a sense, it reflected the disintegration of the compromises upon which that Act rested. The industry had changed, and the New Deal law was now politically obsolete. Badly divided, the Congress had been unable to create new rules, and the problem had fallen in the lap of the Supreme Court.

A divided Court ruled in favor of Wisconsin and consumer interests, reversing the FPC. The FPC, it found, did have the authority to regulate prices set by independent producers for gas entering interstate commerce. The FPC would now be forced to govern thousands and thousands of sales by producers, small and large. More importantly, these sales would for the first time be within the political "reach" of consumers. The era of compensatory regulation had begun.

In a structural sense, the *Phillips* decision unified the gas regime by breaking the barrier between federal control of transmission and state management of production—a barrier, incidentally, that the petroleum industry had successfully maintained. Fearful that competition was not protecting their interests, consumers could now appeal to federal regulators to help them. Only the prices of gas sold within the state where it was produced, or sold directly to industrial users across state boundaries, would be exempt from FPC regulation.

In the energy sector, the nearest parallel to the task handed the FPC by the Court was the one faced by the Bituminous Coal Commission. Unfortunately, the Court seems to have paid little attention to the clear lessons afforded by that historical example.

The *Phillips* decision provoked a burst of political activity aimed at reversing the Court's *dictum*. Arguing that their business was competitive and that the nature of high-risk gas investments made standard regulatory price formulas inappropriate, producers pressed Congress to limit FPC authority. The oil industry, with interests in gas and in limiting the intrusion of federal regulators into state affairs, joined the campaign. Arrayed against these were representatives of Northern cities and consuming states, as well as their public service commissions.

Not surprisingly, the producers prevailed, and in 1956 Congress passed the Harris-Fulbright deregulation bill and sent it to President Eisenhower for his signature. At the last minute, however, Eisenhower announced that he would not sign the bill—despite his philosophical support for deregulation—because it had been tainted when an oil-company lobbyist sought to influence the outcome by making a campaign contribution to Senator Francis Case of South Dakota. Eisenhower's veto took the steam out of the deregulation drive. In subsequent years Congress considered many bills designed to achieve the same goal, but none passed.

In the meantime, the structure of the gas market itself became bifurcated. At the intrastate level, where prices were not federally regulated, prices and production incentives diverged from those that obtained for gas destined to be sold to the regulated interstate market. This bifurcation gradually worsened as the federal regulatory system took hold.

While the Congress and the President struggled over whether to let the Court's decision stand, the FPC itself began to sink into an administrative quagmire from which it never really recovered. Faced with the task of setting prices for many thousands of separate gas sales, it began in 1954 by suspending rate increases until it could complete studies of the matter. By 1957, three years later, it had completed its analysis of only a fraction of the changes requested by producers. Clearly, the agency was not equipped to handle the new job that had been thrust upon it.[22]

But the problem was even more serious. The standard approach to utility price regulation was to estimate an average cost of production and to set prices to allow investors to recover these costs and earn a just and reasonable rate of profit. For a few very large companies with lots of fixed capital, like pipeline companies, this was difficult but manageable. For thousands of investors of different sizes, with different ratios of gas-to-oil and different degrees of risk, regulation in this fashion was, quite literally, impossible. Even in theory, the separate costs and profits of joint products like oil and gas could not be separated out by any noncontroversial means.

The FPC struggled with this dilemma and finally decided that the only way it could manage was by setting broad regional ceiling prices that reflected average costs of production for the areas of the country involved. Accordingly, in 1960 it set interim prices based on the highest prices obtaining in regional markets and began to determine if average costs were such as to justify increases or decreases.[23] This approach was challenged in court by producers on the grounds that an average cost approach made no sense in an industry with such large elements of risk, but the Supreme Court, caught now in a web of its own spinning, upheld the FPC.

Although the new approach was administratively more manageable, it was a clumsy and heavy-handed way to regulate an industry with such an enormous variety of producers and cost and profit conditions. Most importantly, it did not respond to the need for higher prices to bring forth new gas reserves as the old ones became depleted. As Paul MacAvoy has characterized the problem: "Market-clearing prices—those bringing forth more reserves from producers equal to the buyers' demands for more reserves—are set by the marginal costs for more gas, not the average costs used in finding the ceiling prices. . . . The marginal costs of additional supply exceed the average cost in a competitive market for a wasting resource so that market-clearing marginal cost prices exceed the regulatory ceiling prices."[24] Put succinctly, any approach that does not assure the possibility of increasing prices for new reserves will tend to stifle exploration for them. Average price ceilings, no matter how high, cannot approximate such prices. Nor can they provide incentives for new investments in marginal areas where higher risks are involved.

When the FPC finally began to set area prices—first in the Permian Basin in the Southwest and then in southern Louisiana—it acknowledged this problem and adopted a multitiered method that set higher prices for "new" gas in order to provide incentives for discovery without allowing the higher prices paid for new reserves to be passed back to those already discovered.[25] But even these "new" gas prices were based on average cost calculations and would necessarily tend to lag behind those that might have been obtained in competitive markets.

To complicate matters, the political climate changed abruptly with the election of John Kennedy in 1960, and the FPC changed its orientation to accommodate the pro-consumer outlook of the new President and the new Democratic Congress. Using the area prices as an instrument, the Commission now began to hold prices down well below the market-clearing levels that obtained in the unregulated intrastate market (which still accounted for about one third of the sales of gas). In several instances, once the area rates had been determined, the Commission even ordered companies to make refunds to customers.[26]

By integrating the industry within one governing framework, the change in the gas regime forced by the Supreme Court made it possible for consumer interests to use the FPC and price controls as a means of redistributing income from one region of the country to another. In her careful study of natural gas regulation, Sanders has clearly documented this process.[27] Within the industry it was the producers and the producing regions that bore the brunt of this change. Pipelines continued to prosper, passing the lower gas prices on to their customers. And the local distribution utilities, though somewhat troubled by demands for gas that they could not meet, for the most part continued to work in comfortable relationships with their regulators.

The stakes were high. If we assume, for example, that without FPC control intrastate prices would have been representative of market-clearing prices at the interstate level, then a difference of three cents per thousand cubic feet (which was in fact exceeded by 1970) would have signified between 400 and 500 million dollars per year.

Although the shift to compensatory regulation within the gas regime clearly benefited consumers in the short run by lowering the price of gas for homeowners and commercial users, it also sent the producing industry into decline. The symptoms of this decline gradually accumulated in the 1960's. The clearest was a shortage of gas reserves. Annual discoveries of new gas had dropped from 6.6 trillion cubic feet in 1960 to less than 4 trillion in 1969.[28] By 1970, more was being consumed every year than was being added to reserves. More importantly, the reserves-to-production ratio, which in the 1950's stood at twenty or higher—reflecting the historic standard set by pipelines of twenty years guaranteed supply for new markets—by 1969 had dropped to just over thirteen.[29] This reduction occurred during a period of rapid growth in demand, which increased by 60 percent in the decade after 1960.

The trouble in the industry was at first difficult to perceive by consumers since they were drawing on multiyear contracts for reserves, and hence experienced no interruption of supplies. But communities seeking new gas service found it increasingly difficult to obtain. In Chicago, Pennsylvania, and New Jersey, customers were denied gas hookups by pipelines unable to purchase reserve commitments even though they were willing to pay higher prices for them.[30] As might be expected, producers also increased their intrastate sales, taking advantage of the higher, unregulated prices in these markets. By 1970, 77 percent of new gas sales were being made within the producing states themselves.[31]

The precise causes of the decline in the gas-producing industry became the subject of intense political conflict and technical disagreement. Economists pointed out the difficulties inherent in the regulatory system, explaining the shortage as the logical consequence of "artificially" low prices. Supporters of regulation countered by noting that the gas reserves were still very large, and that the FPC had made a special effort to provide incentives for the discovery of new gas. They also charged that producers had good reason to postpone investments and hold back reserves because they expected that the "crisis" in gas would force the FPC to allow higher prices.[32]

In the event, all these explanations were correct. It was certain, as MacAvoy noted, that the structure of prices set by the FPC would tend to deter marginal investments in exploration and drilling, especially in the more risky areas. And once the decline of the industry began, it quickly became self-reinforcing as it became evident that the FPC would soon have to raise prices. No collusion was necessary. More and more producers found it expedient to postpone investments or hold reserves off the market. Thus if the incentives to find and produce new gas were insufficient at the outset, they became increasingly so as the crisis worsened.

Insofar as production was concerned, the gas regime by 1970 had reached the point where accommodation was imperative. The price of gas had become embroiled in a complex bargaining process between consumers and producers, with the FPC caught in the middle. Moreover, the country was so sharply split, geographically, that Congress was paralyzed. New deregulation bills were introduced, but none could pass. Consumer interests, taking advantage of the Supreme Court's action, succeeded in holding prices down. Producers responded by withholding investment and, where possible, reserves. The result was a shortage of the nation's principal domestic energy source.

The prospects for political compromise seemed good. The arrival of the Nixon Administration in 1969 brought a political climate more supportive of producer interests. Consumers unable to obtain gas were willing to pay higher prices. The FPC responded by reopening rate proceedings in several key areas, with a view to permitting higher prices for new gas, and took a number of administrative steps that allowed increased prices in return for greater supply for interstate pipelines.[33] In sum, the conditions seemed ripe for price adjustments that would, in turn, improve incentives for exploration, drill-

TABLE 2

Natural Gas Wellhead Prices, 1950–85

($/1,000 cu. ft.)

Year	Current prices	Constant prices[a]	Year	Current prices	Constant prices[a]	Year	Current prices	Constant prices[a]
1950	0.07	0.29	1962	0.16	0.50	1974	0.30	0.56
1951	0.07	0.28	1963	0.16	0.49	1975	0.45	0.76
1952	0.08	0.31	1964	0.15	0.46	1976	0.58	0.92
1953	0.09	0.35	1965	0.16	0.47	1977	0.79	1.17
1954	0.10	0.38	1966	0.16	0.46	1978	0.91	1.26
1955	0.10	0.37	1967	0.16	0.45	1979	1.18	1.50
1956	0.11	0.39	1968	0.16	0.42	1980	1.59	1.86
1957	0.11	0.38	1969	0.17	0.43	1981	1.98	2.11
1958	0.12	0.40	1970	0.17	0.40	1982	2.46	2.46
1959	0.13	0.43	1971	0.18	0.41	1983	2.59	2.49
1960	0.14	0.45	1972	0.19	0.41	1984	2.66	2.46
1961	0.15	0.48	1973	0.22	0.44	1985	2.48	2.22

SOURCE: United States [23], 1985:155.
[a]Constant prices are in 1982 dollars.

ing, and the sale of reserves. Having reached a stalemate, the parties at interest had realized that they had to come to terms. And in fact prices, on the average, soon began to creep upward. (See Table 2).

Conclusions

Like coal and oil, the natural gas industry was born vulnerable to market instability. Unlike these fuels, however, its status as a natural monopoly at the point of sale brought consumers into the gas regime as participants from the outset. The first arrangements to control competition proved unsustainable: monopolization via holding companies succumbed to widespread hostility and federal intervention; state-based prorationing and pricing independence gave way to federal regulation fueled by consumer political pressures.

In political terms, gas producers benefited heavily for many years from their association with the petroleum industry. Not only did they receive many of the same subsidies, but their success in maintaining the barrier between state-based supply regulation and price regulation at other stages was possible only because of their ties with oil. But, as a regime, gas evolved separately, and its regionalization, structural decomposition, and sheer growth in importance increased its vulnerability to compensatory intervention as the political climate changed.

The outcome of this process was the emergence—following the

Supreme Court decision to extend FPC authority to the regulation of field prices by independent producers—of one of the least satisfactory arrangements for governing economic life to emerge in any major industry in the United States. To begin with, it created a host of unproductive and illogical distortions in resource allocation. Such distortions exist in most areas of economic activity, and are often the result of public intervention. Though they are undesirable on efficiency grounds, they may be justified as a means of attaining other, legitimate goals of public policy. But in the case of gas producers these distortions more often than not made no sense; on the contrary, they reduced the country's capacity to attain the very goals in behalf of which the system had been established and was operated—to assure plentiful supplies at the lowest possible cost over the long term.

The clearest example of this is the price controls maintained in behalf of consumers. Although these reduced prices to levels below those they might have otherwise reached, they also stimulated demand and reduced incentives to find and sell more gas. Those able to buy gas often used it in ways that were economically inefficient because the price signals they received were misleading; those without gas but willing to pay higher prices for it could not get it and used other fuels instead, thereby distorting the market for the products produced with them. In the short run, some consumers—those with hookups—benefited (unless their supplies were interrupted), but in the long run all consumers suffered because of the decline in the industry and because the bargaining process created by regulation almost certainly resulted in higher prices for new gas than would have been required under competitive conditions.

To make matters worse, these efforts to help consumers took place within a broader framework of economic distortions of other kinds. Recall that gas and oil are, to a significant extent, substitutes as well as co-products. This means that the system of controls designed to raise and stabilize the price of oil, including such things as prorationing arrangements and import controls, had an impact on gas as well. Insofar as substitution decisions were based on oil prices, gas demand was artificially stimulated and sellers could receive a higher price.

Finally, there is the impact of tax incentives and subsidies to consider. Generally speaking, subsidies received by the oil companies were also available to gas producers, including the depletion allowance and the expensing of intangible drilling costs. To the extent that these were consumed as profits, they did not decrease prices but did attract investors to gas development (along with petroleum), resulting in a faster depletion of the nation's resources; to the extent that they were used to lower prices, they once again distorted the use of resources in ways that had little relationship to broad public-policy objectives.

The precise impact of this jumble of controls, restrictions, subsidies, and incentives is hard to measure with any accuracy. The point here is that there was little or no coherent relationship between the objectives of the regulatory process and the economic results attained. The allocation of resources was altered in significant ways, with the attendant economic inefficiencies, but in a manner that was difficult to measure and that almost certainly made no sense. Those who were supposed to benefit did not, or did so in ways that were inequitable or temporary.

Among the energy experts who have studied the regulation of natural gas there has been a tendency to "blame" government intervention for distortions of the kind just described. And it is true, as we have seen, that the regulation of producer prices, imposed despite the opposition of the industry, was important. However, of the kinds of distortions mentioned—price regulation, production controls supporting oil (and gas) prices, and subsidies—two were of the industry's own design and were carefully cultivated and protected by the interests involved. These distortions, while contributing to the welfare of the oil and gas industry at the expense of energy efficiency, were less "visible" than price controls but might easily have been more costly to the country in economic terms. Subsidies and supply control "work" because they disappear from the public mind and are not likely objects of political conflict. Subsidies require no ongoing political process; and supply controls require one that is limited to consenting partners. Controlled prices, in contrast, must be set again and again, and are thus more visible and more accessible to political interests.

The gas regime also suffered from a problem that was more serious than that of purposeless inefficiency in resource allocation. It had built-in self-destructive tendencies that created recurrent episodes of malaise in the industry. The source of these was the complex bargaining process between consumers and producers, mediated by the FPC, which was suffused with mistrust. Consumers had a strong immediate interest in low prices, and were capable of securing these in a political process that increasingly favored them as the gas industry expanded. Producers, however, had bargaining power of their own—they could withhold investments and refuse to commit reserves. Over time, as stakeholders exercised their power, a compromise became mandatory.

In 1970 the industry had reached the culmination of an episode of this kind, and compromise on price had already begun. But the industry had suffered as a result. Political tensions mounted, as did levels of mistrust. Compromises, when they came, could not make up for the losses associated with industry stagnation, nor could they prevent the onset of still another "round" of conflict as costs of production went up, resources became depleted, and producers again found prices unsatisfactory.

Built-in conflict, in other words, created a kind of degenerative instability in the gas industry, one that could be expected to continue in the future. Ironically, the same polarization that created this interregional conflict also paralyzed Congress, the only institution with the power to restructure the regime itself. As is the case with the direct price distortions created by price regulation and subsidies, the economic consequences of this degenerative process are impossible to estimate with any precision, but they are certainly very large. So are the political costs.

The experiences of the gas regime are extremely important to the study of energy governance in the United States. They illustrate clearly the pressures that lead to private and public market management. And to a considerable extent, the problems with compensatory regulation in gas, clearly visible in the decade before the energy crisis, also represent a preview of the difficulties and failures that would mark the government's effort to fashion a similar system for petroleum after 1973. Even more importantly, many of the conditions that made such unproductive, indeed destructive, compensatory regulation likely in the gas regime are sure to recur in the future in all the energy regimes. These include market instability, interregional conflict, consumer assertiveness, and the propensity of the government to respond to demands for protection in a manner that is ad hoc, incremental, and uninformed by any coherent principles concerning the governance of the economic system.

CHAPTER 5   Electricity

There is probably no better measure of technical advancement in the modern world than the spread of the secondary form of energy that we call electricity. Although many of us take electricity for granted, many older Americans remember clearly the changes in family and community life that came with electricity. They recall when power lines brought light to their towns and made possible the use of so many valued appliances and services. The availability of electricity, in America and the rest of the world, has been intimately associated with the industrial revolution, economic growth, and the improvement of living standards.

Between the 1880's, when the first municipal distribution systems were set up by Charles Brush and Thomas Edison, and the early 1970's, the electricity industry in the United States grew steadily in size, technical sophistication, and importance for the operation of the rest of the economy.[1] And it grew in a very "American" style: at first in many small pieces, owned and managed in different ways and regulated by cities; then under the sway of financial barons seeking to bring "order" and "stability" while collecting handsome rewards; and finally with the increasing, but far from systematic, involvement of both state and federal authorities seeking to assure compliance with broader public objectives.

Reflecting this pattern of historical development, the governance of electricity today is a complicated mosaic. Unlike the other energy regimes, it is made up entirely of franchised monopolies in which price and supply are formally regulated by government agencies. Although privately owned utilities predominate, cities and the federal government are also significant participants in production and distribution. Market relationships play very little part in decision-making within the regime. Electricity competes with other fuels, but vendors rarely compete directly with one another for customers.[2] The legal authority to regulate electric monopolies rests primarily in the hands of state authorities, but over the years the federal government has taken an ever more important part in shaping the evolution of the industry, first through the New Deal's promotional policies and federal power projects, and later through the push to assure the rapid growth of nuclear power in the United States and abroad.

In the first years after the Arab oil embargo, the electricity industry appeared to be less vulnerable to the crisis than the other energy industries. It was, in many respects, less directly affected by petroleum price increases, since electricity did not compete with oil in the way that natural gas and coal did, and many people expected that the higher costs imposed by price increases in fuels used to generate power would simply be passed on to consumers. It has since become clear that this optimism was unjustified. For a variety of reasons, technical as well as institutional and political, the crisis shook the regime to its very foundations, leaving a legacy of financial insolvency, technological uncertainty, and political tension that persisted long after the decade of crisis ended.

The Role of Capital and Technical Innovation

There are important structural reasons for the electricity industry's vulnerability. To begin with, electric utilities are the most capital-intensive industry in the country. This means that utility companies hold and manage more capital assets, and draw upon more of the country's available investment funds, than any other sector of the economy. In 1982, for example, the industry committed more than $31 billion to construction, an amount that represented 9 percent of the nonresidential fixed business investments in the domestic economy.[3] Its capital-intensive nature also means that the industry as a whole is unusually sensitive to changes in the availability of investment funds and the risks involved in using them to build such things as power plants, substations, and transmission lines. Such factors as investor confidence, inflation, interest rates, technology, and construction schedules all have to be taken into account. Furthermore, the approach chosen by regulators to calculate earnings for utilities, a set rate of return on capital investment, creates a strong incentive for utilities to meet demand by continuing to invest in large-scale plants, thereby accumulating even more capital assets.[4]

A second feature of the electricity industry that has shaped its ability to adjust to the changes that occurred after 1973 is its history of technical innovation and the institutional incentives to which this gave rise. Improvements in the generation, transmission, and use of electricity contributed, for nearly a century, to the rapid growth of the industry by reducing the cost of electric power to the user. The real price of electricity, in fact, declined over the entire history of electric generation until the early 1970's (See Fig. 2).[5] Most notable of these technical changes, especially in the years after the Second World War, were the increases in scale efficiency that made it possible for companies, by building bigger and bigger generating plants, to produce cheaper electricity. As the economist Duane Chapman put it: "For approximately 80 years, larger size meant lower cost of generation. In 1893, General Electric built two 0.8-megawatt generators. In the 1980's, 1,000-megawatt facilities are common."[6]

This meant that nearly everyone involved could benefit from a rapid increase in consumption and the resulting expansion of the industry's generating capacity. Consumers would enjoy cheaper power; managers of the utility companies could increase revenues and reap the rewards of organizational growth and expansion; investors would prosper; and the economy as a whole would expe-

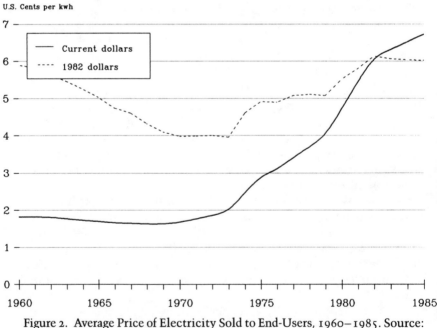

Figure 2. Average Price of Electricity Sold to End-Users, 1960–1985. Source: United States [23], 1985: 201.

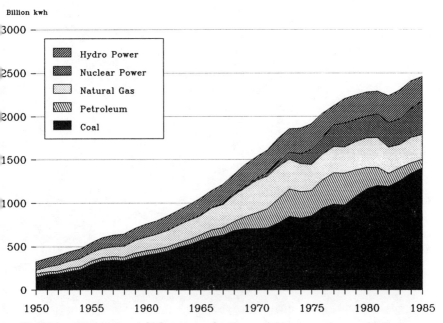

Billion kwh

Hydro Power
Nuclear Power
Natural Gas
Petroleum
Coal

Figure 3. Generation of Electricity by Energy Source, 1950–1985. Source: United States [23], 1985: 185.

rience declining cost for this increasingly important factor of production. Accordingly, policies promoting growth in consumption were adopted by utilities and their regulatory agencies everywhere. Declining block rates for very large users created incentives for industrial consumption, while advertising campaigns and the introduction of new products using electricity—from tooth brushes and carving knives to entire "electric homes"—boosted demand among individual users. (See Fig. 3 and Table 3.)

Declining prices and technical advances also created a distinctive set of managerial attitudes in the electricity industry. One of these was a kind of technological optimism, born of so many years of incremental improvements. This almost certainly contributed to the willingness to accept flawed predictions, in the 1950's and 1960's, about the lower prospective costs of nuclear power plants.[7] Another involved attitudes toward uncertainty. The markets involved remained steady and predictable: hydroelectricity costs, once dams were built, did not increase; and the prices of coal and oil, heavily influenced by the latter as the marginal fuel, held steady or declined for decades. Electricity demand and production expanded steadily,

TABLE 3
Net Generation of Electricity by Energy Source, 1950–85
(Billion kwh)

Year	Coal	Petro-leum	Natural gas	Nuclear power	Hydro power	Geother-mal[a]	Total
1950	155	34	45	0	96	0	330
1951	185	29	57	0	100	0	371
1952	195	30	68	0	105	0	398
1953	219	38	80	0	105	0	442
1954	239	32	94	0	107	0	472
1955	301	37	95	0	113	0	546
1956	339	36	104	0	122	0	601
1957	346	40	114	0	130	0	630
1958	344	40	120	0	140	0	644
1959	378	47	147	0	138	0	710
1960	403	48	158	1	146	0	756
1961	422	49	169	2	152	0	794
1962	450	49	184	2	169	0	854
1963	494	52	202	3	166	0	917
1964	526	57	220	3	177	0	983
1965	571	65	222	4	194	0	1,056
1966	613	79	251	6	195	1	1,145
1967	630	89	265	8	222	1	1,215
1968	685	104	304	13	222	1	1,329
1969	706	138	333	14	250	1	1,442
1970	704	184	373	22	248	1	1,532
1971	713	220	374	38	266	1	1,612
1972	771	274	376	54	273	2	1,750
1973	848	314	341	83	272	2	1,860
1974	828	301	320	114	301	3	1,867
1975	853	289	300	173	300	3	1,918
1976	944	320	295	191	284	4	2,038
1977	985	358	306	251	220	4	2,124
1978	976	365	305	276	280	3	2,205
1979	1,075	304	329	255	280	4	2,247
1980	1,162	246	346	251	276	6	2,287
1981	1,203	206	346	273	261	6	2,295
1982	1,192	147	305	283	309	5	2,241
1983	1,259	144	274	294	332	6	2,309
1984	1,342	120	297	328	321	9	2,417
1985	1,401	100	292	384	282	11	2,470

SOURCE: United States [23], 1985:185.

[a]Geothermal includes an unspecified category of "other" sources, of very minor importance.

doubling every decade.[8] Utilities even maintained a favorable place in financial markets, chiefly owing to their status as publicly regulated monopolies with guaranteed rates of return, and thus had little difficulty obtaining funds. Under these circumstances, it is not surprising that industry leaders settled into conservative administrative routines that emphasized engineering feats rather than risk management. The principal measure of success came to be the ability of utility executives to plan, build, and bring on line new capacity.

Although technical improvement continues today in the generation, transmission, and use of electricity, it appears that the limit to scale efficiencies was reached in the late 1960's and early 1970's. For steam-driven generators, plants in the 500- to 1,000-megawatt range now represent the largest installations that can be built before costs cease to decline. This means that the historic formula of profits and price reductions through growth in scale, which served the industry so well, is no longer appropriate—nor are the attitudes and managerial approaches that went with it.

The Structure and Evolution of the Electric Utility Industry

Electric power in the United States is supplied to customers by more than 3,400 separate entities, which, all told, have an installed capacity of some 620,000 megawatts and sell, to more than 90 million customers, about 2.3 trillion kilowatt hours of electricity.[9] (See Table 4.) The entities are of many kinds and exist in a variety of configurations in different states and regions of the country. They include private, investor-owned utilities; cooperatives; publicly owned utilities; federal power agencies; power pools; and electric reliability councils. These primary actors, in turn, support a large industry specializing in the production of equipment for generation, transmission, distribution, and consumption of electricity.

As Table 4 makes clear, the large, private, investor-owned utilities dominate the business. Though few in number, the 217 private utilities account for more than three-fourths of the business, whether measured by installed capacity or customers served. The largest six of these companies in 1979 accounted for 26 percent of the sales of all investor-owned utilities.[10] And the degree of concentration of control in the industry has been increasing in the last two decades.[11]

As was the case with coal, oil, and natural gas, the first years of the electric utility industry were marked by vigorous competition among companies seeking to provide service to new customers. But as the industry grew, it rapidly came under the control of enterprising individuals quick to sense opportunities for profit in consolidation. Weak federal oversight, coupled with decisions by municipalities, and later by states, to treat utilities as "natural monopolies" (the costs of duplicate distribution systems being uneconomical), facilitated the process. Financial control groups, the most notorious

TABLE 4

U.S. Electric Power System Statistics, 1980

Type of system (and number)	Installed capacity		Kwh generation		Customers		Electric operating revenues		Net electric plant investment[a]	
	Megawatts	Percent	Millions of kwh	Percent	Number	Percent	Millions of dollars	Percent	Millions of dollars	Percent
Local public systems (2,248)	67,568	10.9%	204,880	9.0%	12,467,700	13.5%	$12,224	10.8%	$34,100	11.9%
Privately owned systems (217)	476,979	77.1	1,782,545	78.0	70,620,300	76.2	87,062	76.9	207,555	72.4
Rural electric cooperatives (924)	15,425	2.5	63,557	2.8	9,523,600	10.3	9,707	8.6	23,892	8.3
Federal power agencies (8)	59,078	9.5	235,051	10.3	13,300	0.01	4,238	3.7	21,100	7.3
Total	619,050	100.0%	2,286,033	100.0%	92,624,900	100.0%	$113,231	100.0%	$286,647	100.0%

SOURCE: United States [10]:55, from "Public Power Directory," *Public Power*, Jan.–Feb. 1982.
[a]Does not include nuclear fuel.

under the direction of utility magnate Samuel Insull, assembled vast and complicated holding companies that then engaged in a wide variety of duplicitous schemes to increase their profits.[12]

By the time the movement to consolidate utilities in paper empires had reached its peak in the late 1920's, control had become highly concentrated. As a federal investigation into the problem reported: "By 1932, thirteen large holding company groups controlled three-fourths of the entire privately owned electric utility industry, and more than forty percent was concentrated in the hands of the three largest groups—United Corporation, Electric Bond and Share Company, and Insull."[13]

At the same time that it restructured the natural gas industry, the Securities and Exchange Commission (SEC) reorganized the electric utility industry. The onset of the Great Depression brought many of the abuses of holding company schemes to light, and investors, consumers, and politicians concurred in the need for regulation. As it turned out, the Holding Company Act and the work of the SEC in succeeding years still represent one of the most decisive campaigns by federal regulators to reshape the structure of a sector of the economy. (The court-ordered divestiture of the petroleum industry, of course, represents another instance, and it remains to be seen if the deregulatory efforts of the 1970's and 1980's will bear similar fruit.) Though the total number of private power systems continued to decline, the SEC succeeded, over several decades, in breaking up the control of the holding companies and reducing the abuses that had come to plague the industry.[14]

The federal government changed the structure of the electricity industry in other ways during the New Deal. Drawing on his experience with public ownership and promotion of electric power development in New York State, FDR created the Tennessee Valley Authority (TVA) and the Bonneville Power Administration (BPA), the former to manage what would become the country's most ambitious regional development experiment, and the latter to distribute power generated by dams built by the federal government in the Northwest.[15] These established a federal presence in the generation and transmission of electricity that would later expand to include the Southwestern, Southeastern, Alaska, and Western Area Power Administrations.[16]

Roosevelt also created the Rural Electrification Administration (REA) and gave it the job of subsidizing the distribution of cheap electricity to the rural areas of the country—areas the utilities often neglected because of the high cost of transmission lines. The lending policies of the REA in turn stimulated the growth of the rural electric cooperative movement, still another institutional alternative to the privately owned utilities. The cooperatives proved an effective instrument in the enlargement of rural electric distribution.[17]

By the mid-1940's the industry had acquired most of the structural diversity that now characterizes it. Two additional components, however, were added in the years before the crisis. The first of these was a set of "power pools" and regional electric reliability councils, and the second was the nuclear power industry. Power pools are agreements between utilities designed to permit sharing of power and coordination of supply. They became increasingly important as the scale of facilities increased, making it necessary for utilities to cooperate in building generating capacity. They resulted in the formation of service networks, or grids, that were much larger than the districts served by individual utilities.

The interdependent grids created by power pools, however, also increased the vulnerability of electricity systems to large-scale blackouts, a problem that became evident in a dramatic fashion with the massive power failure of 1965.[18] The blackout, which cut off an area extending from New York City all the way to southern Canada, led to the formation of nine regional electric reliability councils and one overarching national council. Their job was to assure more careful planning among utilities. The councils are voluntary in nature, but have become increasingly important in coordinating the activities of individual utilities.

The nuclear power industry was the offspring of military research and development work in atomic energy after the Second World War. The first American prototype civilian power reactor was built at Shippingsport, Pennsylvania, and began supplying power to the grid in 1957.[19] Then, beginning in the mid-1960's, first General Electric and then Westinghouse and several other manufacturers began to build reactors for the generation of electricity. As the number of new orders grew in the next few years, it began to appear that nuclear plants would rapidly replace oil- and coal-fired power facilities as the preferred technology. By the late 1960's, utilities had ordered nearly fifty plants with a generating capacity of about 40,000 megawatts.[20]

The sudden emergence of the nuclear industry, an emergence that was possible only because of government promotion and subsidy—a theme to which I will return—added a complex new dimension to the political economy of electricity. Nuclear power depends for its success on the transformation and management of a dangerous and exotic fuel, which in turn requires a series of expensive and technologically complex operations—stages in what is known as the "nuclear fuel cycle." Uranium has to be discovered, mined, processed, enriched, transported, and, after use in expensive and complex power plants, stored and then reprocessed. Waste products have to be disposed of in such a way as to inspire confidence that public safety will be protected.[21]

The different stages of the nuclear fuel cycle have different structural attributes, and the role of competition among the key actors has from the outset been heavily influenced by the presence of the federal government. Overall, the nuclear power industry is highly concentrated, but the part with the most diverse membership—involved in the mining and milling of uranium ore—is dominated by petroleum companies. More than half of the milling capacity in the United States is directly owned by petroleum companies, and the remainder is owned by companies affiliated with them or also owning oil production facilities.[22]

As was the case in the early years of the petroleum industry, an effective (albeit illegal) international cartel emerged in the early 1970's to manage the market for uranium ore. In meetings in the capitals of producing countries, eighteen corporate groups allocated quotas and set prices in an effort to control competition. As a result, prices rose sevenfold in a few years.[23] An interesting feature of this cartel is that the governments of several countries—among them Australia, South Africa, France, and Canada—were active participants. The major American conspirator, Gulf Oil Corporation, was eventually caught and forced to make restitution to some of the customers damaged by its actions.[24]

The other stages of the nuclear industry are much more concentrated: in 1980 four or fewer corporations controlled the entire activity in each. In one of these, the reactor construction business, competition for sales became extremely intense during the 1960's when it appeared that the industry was headed for continuing growth. As the analyst I. C. Bupp has noted, this competition, to an extent promoted by government policies, resulted in a kind of "bandwagon" market in which the dominant firms—General Electric, Westinghouse, Babcock and Wilcox, and Combustion Engineering—sought to outbid one another, giving generous supplemental guarantees and repeatedly revising downward their estimated costs of nuclear electricity.[25] This was important because the existence of major capital commitments to nuclear facilities, after the onset of the energy crisis, was a principal source of trouble for the electricity regime.

The Politics of Regulation

If there is a single word that characterizes the impact of regulation in the electricity regime in the years before the energy crisis, it is "promotion." Though some municipalities took the lead in utility regulation, electricity producers, as the industry grew, nearly all eventually came under the jurisdiction of state authorities, usually in the form of state public utilities commissions.[26] These determined the right to provide service—usually by requiring certificates of public convenience and necessity—as well as the rates that could be charged. Private utility companies tended to favor the imposition of state regulation as a means of controlling rampant competition and avoiding municipal ownership.[27] Furthermore, state commissions proved easy to dominate: they were no match, politically and financially, for the holding companies. As in the case of natural gas, legal disputes over the accounting methods used in determining fair rates of return also weakened regulatory authorities. Regulatory commissions were able to influence company behavior with confidence only after the Supreme Court in 1944 concluded that judicial involvement was inappropriate so long as the effect of rate decisions was "just and reasonable."[28]

Even as state commissions gradually became more assertive in exercising regulatory functions, however, the general orientation of regulation remained promotional. Rates were set to expand markets by encouraging the use of electricity and the construction of new facilities. The reason for this, as noted earlier, was that the collective interest of the parties involved was the same on this point. Declining marginal costs resulting from technical innovation and economies of scale meant that growing consumption resulted in reduced prices, greater profits, and solid returns to investors. These conditions made for surprisingly harmonious regulatory politics in the electricity regime, a situation that lasted for nearly three-quarters of a century. What conflicts did arise over the governance of electricity had more to do with the respective roles of different forms of economic organization in the expansion process itself. Here the intrusion of the federal government played an important part, beginning with the New Deal.

Federal involvement in electricity regulation in the years before the crisis remained much more limited than was the case with natural gas, despite the fact that they were both clearly designated "natural monopolies." The reason for this is that federal authority was never extended to the regulation of production and prices at state and local levels, as it was after the *Phillips* decision in natural gas. State public utility commissions thus retained their role as the principal institutions in the setting of rates and the licensing of new facilities.

This said, it must be added that federal influence in the electricity regime has expanded greatly in the years since the Great Depression. The role of the Public Utilities Holding Company Act of 1935 in restructuring the industry has already been mentioned. In that same year the government established the Federal Power Commission (FPC) and gave it the authority to regulate the rates and services of utilities selling electricity for transmission across state borders.[29] By the mid-1930's this amounted to nearly one-fifth of all electricity sold. A growing federal involvement, through the FPC, in planning and coordinating interstate and regional transmission and development programs was a natural result.

As noted earlier, Roosevelt was strongly committed personally to the electrification of the country, and especially to the extension of electric service to rural people, an attitude that led to the aggressive promotion of public power systems such as the TVA and the Bonneville Authority and to the Rural Electrification Administration. The growth of federal generation, promotion, and sale of power exacerbated one of the most persistent conflicts in the electricity system—one that focused on the relative merits of private, public, and cooperative institutions as providers of power. Investor-owned utilities, not surprisingly, viewed public power and cooperatives as a direct threat. Public power advocates, on the other hand, argued that natural monopolies could be operated as efficiently by the public as by the private sector, with the profits going to the consumer. They also argued that public power systems, whether municipal, state, or federal, could serve as a useful check on private greed by demonstrating the true costs of electricity production.

Neither side really won in this struggle, but the expansion of public power generation quickly lost momentum after the end of the New Deal. No more TVAs—regional development programs with a comprehensive scope—were seriously proposed, and public generation of electricity was limited to the exploitation of hydroelectric sites, traditionally a federal responsibility. By the late 1940's, therefore, the issue had become, for practical purposes, moot. Private, investor-owned utilities continued to control the lion's share of the business in the country, though other institutions, ranging from federal generation and distribution facilities to rural electrification cooperatives, retained a hold. In economic terms, it appears that no institutional arrangement is clearly superior—at least in the light of available evidence. However, government support muddies the water. Public utilities are often highly efficient, but they benefit from tax-exempt status; private utilities are often quite efficient, too, but they also receive a variety of tax subsidies.[30] The clearest conclusion seems to be that the quality of management is the critical variable, and this is determined by many things, of which ownership pattern is but one.

The emergence of nuclear power resulted in a very dramatic enlargement of federal involvement in the affairs of the electricity regime. Here, too, the government played a critical role in promoting power generation, but with results that were far less auspicious. Because of its military origins, atomic energy began as a closely held government monopoly, shrouded in secrecy. The Atomic Energy Act of 1946, which set the terms for research and military applications of atomic energy, placed responsibility in the hands of a civilian agency, the Atomic Energy Commission (AEC), which in turn operated under the close supervision of Congress's Joint Committee on Atomic Energy (JCAE). The AEC proceeded to invest many billions of dollars in research and development for military applications, relying almost exclusively on private contractors to do the actual work.[31]

The transition from military to civilian power was critically important in shaping the character of the industry. There was little economic pressure for civilian reactor development, since energy costs from conventional fossil sources were low and had been decreasing for years.[32] For political reasons—chiefly the desire to demonstrate "peaceful" uses of the atom—the JCAE in the early 1950's began pressing the AEC to move ahead with a civilian reactor program. In 1954 the Atomic Energy Act was revised to permit private-sector involvement in reactor development (although Congress chose to retain ownership of the fuel itself). It also established the AEC as the agency that would oversee reactor construction and use, thus stipulating that nuclear electricity would be regulated in a manner different from electricity produced from conventional power plants— and that it would be regulated by the same agency that had the job of promoting the expansion of nuclear power.[33]

The development of civilian nuclear power thus took place under comprehensive federal supervision. Early prototypes were modeled on reactors originally developed for military uses—the Shippingsport reactor, for example, was designed originally to power an aircraft carrier.[34] There was little competition, and little concern for cost. Indeed, the promotion of civilian applications continued even after early evidence showed that the costs would be much higher than expected. The companies involved were chosen by the government, and, not surprisingly, the handful that came to dominate the industry were in most instances the same ones that had been selected, in noncompetitive decisions, to do the military work for the AEC in previous years. Those building reactors also received large subsidies: the government provided the fuel free; contributed research results; bought back information generated by the reactors; and even undertook to protect utility companies by limiting their liability to offsite claims in case of nuclear accident.[35]

In sum, it is clear that, without government promotion and subsidy, there would have been no civilian nuclear power industry. Furthermore, the government's involvement was critical in shaping the character of the industry that did emerge. Federal policies assured the transition from public monopoly to private oligopoly, determined the character of the technology that was eventually deployed, and promoted the growth of the industry long before economic conditions made it attractive to private investors.

These circumstances are important because they represent a type of public involvement in the emergence of an energy industry that is very distinctive. In no other regime were market forces and competitive processes so systematically set aside, even in the determination of which among many technical alternatives would predominate. Where competition did finally arise, it was over who would get a chance to profit from the construction of a technical system developed under government direction—and under strong political pressures to produce something of civilian and peaceful value from military-oriented research—not over which company and which technology could provide the most economical means of generating electricity.

As a consequence, nuclear power came into existence in a manner that can only be characterized as hasty and premature. Not only were the costs unclear and the technology unseasoned, but as I. C. Bupp has noted, reactors themselves were ordered and built before the complex support system they would need, in the rest of the fuel cycle, had become established and was working. It was, as he put it, "an incomplete system."[36] Many of the problems the nuclear industry suffered in the 1970's and 1980's must be attributed to the fact that the set of technologies involved were rushed to commercialization in this manner.

Conclusions

The political economy of electricity is different, in many respects, from that of the other energy forms examined in this volume. Unlike coal and oil, electricity was established early on as a system of legal monopolies in local service districts. This meant that the problem of supply management, as a means of controlling competition, was not a central concern after the first few years. Until the late 1960's, the electrification of the country grew rapidly, but the governance process was largely free of the kinds of compensatory conflicts that encumbered the natural gas regime. The technical and economic attributes of the industry made its relationship with regulatory authorities more cooperative than conflictual—in effect, it made the maintenance of proprietary regulation at the state level both convenient and uncontroversial. The key to this was declining prices stemming from technical innovation, declining fuel costs, and increasing scale economies. This meant that those with an interest at stake—investors, managers, and consumers—could all benefit from growth, especially growth that involved the construction of new and larger facilities for the generation of power, while avoiding conflicts with one another.

Two problems arose to disturb this tranquillity: first, private efforts to secure monopoly profits through structures of financial control that were beyond the political and legal reach of state regulatory agencies; and second, the challenge to privately owned utilities posed by the advocates of public power. The former was put to rest by decisive federal action, which dismantled most holding company empires and controlled the abuses of others, and the latter eventually became moot as the existing mix of public, cooperative, and private power systems came to be generally accepted. A third problem, that posed by the demands of environmentalists, had begun to emerge by the late 1960's, but it had not yet become so serious that it threatened the basic character of the regime.

Reflecting the technical and economic incentives that obtained, regulatory authorities adopted a strongly promotional attitude toward electric power. Rate structures encouraged the growth of demand; siting policies encouraged construction; tax policies gave the industry (the most capital-intensive of all) privileged access to investment funds. These things combined to nurture a very distinctive set of managerial attitudes and orientations, ones that valued skill in assuring predictable increments in supply by bringing on line new and large units, but not necessarily the ability to estimate risk and compare alternative responses to demand and price changes.

The federal government, although less intrusive than it had been in the petroleum and natural gas regimes, expanded its role as supply networks reached beyond state boundaries and as federal power generation from hydroelectricity entered the grid in larger quantities. The decision by federal authorities to promote the rapid introduction of nuclear power suddenly enlarged this intervention.[37] Responding to federal promotion, guarantees, and subsidies, utilities in the middle and late 1960's embraced atomic energy as the most promising incremental energy source, and made significant commitments to nuclear power plant construction. Their assumptions at the time were the standard ones: demand would grow in a steady and predictable fashion; new technology embodied in larger plants would reduce costs; investors, utility managers, regulators, and consumers would all be happy with the result.

As noted earlier, this distinctive history of growth, cost reduction, innovation, regulatory promotion, and government subsidy made the electricity regime unusually vulnerable to the energy crisis that shook the nation in 1973 and in the years that followed. Not only did fuel costs increase with the crisis, but demand patterns changed, inflation increased the costs of construction, soaring interest rates undermined the viability of projects requiring long lead times, and technical economies of scale all but disappeared. To make matters worse, changing public opinion and patterns of political representation increased the influence and access of a growing cadre of consumer interests, environmentalists, and antinuclear activists. As we shall see in Chapter 9, the result was a profound transformation: the quiet world of cooperative, proprietary regulation gave way to the chronic instability and conflict of compensatory regulation.

PART TWO   Crisis and Response

CHAPTER 6

Nixon, Ford, and
the Arab Oil Embargo

For most historic changes we mark an event that divides time into "before" and "after." In energy, the Arab oil embargo of October 1973 serves this purpose. Meeting in Kuwait on October 17, just after the outbreak of the Yom Kippur War, the oil ministers of the Arab oil-exporting countries decided to impose production cutbacks in order to demonstrate their market power and to draw Western attention to the Arab cause.[1] In the next few weeks, country after country complied, sending shock waves through Western capitals. Led by Saudi Arabia, the members of OAPEC sought to impose a complete boycott on the United States and several other countries considered friendly to Israel. In the first months, they cut the supply of oil reaching international markets by nearly 15 percent.[2] Spot market prices shot up, and other oil-exporting countries who were members of OPEC quickly agreed to take advantage of the situation by raising their own prices. By the time the Arabs ended the embargo, in March of 1974, prices for world oil had soared from $3 to $12 per barrel.

This was a staggering economic blow; indeed, it was the impact of the price increases and OPEC's determination to retain control of prices, rather than the brief shortages experienced by several countries, that had the most telling effect. Middle East expert Dankwart Rustow characterized it as a "$100 billion tax on the global economy—the most gigantic reallocation of income in history."[3] Even in the United States, where imported oil accounted for only 18 percent of energy consumption, the shock to the economy was enormous. Economist Thomas Schelling estimated that the cost to the United States alone, extrapolated to the future, would be "equivalent to a deadweight tax of up to five percent on our GNP in perpetuity."[4]

Origins of the Crisis

As with so many historic thresholds, a closer examination reveals that the change in national and world affairs was not nearly as sudden as it appears to have been. In the years immediately preceding the embargo the United States was already suffering, for the first time in decades, from energy problems—most notably shortages of natural gas and some petroleum products. Indeed, the policies adopted to respond to those problems, especially in the oil industry, actually tended to increase our vulnerability to the crisis. They also set the pattern for the policies that were adopted once energy problems were transformed into a full-blown national security emergency.

The difficulties experienced by the petroleum industry were at least partly the result of an ill-fated intersection of economic and political trends. In 1971 and 1972, just before the crisis, the industry underwent a number of far-reaching changes. The peaking of domestic production capacity and the gradual increase of international prices made the apparatus set up to control production and protect the industry against imports unnecessary. Accordingly, state prorationing agencies gradually raised "allowables" to 100 percent, and the federal government eased import quotas until they, too, were no longer an impediment to the entry of petroleum and products. In April 1973, the government abolished the mandatory import-control system entirely and instead set a small fee for imports. These changes made perfect sense from the perspective of the industry. Indeed, it is a testimony to the flexibility and adaptability of the control system that changes of this magnitude could be accommodated, quietly and efficiently, in so short a time.

As it happened, however, the early 1970's was also a time of serious economic problems in the United States, problems that could be traced to the economic and budgetary effects of the Vietnam War and Lyndon Johnson's Great Society domestic programs. Inflation came first, engulfing the nation in the late 1960's. Nixon's efforts to stem rising prices brought recession and unemployment; but to the surprise of most economists, inflation did not subside—instead, the country experienced its first serious episode of stagflation. Fearing an election year with the country's economy in the doldrums, Nixon in 1971 decided on a radical alternative: he instituted an economy-wide wage and price freeze. Because the price of petroleum was rising, and because the oil industry was, as always, politically suspect, the government was especially strict in its control of the petroleum marketplace.

Although the precise impact of Nixon's price regulations differed during various phases of the program, it is possible to draw some broad conclusions about what they meant for the industry. To begin with, they almost certainly helped create periodic shortages of petroleum products, most notably heating oil and, later, gasoline. They did so partly because regulators were inflexible and did not accommodate seasonal shifts in demand for refinery output, and partly because, in combination with quotas, the regulations discouraged importation of quantities of crude and products sufficient to meet rising demand.[5]

The controls also exacerbated intra-industry tensions and conflicts, especially between the larger integrated companies and independent producers, refiners, and distributors. Differential access to foreign supplies and complex regulations concerning where profits could be taken, along with the general tightening of crude supply, led the larger companies to cut supplies to the independents and "private branders" that had become increasingly popular as retail outlets for gasoline and products.[6]

Shortages and distortions in the distribution of crude and products in turn led to growing demands for government allocation of supplies. As we have seen in the coal and natural gas industries, price controls, by creating shortages, also create the political need for authorities to choose those who will gain access to available supplies. The government responded first with a "voluntary" allocation program and then with a mandatory one.[7]

Thus the general economic policies of the early 1970's added to the already complex controls that affected the energy system of the country. Nixon's wage and price freeze was supposed to be temporary. And for the rest of the economy, controls were lifted in the course of 1973. But for the petroleum industry, the freeze became a trap. By contributing to the shortages of products, controls drew attention and public hostility to the industry. More importantly, because the system of controls was already in place when the embargo occurred, it set the pattern for the legislative response to the crisis when world prices began to soar. Despite its political influence, the petroleum industry could not avoid being included in a program of economywide controls; after the embargo, the crisis made it politically impossible to dismantle that program.

Energy problems, then, did not begin with the embargo. The oil industry was already changing as a result of the peaking of domestic production capacity and the gradual rise of international prices in the years after 1970. When it came under government controls—

first of prices and then of supply—as part of Nixon's stabilization program, the controls themselves created shortages and intra-industry conflicts. They also provided a convenient precedent for new and more permanent controls which were imposed when the embargo made them politically unavoidable. As noted earlier, the gas industry was also suffering shortages at this time, the result of the stalemate in bargaining between consumers and producers over regulated prices. And the coal regime was also in a time of transition, as the union-management alliance that had brought stability for nearly two decades was nearing collapse. Thus the American energy system, by the time of the embargo, was already in a minor crisis of its own; the Arab embargo caught the system and its principal regimes at a point of critical transition and adjustment.

Nixon: Damage Control

If a word had to be chosen to characterize the national political response to the OAPEC embargo of October 1973, it would almost certainly have to be "confused." Energy was already a political issue; both Congress and the Executive were struggling to find acceptable ways of handling the shortages created by the administration's price controls. The embargo added a new dimension to this problem, but there was no consensus about how serious the new threat was. How long would the embargo last? Could OPEC continue to hold prices at their new levels, or would the cartel fail? What would price increases do to the economy? Whom would they hurt, and whom would they benefit? Conceptually as well as politically, we were, as Martin Greenberger has characterized it, "caught unawares."[8]

There was widespread agreement that decisive action was necessary; the stakes were too high, the challenge too direct. Because of the confusion and disagreement about the nature of the crisis, however, only "temporary" and incremental measures could win approval.[9] As is so often the case, these gradually became permanent. Indeed, it is surprising to what degree the basic outline of the nation's response to the energy problem was set in place during the first hectic months of the second Nixon Administration. And this was done not by the passage of a sweeping "plan," but by a series of steps each of which, for lack of broadly acceptable alternatives, eventually became a key element in the national "solution." Also surprising is the degree to which the historical record reveals a continuity in the actual steps taken in response to the problem, in Congress as well as the Executive Branch, across the three administrations of Nixon, Ford, and Carter, despite significant differences in philosophical orientation on the part of the presidents and their advisers, and despite marked differences in the broad "plans" that they proposed as solutions.

Just three weeks after the Arab embargo, Nixon went before the nation and delivered the first of what would be a long list of presidential energy statements. After exhorting the American people to conserve energy in the coming winter months, he outlined a bold plan, which he named Project Independence, to make the country self-sufficient in energy by 1980. We know now that Project Independence was based on very little careful analysis, and the goals it set forth had little chance of realization.[10] Nixon himself would soon leave office in disgrace—in fact, his energy address was marred by a pleading defense of his personal integrity. But the speech did set the tone for what became the basic Executive Branch approach to the crisis. The problem, as the President defined it in his next address in January 1974, was the vulnerability created by America's link to outside supplies of energy. This was a long-term challenge, belatedly recognized, and required national efforts, led by the government, to restore energy self-sufficiency:

We must also face the fact that when and if the oil embargo ends, the United States will be faced with a different but no less difficult problem. Foreign oil prices have risen dramatically in recent months. If we were to continue to increase our purchase of foreign oil, there would be a chronic balance of payments outflow which, over time, would create a severe problem in international monetary relations. Without alternative and competitive sources of energy here at home, we would thus continue to be vulnerable to interruptions of foreign imports and prices could remain at these cripplingly high levels. Clearly, these conditions are unacceptable.[11]

The threat to the economy and to the nation's security required the government to step in and find a solution, a "blueprint" as the administration's planners called it, to assure self-sufficiency. This would entail a major commitment to increased production of domestic oil (which at the time was still considered abundant), coal, and nuclear power, as well as research and development to discover and develop new energy alternatives.

In Search of Collective Security

Although the economic damage caused by the embargo and price increases was the principal concern of most policymakers, the crisis also created some important foreign-policy problems for the United States. The successful Arab use of the "oil weapon" constituted a potent, if unexpected, challenge to the administration's broad international objectives, particularly in the Middle East. It also precipitated some very troubling tensions within the Western Alliance itself.[12] The embargo targeted the United States and the Netherlands, countries the Arabs considered key supporters of Israel in the Middle East War. The other EEC members, excepting Britain and France, were subjected to a progressive "squeeze" of their oil supplies from OAPEC members of 5 percent per month.

The first reaction of many of the European governments was to protect their own interests, even at the expense of their Western allies. This set off a round of bitter charges and countercharges. The French and Japanese urgently sought bilateral guarantees of supply from producer governments. The French and British refused to assist the Dutch, ignoring EEC regulations in the process, and relented only when the Dutch threatened to cut off shipments of natural gas to France and other members of the Community.[13]

In one of the most decisive and successful initiatives of the energy crisis, Secretary of State Kissinger moved quickly to control the damage and reassert American leadership. His solution was to form a protective association of the industrialized oil-importing countries. To that end he brought them together for an emergency meeting in Washington in February 1974 and got them to agree to form an Energy Coordinating Group to set up a mechanism for dealing with the crisis.[14] This led, in succeeding months, to the formation of the International Energy Program (IEP) and the International Energy Agency (IEA), the latter responsible for the administration of the Program. Eventually twenty countries, including Canada, New Zealand, and Japan, joined in.[15]

The heart of the IEP system was a series of mechanisms designed to blunt the effectiveness of any future embargoes. By joining, members agreed: (1) to set up stockpiles of oil equal to 60 (later 90) days of net imports; (2) to have ready "demand restraint" policies for use in emergencies; and (3) to follow a preset formula for sharing oil among themselves in case of an embargo. They also agreed to work together in the future to promote conservation and the development of alternative energy sources.[16]

The Congressional Response

American success in energy statecraft abroad, unfortunately, was not matched at home, where disagreement held sway concerning the nature of the threat, and where the benefits of collective action were less evident to the interests involved. A few weeks after the embargo, Congress passed and sent to the President two pieces of legislation, the Alaska Pipeline Act and the Emergency Petroleum Allocation Act (EPAA). The appearance of decisiveness is misleading, however: both bills had been working their way through the legislature since spring, and neither was designed with the international crisis in mind.[17]

The EPAA was the more important of the two bills; indeed, in many ways it was the most influential piece of legislation passed during the decade. In the name of equity, it set in place a host of controls over petroleum prices, production, and marketing that, in turn, (1) froze key relationships in the energy economy, and (2) quickly created an ensemble of stakeholders in the regulatory system itself. Though Congress intended the controls to be temporary, the arrangements the EPAA mandated, as implemented by the Executive Branch, remained in force for many years.[18]

When they began work on the EPAA, most legislators were concerned mainly with fairness and, in particular, with assuring an equitable distribution of petroleum and products. Prices were already controlled under the authority of the Economic Stabilization Act, and pressure had been building from independent distributors and refiners for government allocation of scarce supplies. As might be expected, the major oil companies opposed any arrangement that would result in mandatory allocation of products. Reluctant to extend government controls further, Nixon had tried a "voluntary" allocation scheme; not surprisingly, it failed. Congress then decided to step in and force the President's hand. All of this occurred before October 17, 1973. Significantly, although the bill did provide for price controls, prices were not the principal issue, since they did not begin their rapid rise for several months.

The EPAA required that the government control the prices of crude oil and products, and that it allocate scarce supplies to those relying on them. The bill also contained provisions favoring small and independent refiners, requiring that regulators give them shares proportionate to those they received in the base year 1972. Finally, it stipulated that the President could neither decontrol prices nor dismantle allocation regulations without a formal finding that shortages were over—and it granted Congress the right to veto his decision. The bill gave the President 30 days to put the necessary regulations into effect.

The embargo helped convince the administration that it needed the temporary emergency powers embodied in the EPAA, and Nixon signed the bill. At the administration's request, however, Congress then began work on what everyone expected would be a more carefully designed and comprehensive bill—named the Energy Emergency Act—to shape more carefully the government's involvement in energy markets. Although Congress eventually cleared a version of the Emergency Act, Nixon vetoed it, and a substitute measure was defeated on the floor of the House a few weeks later.

An examination of the political career of the ill-fated Emergency Act is instructive, for it illustrates the doctrinal and practical conflicts that were so important in shaping the nation's response to the crisis. The original purpose of the bill was to give the President emergency powers, most of which he had requested in his Project Independence address. These included such things as authority to ration petroleum products, restrict energy use to essential purposes, reduce highway speed limits, control the types of fuel used by industry, and postpone the implementation of environmental standards. But though it had already agreed to grant these to the President in the EPAA (on a temporary basis), Congress could not agree on a permanent substitute without also addressing the problem of wealth redistribution; the nature of the crisis as a redistributive opportunity had become clearer—although consensus on its nature had not—and political pressures to allocate costs and benefits were simply too powerful. At the same time, there was enormous disagreement about the causes and consequences of the crisis, and hence about the appropriate means of assuring a just distribution of costs and benefits. Accordingly, consensus broke down as the Senate and House struggled to find a formula that would provide such a just distribution.[19]

The first version of the bill to reach a vote emerged from conference with a windfall profits provision and with a directive to the President to set prices for crude in such a way as to prevent excess profits. But oil-state senators mounted a successful filibuster against the bill, and the House refused to pass a compromise with the windfall profits provisions deleted.[20] Subsequent efforts to revive the bill succeeded, despite the opposition of an unusual alliance of energy producers and environmentalists—the latter concerned about the reduction or postponement of clean air standards—but this time the bill emerged with a formal ceiling on oil prices (instead of a windfall profits tax) along with additional unemployment provisions for workers displaced by the crisis, both of which the administration's energy managers opposed. By this time, late in the spring of 1974, the embargo was over, the sense of emergency had begun to dissipate, and the administration felt little need for additional legislation. And in any case the EPAA was due to expire in February of 1975. Accordingly, Nixon vetoed the bill.

The effect of the veto was to let the EPAA stand as the legal basis for government action in the energy field. The "solution" it embodied was to freeze distributional relationships—and thus, presumably, equity patterns—in their pre-embargo configuration, making national security and economic efficiency secondary, and to accomplish this by mandating price controls and allocation of supplies, these to be administered by inexperienced and ill-prepared federal regulators.

One of the few areas in which the President and Congress did agree was on the desirability of a national highway speed limit. Nixon proposed a national limit of 50 miles per hour, but protests by trucking interests led Congress to raise this to 55 miles per hour. To force states to go along with the national goal, legislators tacked the mileage provision onto a bill providing federal assistance to state highway programs.[21] As with so many of the energy initiatives passed in these first years of crisis, the 55-mph speed limit was also to be temporary.

The Regulators

Within the Executive Branch, the last months of the Nixon Administration saw a hasty scramble by newly appointed energy administrators to come to grips with the mounting crisis. The President himself, despite his determination to present the appearance of decisive leadership, became increasingly preoccupied with the Watergate scandal; under him ambitious and energetic administrators vied for influence over policy.[22] Two tasks confronted them: (1) to define and defend a technically plausible set of goals for the nation (a task made necessary by the outline set forth in Nixon's Project Independence speech); and (2) to handle the regulatory tasks imposed by the system of price controls and other regulations contained in the EPAA. The administrators were under intense political pressure. Their response to these challenges, despite deep misgivings on the part of many and some notable ideological and bureaucratic conflicts, set the terms for the nation's response to the energy challenge. Again, the temporary became permanent.

Nixon had created a small Energy Policy Office in the summer of 1973 to review energy options. The Cost of Living Council retained responsibility for price controls. After the embargo, the President by executive order consolidated responsibility for energy matters in a new Federal Energy Office—shortly to be renamed the Federal Energy Administration when Congress gave the reorganization its stamp of approval—and charged it with managing the system of regulations inherited from the Cost of Living Council, designing new allocation mechanisms to comply with the requirements of the EPAA, and carrying forward the planning required to turn Project Independence into a coherent national energy strategy.

Nixon's energy regulators demonstrated a surprising degree of doctrinal agreement. They all recognized that policy had to strike an acceptable balance between several goals, including national security, efficiency, and equity (usually in that order). But almost without exception they felt that the free play of market forces should be harnessed to achieve government objectives, and thus preferred to avoid direct regulatory intervention in the energy economy where possible.[23] It is thus particularly significant, as well as ironic, that it was precisely these men—William Simon, John Sawhill, Frank Zarb, their names familiar still—who found themselves carefully designing and putting into operation one of the most complex and cumbersome regulatory apparatuses ever imposed on an American industry. The solutions they devised were neither their first nor, often, their second choices. The political context within which they worked was simply too overwhelming, the structural constraints too great.

The overriding goal of the EPAA, as stated earlier, was fairness: distributing short supplies equitably among those in the industry who depended on them, and protecting consumers and the economy as a whole from sudden price increases that had no necessary relationship to increases in production costs. In the months that followed the embargo, energy regulators struggled to comply with the Congressional mandate while at the same time responding to hundreds of individual complaints by firms that found themselves in some way hurt by the new arrangements.[24] As they did so, rapid price increases, anticipated by neither Congress nor the Executive, complicated matters greatly. Of particular importance, as prices rose, were growing suspicions, in Congress and among the public at large, that the crisis was directly or indirectly the product of oil-industry machinations. These suspicions made proposals to decontrol prices, even if accompanied by a compensating tax, more and more politically unpalatable as the crisis worsened.

The key to post-embargo regulation was a system of price controls on domestic crude oil that created two "tiers" or levels. One tier, which included domestic oil that had already been discovered and placed into production before the crisis, was tightly controlled at pre-embargo prices (these later were allowed to drift upward in a controlled fashion); the second tier, which included new production, "stripper" oil (from very small or depleted wells), and, of course, imported oil, was uncontrolled.[25] Cost increases could be passed through to retail products, but according to carefully delineated formulae. Regulators addressed the allocation problem by requiring that buyers and suppliers return to the relationships that had obtained in 1972, in effect freezing supply arrangements.[26]

As international prices soared, it quickly became evident that the two-tier system of price controls contained a major flaw: it gave a financial advantage to those refineries with access to lower-priced, domestic "old" crude. Because their feedstock costs were lower, such refineries were in a position to make greater profits. And even if they were forced by regulators to lower their prices, a significant disparity would arise between the prices of the same products produced by different refineries, depending on the amount of imported crude they used. Consumers would then have the costs distributed unfairly among themselves.

To resolve this problem, federal regulators invented the now infamous "entitlements" system. The entitlements system resembled the old import-quota "ticket" system turned upside down. According to the new arrangements, designed in the waning days of the Nixon Administration and implemented in the fall of 1974, each refiner received entitlements "equal to the number of barrels of controlled crude oil that the refiner would have used in the previous month had it operated using the national proportion of controlled to uncontrolled crude oil."[27] Those refineries with access to more than their allotted amount of controlled crude would thus have to buy entitlements from those relying on higher proportions of imported oil. In this way the benefits of access to cheaper oil were distributed equally among refineries. A number of adjustments were made to the program—most notably the granting of extra entitlements to small refineries—but the basic outline remained unchanged until oil prices were decontrolled in 1981.

Ford and Deregulation

Within a few months of taking office, Gerald Ford sought to reassert executive leadership in the energy field. In his State of the Union Address in January 1975, he announced that he was going to refashion the nation's energy policies so that they would harness market forces to achieve energy independence. To begin with, he would levy a fee on imported oil and decontrol the price of domestic crude oil. The import fee would start at $1 per barrel and increase to $3 by April 1, 1975; crude oil prices would be freed from government controls on April 1, 1975.

Having announced his intention to move the country away from increasingly complex regulatory solutions, Ford then challenged Congress to follow his lead and pass the legislation necessary to complement his actions. The list he presented was a long one. Among other things, he asked Congress to deregulate new natural gas, place excise taxes on imported crude and products, and create a strategic petroleum reserve of a billion barrels. Later in the year he also proposed the creation of a $100 billion Energy Independence Authority, a government corporation whose job would be to stimulate the development of new energy sources such as synfuels from shale or coal.[28] To "ensure that oil producers do not profit unduly," he suggested a windfall profits tax—noting that it would have to be in place within ninety days, the deadline he had set for decontrol.[29] He also proposed that revenues collected from higher energy taxes be refunded through the tax system.

Ford's plan, as a plan, never made it out of legislative committee. Although it was more coherent than Nixon's patchwork of proposals—the market- and production-oriented philosophy behind it was more consistently applied in its design—the plan itself and the way it was presented could hardly have been less in tune with the political mood of the Congress and the country.[30]

Ford's administration coincided with a period of growing anger and dismay about the performance of the American government, and the management of energy policy suffered as a consequence. Elections had brought a cohort of "Watergate" freshmen, suspicious of authority and critical of big business, into office. The embargo was past, but prices remained high. Oil company profits had begun to soar. Opinion polls revealed that many Americans did not believe there was a crisis; a surprising number did not even realize that the United States had to import oil.[31] To many in Congress high prices *were* the energy problem; yet the administration proposed a plan that, in effect, said high prices were the *solution*.

On a more practical level, the costs and benefits associated with what now seemed to be permanently high prices remained to be allocated. It was here that Ford made his greatest mistake: he did not make distributional fairness the centerpiece of his program. Instead, he announced that he would unilaterally set aside the EPAA arrangements in favor of more efficient decontrolled prices, on an urgent basis, and left it to Congress to handle the task of distributing the costs and benefits—all within three months.[32] To be fair to Ford, political fragmentation and the mobilization of interests were so extensive that it was unlikely that any plan would have been acceptable; but a plan that seemed to favor oil and gas interests over those of the consumers was doomed at the outset.

However distasteful and impolitic the administration's plan, Congress had to address the energy problem. Not only had Ford threatened unilateral decontrol, but the EPAA itself was due to expire at the end of August 1975. The mobilization of political interests stimulated by Congressional work on energy policy was truly impressive. Stakeholders sensed their vulnerability in the unstable, emotion-laden atmosphere in Washington. Consumers feared they would have to shoulder the costs of energy price increases; environmentalists feared that the energy crisis would be used as an excuse to set aside hard-won restrictions on emissions from cars and power plants; producers of various kinds struggled to defend their economic interests in an increasingly hostile environment. Democrats, in the majority, tended to support continued controls; Republicans tended to favor decontrol (but not redistributive tax measures). However, coalitions among groups proved changeable as different proposals emerged from Congressional committees. Oil and gas companies found the environment particularly hostile: in 1975 a vertical divestiture measure in the Senate failed by the narrow margin of 45–54—five votes short of passage—and a bill eliminating the depletion allowance (for all but independent producers) passed by a generous margin.

Ford clashed repeatedly with a badly divided Congress as they struggled, for more than nine months, to agree on what to do about energy. As he realized that he could not force action on his program by issuing ultimatums, Ford began to back down. He extended his deadline for decontrol, delayed the imposition of higher import fees, and then modified his proposal, suggesting instead a phased-in decontrol. He twice agreed to extend, "temporarily," the life of the EPAA. It became quite clear, as the year progressed—and as elections began to loom on the horizon—that Ford was unwilling to move to decontrol without Congressional collaboration.

Within Congress, coalitions shifted daily. In the end consumer interests, with the support of coal interests and a mixed lot of groups and individuals ideologically opposed to the oil and gas industry, were able to block immediate price decontrol. The bill that finally did emerge from Congress, the Energy Policy and Conservation Act (EPCA), bore little resemblance to Ford's proposal. It was an elaborate, omnibus bill, with many provisions that would have a lasting impact on energy relationships in the country. However, insofar as the critical issue of pricing policy was concerned, it amounted to an

extension and elaboration of the EPAA. It provided for eventual decontrol, but not for nearly five years. In the meantime, the price of
oil and gas would remain politically "accessible."

Ford's advisers were divided about whether he should sign the
EPCA. Economic purists in the Council of Economic Advisers
(CEA) and the Treasury Department, worried about the economic
inefficiency associated with price controls, advised him to veto the
bill and move to decontrol—the EPAA expired on the same day,
December 15, that the EPCA was sent to the President. The oil industry and representatives from energy-producing states also urged
a veto. The new Federal Energy Administration (FEA), headed by
Frank Zarb, felt the law was an acceptable compromise, given the
circumstances, and noted that a veto might prove a serious political
liability in the upcoming election.[33] Ford signed the bill.

The EPCA was a complex bill. It retained the overall system of
petroleum regulation, but allowed some price increases and set a
fixed termination date for controls. The bill provided for a continuation of mandatory price controls until June 1979, after which the
President could continue them at his discretion, but only until Sep-
tember 1981, when his authority to do so would expire.[34] It imposed a reduction in the average price of controlled crude (to $7.66
per barrel) and established a more complex, three-tiered system of
prices.[35] It also allowed the President to adjust the average price upward 10 percent to account for inflation and to stimulate new production. Finally, refined product prices could be freed from controls
at the President's discretion. Ford took advantage of the last of these
provisions to lift controls from all products except gasoline, jet fuel,
and propane.[36]

The EPCA's nonpricing provisions, taken together, constituted a
significant extension of the government's involvement in energy
matters. Among other things, the EPCA (1) created an automobile
efficiency program requiring that automakers achieve a fleet average
of 27.5 miles per gallon by 1985; (2) granted the authority needed for
the United States to participate in the recently negotiated International Energy Program (IEP); (3) established the strategic petroleum
reserve necessary for participation in the IEP; (4) enlarged the President's regulatory authority in several nonpetroleum areas (notably
coal conversion and product labeling); (5) granted him a wide array
of standby powers to use in case of emergency, while requiring him
to prepare contingency plans for emergency allocation and conservation measures; and (6) significantly extended the government's authority to collect information about the national energy system and
its participants.[37]

Ford returned to Congress in 1976 with another list of requests. Some of these were the same as those he had advanced a year earlier, including his proposal to deregulate the price of natural gas. Congress agreed to extend the life of the Federal Energy Administration; to renew the liability limitation protecting the nuclear power industry; and to approve a large energy research authorization, most of which went to support nuclear programs. But legislators continued to reject Ford's leadership on the critical matter of price controls; they simply had no appetite for renewed debate on the operation of the energy system and the distribution of benefits and costs it created.

Conclusions

By the time Nixon left office, less than a year after the Arab oil embargo, the basic outlines of what would remain the U.S. response to the energy crisis were already in place. Price controls, allocation of supplies, entitlements, an inexorable enlargement of the government's analytical and regulatory apparatus—all temporary expedients to manage shortages—quickly became institutionalized, bringing into existence an ensemble of stakeholders whose roles would significantly constrain the options of subsequent administrations.

It is tempting, in view of the criticisms that have been leveled against those responsible—criticisms that have come from all directions, but especially from economists concerned with the efficiency losses associated with regulation and failure to rely on markets— to search for a single critical moment, a point at which decision-makers turned away from policies that relied on market forces and turned to ones that would, from an insistence on near-term distributional equity, draw the government more deeply into the regulatory quagmire.

But there was no such single moment. Energy policy was the result of a series of incremental decisions, some taken by regulators, some by Congress, but all heavily influenced by the existing pattern of energy regulation and by political pressures to "right" wrongs imposed by international changes as they worked their way into the domestic energy economy.

To be sure, there were important turning points. Of these, perhaps the most decisive was Nixon's pre-crisis decision to impose economy-wide price controls, because it set in motion the regulatory response that followed. Price controls created a shortage, and thereby a need to allocate supplies; allocation created stakeholders, who in turn perceived a threat in a return to market processes. When Phase III controls were lifted on the rest of the economy, the energy system had already entered a period of crisis (which included gas as well as oil), and the administration found it expedient to retain controls (Phase IV) on the oil industry. These in turn were the basis for the EPAA, Congress's initial response to the OAPEC embargo. Price controls led to allocation, and in time to the entitlements program. And these led to the EPCA.

Another turning point came just after the embargo. It is possible to imagine, for example, a different presidential response to the crisis by Nixon. In the Executive Branch—especially the Treasury and the CEA—a plan based on decontrol, a windfall profits tax, and coupons to redistribute the burden of higher gasoline prices was actively considered.[38] But time was short. Congress had already mandated price controls and allocation, and political pressures from those disadvantaged by the existing arrangements were intense. And, perhaps most important of all, the President was preoccupied and weakened by the growing Watergate crisis. Although he favored deregulation in theory, Ford was a politician first. When Congress refused to accept his leadership and instead presented him with an extension of the EPAA regulatory regime, he signed it because to do otherwise would damage his chances of becoming an elected President of the United States.

In retrospect, each part of the policy response makes historical "sense;" each can be explained as an outgrowth of the last action, a product of circumstances. Thus the response to the crisis was the product not of a key decision, but rather of a sequence of choices deeply influenced by the rules of the political process—above all the prohibition against costly visible redistributions—and by the weight of past decisions, themselves the product of the larger political economy. The fact that these choices were not achieving key objectives—among them reduced vulnerability to international events, and equity in the distribution of costs and benefits—grew increasingly evident as time went by. But policies that would respond to these problems simply could not overcome the deadlock created by those, especially in Congress, who feared they would be worse off under any alternative arrangement.

CHAPTER 7

Carter, Reagan,
and the End of Crisis

Energy policy and its politics were a heavy burden for Jimmy Carter. Like Ford, he came to office alarmed about the government's incapacity to act decisively in this area, and he wanted to provide the leadership needed to change that. He made energy his first priority, hoping to set in place arrangements that would strike an acceptable balance among the competing goals of equity, efficiency, security, and environmental protection. This would free him to concentrate on other vital problems.[1] Instead, he found himself caught in a frustrating battle of competing interests and alternatives that absorbed his time but brought little satisfaction.

From Carter's perspective—and that of most energy experts at the time—the energy picture seemed to have been worsening steadily since 1973, despite the already formidable accumulation of laws and regulations and the thousands of hours of legislative and executive time devoted to it. Higher prices seemed to have done little to dampen consumption, for energy use in the United States had continued to grow rapidly. Since domestic production had leveled off, imports, which were up a shocking 31 percent since 1973, made up the difference. Even more startling, new imports were coming from precisely those Arab countries that had embargoed the United States. Whereas in 1973 only 15 percent of our crude and products originated in OAPEC countries, by 1977 fully 36 percent did.[2] According to a study by the CIA, if American consumption continued to grow, the country's imports would increase from 8 million barrels per day in 1977 to 12–15 million by 1985, with the percentage coming from OAPEC sources, especially Saudi Arabia, continuing to swell. Furthermore, demand would once again closely match supply, creating the conditions for another sudden increase in prices.[3] Measured in these terms, America's vulnerability to embargo and political blackmail had increased enormously.

The longer-term perspective seemed equally dismal. Assessments of reserves of oil and gas remaining in the ground led most analysts to conclude that the country was now moving on the downward slope of the depletion curve.[4] Substitutes for oil and gas, ranging from coal to less familiar renewable energy forms, were more expensive. In sum, it was becoming evident that the energy crisis was best understood not as a short-term foreign-policy problem but as an episode in a long-term transition to a different and more costly mix of energy sources, a transition that would require pervasive, and sometimes unwelcome, changes in the habits and institutions of industrial society.

The National Energy Plan

Carter promised to have an energy proposal ready for Congress within ninety days of his inauguration, and he asked James Schlesinger, former Defense Secretary and AEC head, to assemble a team and prepare it. The resulting document, *The National Energy Plan*, contained very little that was entirely new; most of the changes it proposed had been under discussion in one Congressional forum or another for some time, and some had been proposed by past Presidents.[5] However, it did differ from the Ford Administration's general approach to energy matters in several important respects.[6] First and foremost, it stressed the goal of assuring equity in the distribution of benefits and burdens. The authors carefully justified each proposal in terms of its "fairness" to groups affected by it, and the President stressed this feature repeatedly. Second, it emphasized the attractiveness of "conservation," treating it as a source of new supply that was both domestic (and therefore secure) and less expensive than imported oil.[7] Finally, the Carter plan more carefully articulated the long-term nature of the energy crisis as a problem of resource transition as well as one of efficient resource allocation. Reflecting this emphasis, the *Plan* stressed the importance, along with conservation, of gradually shifting the country to the use of coal and other alternative sources of energy.

In practical terms, the most important difference between the approaches of Ford and Carter was the way they proposed to handle oil and gas prices: Ford at first sought rapid decontrol as a means of allowing domestic prices to rise to world levels; Carter chose instead to retain price controls—at least at first. He asked Congress to allow "new" oil prices to rise gradually to world levels, and he asked for a tax on "old" oil that would bring it also to world levels. Consumers would pay about the same prices for petroleum products as they would under decontrol, but the difference between the decontrolled and the controlled prices would be collected by the government and then rebated (through the tax system) to consumers. Thus oil companies would not be able to collect the difference on oil they had already discovered. He asked Congress to extend the controls on natural gas to cover the intrastate market, but to link the price for new gas to the average price of controlled oil. Gas already in production would remain under control, but its price would be increased.

The National Energy Plan also contained many other proposals. Among the most important were (1) a standby gasoline tax that increased by 5 cents each year consumption levels exceeded targets set by the government, but that would not exceed a total of 50 cents; (2) a graduated excise tax—also known as a "gas-guzzler" tax—on new cars, aimed at increasing the effectiveness of the fuel efficiency regulations contained in the EPCA; (3) several provisions, including an industrial user's excise tax, to encourage the use of coal by industry and utilities and to prohibit the burning of oil or gas in new facilities; (4) tax credits and other measures to promote building conservation and the use of solar hot water and space heating; and (5) reform of utility rate structures to encourage conservation.

Carter also proposed, in separate legislation, the creation of a cabinet-level Department of Energy (DOE) to manage the government's new role in the energy field. The new department would absorb the functions of the Federal Power Commission, the Federal Energy Commission, the Energy Research and Development Administration, plus a variety of other agencies and programs in half a dozen existing departments.[8] Finally, the President advocated a new approach toward nuclear energy. He proposed that the country "pause" and reexamine the desirability of a nuclear program that might contribute to the danger of worldwide nuclear proliferation. In particular, he announced that he would use his authority to defer commercial reprocessing and recycling of plutonium and requested that Congress reconsider its support of the breeder reactor program. His fear was that these programs, as currently planned, would increase the worldwide availability of high-grade plutonium, the fuel of nuclear weapons.

The "Moral Equivalent of War"

It appeared at first that Congress, after three years of struggle over energy issues, was finally willing to accept presidential leadership.

A majority of energy specialists supported the administration's view that the threat posed by imports was urgent, and a ground swell of support for new policies seemed to be building across the country. The time seemed right.

Carter donned a sweater and devoted a "fireside chat" to energy, trying to increase public understanding and support for his proposals. To emphasize the seriousness of the problem, he drew on a phrase suggested to him by his mentor, Admiral Hyman Rickover. The effort to handle energy problems, he said, "will be the 'moral equivalent of war,' except that we will be uniting our efforts to build and not to destroy."[9] Gas shortages, the product of a bitter winter and the reluctance of suppliers to sell to interstate markets at controlled prices, led him to request emergency authority to approve interstate sales at prices higher than regulated levels and, if necessary, to transfer supplies to areas of need. Within two weeks a measure giving him that authority was on his desk.[10] And his proposal for a Department of Energy (DOE), with some changes, was approved before the end of the summer.[11]

The administration's energy package, the *National Energy Plan*, did not fare so well, however. This, after all, embodied Carter's solutions to the sensitive distributional issues raised by energy management. Democrats held a majority in both houses of Congress, and the party's leaders, Tip O'Neill in the House and Robert Byrd in the Senate, made passage of the energy package their first priority. Carter's proposals did surprisingly well in the House, where O'Neill shepherded the legislation carefully through one committee after another. By late summer the House had passed a bill containing all of the key proposals except the gasoline tax.

The Senate, too, acted speedily, but here representatives from energy-producing regions were better placed to influence the substance of the legislation. Accordingly, the bills that cleared the Senate— where the package had been divided into five separate pieces— differed markedly from those passed by the House.[12] Neither the crude oil equalization tax nor the gas regulation provisions made it through; instead, the Senate passed a bill calling for deregulation of natural gas prices. In the end, the differences between House and Senate were so great on these issues that the conference committee could not resolve them; to Carter's enormous disappointment, Congress adjourned without acting on his plan.

The second year of legislative struggle over *The National Energy Plan* was, if anything, even less satisfactory to the President. When Congress returned to work, it gradually became evident that the crude oil equalization tax, the centerpiece of Carter's approach to the problem of oil pricing, could not make it through the Senate. Supporters of the oil and gas industry were too well placed and opposition to major new taxes was too pervasive. Senator Russell Long, a veteran defender of the oil and gas industry, won the agreement of his colleagues on the Finance Committee to a postponement of further deliberations on the tax proposal until the gas issue could be settled.[13] The conference committee on natural gas met, but bogged down immediately.

As it had so many times in the past, gas regulation provoked intense disagreement in Congress. In response to enormous pressures, the FPC after 1974 had repeatedly increased the price allowed for new gas. These price increases, plus the shortages experienced in the winter of 1976–77, intensified the bitter conflicts between representatives of consuming and producing regions of the country. Sentiment favoring deregulation had been growing for several years in the Senate, where many legislators had become more and more convinced that it was necessary to achieve increased production for interstate trade.[14] But the House, with many more direct representatives of the cities and towns of consuming areas in the North and Northeast, remained a stronghold of pro-regulation sentiment.

Conferees struggled with the gas problem for months. Solutions were proposed, discussed, then rejected as one or another interested party found them unacceptable. Determined to achieve some success in the energy field, Carter and Schlesinger followed the internecine struggles carefully, urging agreement.

Legislators finally worked out a compromise, but few were pleased with it. This was because it was a true compromise. It provided, in fact, for both new controls and deregulation. Among the key provisions were (1) the extension of price controls to include the intrastate market (plus some hefty increases in prices); (2) phased deregulation of wellhead prices of new gas, to be completed by 1985; and (3) requirements that "low priority" users, such as industrial facilities, rather than "high priority" users, such as homes and schools, bear a disproportionate share of the new costs as deregulation proceeded. In short, Congress agreed to deregulate, but postponed the day of reckoning and tried to protect key users from deregulation's effects. The "solution," in fact, bore a strong resemblance to the "solution" for oil embodied in the EPAA and EPCA.

It was not until October 1978 that Congress finished work on Carter's plan—what was left of it—and sent it to him for his signature. The crude oil equalization tax was gone, and the gas compromise, originally based on regulated prices tied to fuel oil, had become a program of postponed deregulation. In other words, the real heart of the program, the mechanisms by which costs and benefits in energy would be allocated, had been replaced.[15] On the other proposals, Congress was more accommodating: watered down provisions dealing with coal conversion, utility reform, and the promotion of conservation passed with little difficulty, as did a cluster of taxes, tax credits, and subsidies to promote conservation and the use of solar and other forms of renewable energy. Among the most important of the latter were a gas-guzzler tax; a subsidy for gasohol; a ten-year, $1.5 billion research and development package for solar energy; and a range of grants and tax credits to promote conservation and solar energy use in homes and businesses.

Carter and the Second Oil Shock

In October of 1978, a full year and a half after he asked Congress to approve his energy plan, Carter signed into law a package of bills that represented the result of an enormous expenditure of political and administrative time and effort. Like Ford before him, he took credit for some positive accomplishments. The Department of Energy was in place, and the nation could now boast a number of subsidies and regulations designed to promote conservation and research in the energy field. And it appeared that at least a measure of "fairness" had been assured by the retention of government controls on energy prices. However, the most critical short- and medium-term problem remained: the United States was importing more and more oil from the most insecure sources in the world. Moreover, the system of price controls worsened matters by making imported petroleum seem cheaper than it was.[16] The government had taken a number of steps designed to improve the long-term perspective; but the nation's vulnerability continued to increase. (See Fig. 4 and Table 5.)

Carter knew that the nation had grown weary of hearing about energy problems. He hoped to be able to leave energy behind and concentrate on other pressing issues in the second half of his term. In his State of the Union Address and his Budget Message early in 1979 he barely mentioned energy.[17] But within a few months international events forced him to focus again on the issue. As it turned out, the next two years proved the most eventful, and frustrating, in the country's long struggle with the energy issue.

In the winter of 1978–79 Iran, second only to Saudi Arabia as an

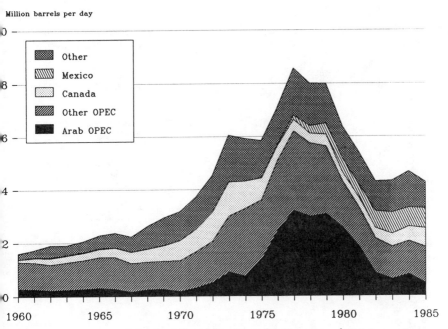

Figure 4. Imports of Crude Oil and Products by Country of Origin, 1960–1985. Source: United States [23], 1985: 113.

oil exporter at the time, collapsed in revolutionary turmoil. The effect on its oil industry was crippling: exports originally in excess of five million barrels a day dropped because of strikes and attendant technical difficulties until, by the end of 1979, shipments stopped completely.[18] Teheran eventually resumed exports, but at levels nearly two million barrels per day below its 1978 average. As supplies of oil fell, prices on the spot market began to rise rapidly. Oil companies, anticipating additional price increases, hurried to build their stocks, further tightening the market.[19] Sensing the opportunity, OPEC members agreed to a formula that would increase average prices by nearly 15 percent over the year, and pressure quickly mounted for still greater increases.

Finally, beginning in April 1979, the second crisis struck home in the United States: gasoline lines appeared, first in California and then on the East Coast.[20] To many energy experts, in government and out, it seemed like a nightmare come true. The country's energy vulnerability, actually worsened by poor and ineffective policies, had once again resulted in serious economic dislocation.

TABLE 5

Net Imports of Crude Oil and Petroleum Products by Country of Origin, 1960–85

(1,000 barrels/day)

Year	OPEC						Non-OPEC					Total Imports	U.S. dependence on OPEC		
	Nigeria	Saudi Arabia	Venezuela	Other OPEC	Total OPEC	Arab OPEC	Canada	Mexico	United Kingdom	Virgin Is./ Puerto Rico	Other non-OPEC		Total imports as pct. of consumption	OPEC imports as pct. of total imports	OPEC imports as pct. of consumption
1960	0	84	910	317	1,311	292	86	-2	-12	34	195	1,613	16.5%	81.3%	13.4%
1961	0	73	878	333	1,283	284	167	27	-10	42	232	1,743	17.5	73.6	12.9
1962	0	74	905	232	1,210	241	229	35	-6	40	405	1,913	18.4	63.3	11.6
1963	0	108	899	274	1,282	258	243	29	-7	43	325	1,915	17.8	67.0	11.9
1964	0	131	932	296	1,359	293	272	23	-9	45	368	2,057	18.7	66.1	12.3
1965	15	158	994	308	1,475	324	297	21	-11	45	454	2,281	19.8	64.7	12.8
1966	11	147	1,018	295	1,470	291	352	6	-6	58	494	2,375	19.6	61.9	12.2
1967	5	92	937	224	1,258	177	400	13	-51	89	521	2,230	17.8	56.4	12.2
1968	9	74	886	332	1,302	272	468	15	13	143	668	2,609	19.5	49.9	10.0
1969	49	65	875	346	1,336	276	564	10	7	186	831	2,933	20.8	45.5	9.7
1970	50	30	989	274	1,343	196	736	9	-1	270	804	3,161	21.5	42.5	9.4
1971	102	128	1,019	422	1,671	327	831	-14	-1	365	848	3,701	24.3	45.2	9.1
1972	251	189	959	662	2,061	529	1,082	-20	-1	428	969	4,519	27.6	45.6	11.0
1973	459	485	1,134	913	2,991	914	1,294	-28	0	426	1,343	6,025	34.8	49.6	12.6
1974	713	461	978	1,125	3,277	752	1,038	-27	1	475	1,127	5,892	35.4	55.6	17.3
1975	762	714	702	1,421	3,599	1,382	824	29	7	484	904	5,846	35.8	61.6	19.7
1976	1,025	1,229	699	2,110	5,063	2,423	571	53	24	488	891	7,090	40.6	71.4	22.0
1977	1,143	1,379	689	2,978	6,190	3,184	446	155	117	560	1,097	8,565	46.5	72.3	29.0
1978	919	1,142	644	3,042	5,747	2,962	359	291	173	436	996	8,002	42.5	71.8	33.6
1979	1,080	1,354	688	2,510	5,633	3,054	438	418	196	353	948	7,985	43.1	70.5	30.5
1980	857	1,259	478	1,699	4,293	2,549	347	506	169	256	794	6,365	37.3	67.4	30.4
1981	620	1,128	403	1,165	3,315	1,844	358	497	370	169	693	5,401	33.6	61.4	25.2
1982	512	551	409	663	2,136	852	397	632	442	154	538	4,298	28.1	49.7	20.6
1983	299	336	420	788	1,843	630	471	802	374	178	644	4,312	28.3	42.7	14.0
1984	215	324	544	953	2,037	817	547	714	388	184	820	4,688	29.8	43.4	12.1
1985	287	167	606	756	1,815	473	694	754	299	114	588	4,264	27.2	42.6	13.0

SOURCE: United States [23], 1985:113.

As the crisis worsened, Carter tried to work with the IEA and leaders of the other major consuming countries in shaping the U.S. response, but found that this was a two-edged sword. Since the shortfall caused by the loss of Iranian production did not formally exceed the "trigger" level of 7 percent for any of the members, the IEA emergency arrangements—mandatory conservation, stock-drawdown, and sharing of petroleum—did not come into effect.[21] But the IEA, in periodic ministerial-level meetings, had become a forum for the discussion of energy issues between the United States and the other consuming countries. Among other things, the members had agreed to a common target for oil imports in 1985, and the Secretariat of the Agency had begun preparing annual reviews of the performance of member countries in achieving common objectives. Not surprisingly, these revealed that the United States had accomplished very little as far as collective goals were concerned.

In response to the Iranian shutdown, the IEA Governing Board agreed that members would reduce their demand for imports by about 5 percent. Although the agreement did not set forth individual targets for countries, the Carter Administration interpreted this as an obligation to reduce imports by about a million barrels per day.[22] European leaders, in their annual summit meetings with the U.S. President, also urged him to take action, pointing out that American consumption accounted for fully half of all the oil consumed by the IEA countries and that the continued growth of demand in the United States was a major cause of the tightening world market for petroleum.[23] They came very close, in fact, to blaming the United States for making the current crisis possible.

Under growing pressure at home and abroad to "do something," Carter on April 5, 1979, once again went before the American people with a package of energy-policy proposals. Warning that the country's security was "dangerously dependent on a thin line of oil tankers stretching halfway around the earth," he announced that he would use his authority under the amended EPAA to begin decontrolling the price of domestic oil. To cushion the shock, he said he would do this gradually, over a period of 28 months, beginning June 1, 1979. He then proposed that 50 percent of the increase be captured by a special excise tax—the Windfall Profits Tax (WPT)—the proceeds of which would be used (1) to promote production of alternative energy sources (funds to be placed in a special Energy Security Fund), (2) to protect low-income persons from economic hardship stemming from price increases, and (3) to build more mass transportation systems. In asking for a windfall profits tax he made a special appeal to the public for support in Congress, revealing a growing cynicism about the legislative process.

First, as surely as the sun will rise, the oil companies can be expected to fight to keep the profits which they have not earned. Unless you speak out, they will have more influence on the Congress than you do. Second, the inevitable scrambling by interest groups for a larger share of these revenues can leave the Congress divided, bogged down, and unable to act. Unless your voice is heard, once again the selfishness of a few will block action which is badly needed to help our entire nation.[24]

Carter went on to announce other actions, most of them administrative in character, to accelerate production and promote conservation. He exhorted the American people to drive less during the crisis. He also promised a more extensive program to accelerate the use of solar energy in the country.

Carter did not tie decontrol to the passage of the Windfall Profits Tax. Although he proposed them both as solutions to the new crisis, he made it clear that decontrol would go forward independently— and it did, beginning June 1, 1979. Like Ford before him, he hoped that the prospect of accelerated price decontrol, even though phased in over more than two years, would provide a powerful incentive for Congressional action to assure fairness in the distribution of the resulting profits.[25] It is clear too that, because of the second crisis, Carter and his advisers now felt a more urgent need for price increases to promote new production and cutbacks in consumption.

The spring and early summer of 1979 was a difficult time for the Carter Administration, mainly because of energy problems. Gasoline lines continued to plague the country, and the government had a hard time explaining them. Carter's standing in public opinion polls dropped to the lowest levels he had experienced as President. At the end of March a partial meltdown of the core in the power plant at Three Mile Island raised serious doubts about the adequacy of federal regulation of nuclear energy. Congress complained that Carter had prepared no standby rationing plan for gasoline, as required by the EPCA, but when he submitted the plan for approval, the House rejected it on the grounds that it favored rural residents.[26] Congress did begin work on Carter's proposals for a windfall profits tax and for ways to use the resulting revenues, but with no urgency—discussions would last into the following year. And in any case these measures could be expected to have little immediate impact.

There was, in fact, not much that the President could do about the worsening energy situation, or at least not much that would really

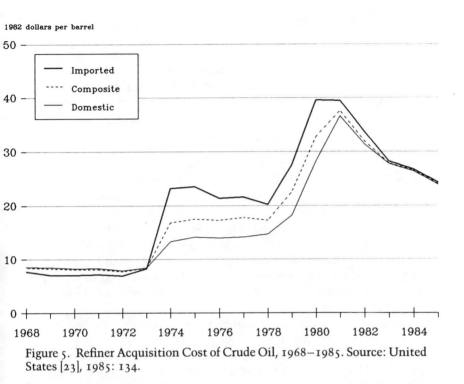

1982 dollars per barrel

Figure 5. Refiner Acquisition Cost of Crude Oil, 1968–1985. Source: United States [23], 1985: 134.

affect the short-term prospects and project the image of leadership he so badly needed and desired. As it was, many of the measures he took—lowering the temperatures of government buildings, asking people to drive fifteen fewer miles per week—seemed petty or insignificant to many in the face of the "real" issues: the high price of energy, the shortage of gasoline, the power of far away Arab and Iranian leaders.

By early summer Carter decided that he must again take action, and he reluctantly scheduled another address to the nation for July 5. He had already announced the results of his special review of the potential of solar and other forms of renewable energy, and had set a goal of obtaining fully 20 percent of the nation's energy from these sources by the turn of the century.[27] The week before his scheduled talk, Carter met in Tokyo with the leaders of the six other industrial consumers—Japan, Canada, Britain, France, Germany, and Italy—and pledged, as part of an overall agreement to reduce demand, that the United States would hold its imports for five years to 8.5 million barrels per day. As it happened, OPEC met at the same time and increased prices again (see Fig. 5).[28] Pressure mounted.

At the last minute, Carter canceled his scheduled address. Explaining that he wanted time to think, he retreated to Camp David and scheduled an intensive seminar on the nation's problems and on the effectiveness of his own administration. To it he invited nearly a hundred leaders, experts, and friends. It took the form of small group discussions that went well beyond energy matters. Although the move upset several of the President's advisers, it was in one sense quite characteristic: after he was elected, Carter tended, often to his own political disadvantage, to place substance before appearance. Problems were accumulating, and he was unsure that still another "energy emergency" speech would be useful.[29]

In the end, Carter decided to go ahead with his energy address. As a result of the Camp David talks, however, he expanded the topic to include broad observations on the general malaise he felt the country was suffering from. He apparently hoped that, by broadening the conceptual framework of the problem, he could then convince the people—and even Congress—to accept his leadership in energy as a means of bringing the nation together and overcoming an even deeper crisis of confidence.

Carter's new proposals contained no real surprises. He announced that he was imposing a quota on imports for 1979 of 8.2 million barrels per day—about the figure they were expected to reach anyway—and that in no future year would he allow imports again to exceed the 1977 average of 8.6 million barrels per day.[30] This fit with commitments already made to the other members of the IEA. He also asked Congress to authorize a new Energy Security Corporation to promote the development, by private enterprise, of synthetic fuels to replace petroleum. These included, among others, liquids from oil shale, coal, and biomass (such as alcohol). He suggested the Corporation be authorized to spend up to $88 billion dollars over the next decade, most of it drawn from the windfall profits tax he proposed in April. To speed the production of domestic energy sources of all kinds, he also proposed the creation of a special Energy Mobilization Board with the authority to cut through the tangle of government restrictions that so often added years to the time needed to complete new projects.

The idea of a synfuels corporation, like the windfall profits tax, had already been advanced unsuccessfully by Ford. The growing sense of frustration caused by price increases and gasoline lines, however, had led to renewed Congressional interest in alternative domestic sources of liquid fuels. Needless to say, there was considerable support for this from private industry. Indeed, the synfuels bandwagon had already gained such momentum that some subsidy arrangement would probably have passed Congress without presidential initiative.

The Windfall Profits Tax and Other Measures

Congress worked on Carter's proposals—and on a large number of other energy measures introduced by individual senators and representatives—throughout 1979. The windfall profits tax caused the greatest struggles. Critics of the oil industry, mostly Democrats, sought a stiffer rate than Carter's proposed 50 percent; industry supporters proposed an exemption from the tax entirely if the profits were reinvested by companies in the discovery and production of new energy sources. Legislators also differed on how to use the proceeds—estimates of which grew dramatically with the escalation of world oil prices. As the debates proceeded, many oil and gas representatives concluded that some tax was inevitable, especially if price controls were to continue to be lifted.[31]

During the spring and summer of 1980 Congress sent Carter the results of another year and a half's work on energy: two more large and detailed bills, one dealing with taxes and the other with synfuels development (the Energy Mobilization Board proposed by the President died in committee). As it turned out, these were the last major pieces of legislation to result from the energy crisis. The first of the two bills was a compromise version of a windfall profits tax. The bill set different rates for different classes of oil, with oil from wells producing before 1979 bearing the heaviest burden of 70 percent, oil from new wells set at 30 percent, and oil produced by independents (the first thousand barrels) paying 50 percent.[32] In all cases the tax was to be paid on earnings above a base price that itself would be adjusted upward to account for inflation. The goal, of course, was to capture a portion of the earnings that stemmed from the action of OPEC and that were therefore "unearned" in the sense that they were in excess of the returns expected by the companies when they originally invested.

Congress estimated the tax would bring in a total of $227.3 billion but rejected Carter's proposal that the money be dedicated to the Energy Security Fund. Instead, the proceeds were to go into the pool of general revenues collected by the government. Congress also set an expiration date on the tax, either the end of 1990 if the full $227.3 billion had been collected, or the end of 1993. Finally, legislators included in the tax bill a bundle of new credits and incentives to promote residential and commercial conservation and the production of synfuels (including gasohol). They also included a section providing $3 billion in grants to state agencies to help low-income families cope with rising fuel bills.[33]

The second of the two bills, and the last major energy bill to reach Carter's desk, was the Energy Security Act, also known as the "synfuels bill." This bill called for the creation of an independent government corporation, called the Synthetic Fuels Corporation (SFC), that would administer a program of government incentives to promote the production of synthetic fuels from coal, shale, and tar sands. The Corporation would operate much like an investment bank, drawing on funds held in the U.S. Treasury. It could offer price or loan guarantees, or promise to purchase fuels produced; if necessary it could even enter into joint-venture agreements with private companies.[34] The goal was 500,000 barrels per day (oil equivalent) by 1987 and 2 million by 1992. Congress authorized the expenditure of $20 billion to 1984, at which time the SFC would have to return to the legislature with a plan for future activities.[35] At that time, according to the bill, an additional $68 billion might be added to the SFC's funds, for a total of $88 billion. Like the windfall profits tax, the SFC was to have a limited life span: its authority to make awards would terminate in 1992, and it would go out of business in 1997.

The Energy Security Act also contained additional, but far less ambitious, incentives for the production of biomass fuels and solar energy, and for the promotion of energy conservation. Among other things, it authorized the creation of a Solar Energy and Conservation Bank within the Department of Housing and Urban Development to provide subsidized loans to individuals and businesses seeking to invest in solar equipment or reduce their consumption of energy by making conservation improvements.

As the Carter Administration drew to a close, the energy crisis quietly slipped from people's minds. Imports leveled off and then began to decline as the economy moved into recession and as investments in smaller cars, insulation, and fuel-efficient equipment (as well as new habits), finally began to reduce the volume of petroleum required to satisfy the needs of the economy. Prices, too, began to weaken as the tight international market gave way to one in which oil offered for sale exceeded demand by larger and larger amounts.

It is clear in retrospect that the years of crisis were deeply frustrating ones for the country: energy problems were inherently divisive in nature, and they frustrated the efforts of presidents who tried valiantly to provide strong leadership and draw from the experience a sense of national accomplishment and unity. Carter's assessment, two years later, could almost certainly be the words of Nixon and Ford as well: "In looking back on the 'moral equivalent of war' against energy waste and excessive vulnerability from oil imports, I see nothing exhilarating or pleasant. It was a bruising fight, and no final clear-cut victory could be photographed and hung on the wall for our grandchildren to admire."[36]

Reagan and the End of Crisis

In sharp contrast with his predecessors, Ronald Reagan refused to acknowledge the energy crisis. He charged that the only crisis was the one created by the government policies that had held back the development of the country's abundant energy resources. The solution, therefore, was to reduce the government's involvement and let "the market" decide what energy forms should be developed, what they should cost, and how the resulting losses and benefits should be allocated.[37] Among other things, he promised to abolish the Department of Energy—to him the symbol of the red tape slowing energy projects—and to accelerate the deregulation of prices.

After the election, Reagan's new energy team set to work trying to implement this approach. His Energy Secretary, James B. Edwards, came to Washington with the understanding that his job was to dismantle the energy bureaucracy, remove barriers to production, and return to private life as quickly as possible. The first major energy policy statement of the administration, the *National Energy Policy Plan*—the word "policy" was added to make the annual report, required by law, seem less like a planning document—stressed that the administration wanted to make a "clean break" with the regulatory, interventionist approach of the past, abandon futile efforts to protect consumers from inevitable price increases, and let the market take over.[38] The only clear-cut exception to this approach was the administration's pledge to revitalize the nuclear industry. This apparently stemmed from the belief, shared by both Reagan and Edwards, that nuclear energy was economically competitive but had been so burdened by regulations and the antinuclear movement that its development had been stymied.

Like the energy managers of previous administrations, however, Reagan's team found, first, that they still had a lot to learn about the government's role in the energy business, and second, that that role had a powerful momentum of its own, a momentum that reflected hard-won political compromises between consumers and producers

TABLE 6

Average Gasoline and Heating Oil Retail Prices, 1960–85

($/gallon)

	Gasoline		Heating Oil			Gasoline		Heating Oil	
Year	Current prices	Constant prices[a]	Current prices	Constant prices[a]	Year	Current prices	Constant prices[a]	Current prices	Constant prices[a]
1960	0.31	1.01	0.15	0.49	1973	0.39	0.78	0.23	0.46
1961	0.31	0.99	0.16	0.50	1974	0.53	0.99	0.36	0.67
1962	0.31	0.96	0.16	0.49	1975	0.57	0.96	0.38	0.64
1963	0.30	0.94	0.16	0.49	1976	0.59	0.94	0.41	0.64
1964	0.30	0.92	0.16	0.49	1977	0.62	0.92	0.46	0.68
1965	0.31	0.92	0.16	0.47	1978	0.63	0.87	0.49	0.68
1966	0.32	0.92	0.16	0.47	1979	0.86	1.09	0.70	0.90
1967	0.33	0.93	0.17	0.47	1980	1.19	1.39	0.97	1.14
1968	0.34	0.89	0.17	0.46	1981	1.31	1.40	1.19	1.27
1969	0.35	0.87	0.18	0.45	1982	1.22	1.22	1.16	1.16
1970	0.36	0.85	0.19	0.44	1983	1.16	1.11	1.08	1.04
1971	0.36	0.82	0.20	0.44	1984	1.13	1.04	1.09	1.01
1972	0.36	0.78	0.20	0.42	1985	1.12	1.00	1.05	0.94

SOURCE: United States [23], 1985:139.
[a]Constant prices are in 1982 dollars.

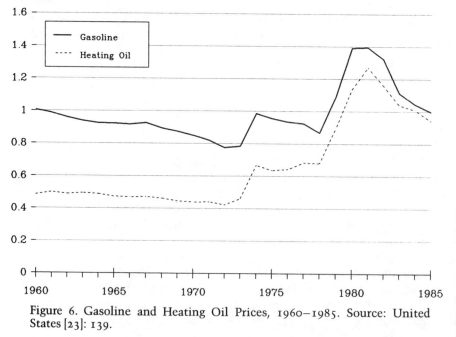

Figure 6. Gasoline and Heating Oil Prices, 1960–1985. Source: United States [23]: 139.

and between different regions of the country. They also discovered that the crisis had created influential stakeholders who would resist any changes in existing arrangements. Thus although they tried hard, especially in the first two years, to impose a "clean break" with the past, they had very little success. Edwards eventually did return home, but he left behind an intact Department of Energy, regulated natural gas, an ailing nuclear industry, and (despite an increase in exploration and drilling) an oil industry whose domestic production was continuing to decline.[39]

Unlike the three Presidents before him, Reagan was really very lucky when it came to energy. During his first term, he faced no crises, no public and Congressional clamor for action, no challenge to his leadership from events beyond his control. He could, and for the most part did, simply ignore energy matters. The fact that he did not fully understand the energy challenge, or the political consequences of a purely "market" approach, did not end up causing problems for him or his administration.

The reason for this was that changes in the world oil market and in the national economy and energy system—changes that had little to do with government policy—turned scarcity into abundance and began to force prices downward, despite OPEC's best efforts to hold them up. As noted earlier, many of these trends had already become visible toward the end of the Carter Administration. Worldwide recession reduced demand, and high prices, along with growing anxiety about future price increases, had led to more efficient uses of energy throughout the economy. In fact, before Reagan's first term was half over, price *reductions* were the principal worry of many experts, as a glut of oil on world markets led several OPEC members—as well as one "observer," Mexico, and several nonmembers, including Britain and Norway—to break ranks with the cartel. A measure of the magnitude of this change is provided by average gasoline prices in the United States, probably the most politically important indicator of the state of the energy economy. As Table 6 and Fig. 6 reveal, gasoline prices, after climbing steeply for years, dropped by 9 cents a gallon between 1981 and 1982.

Price Deregulation

Shortly after his inauguration, Reagan advanced the scheduled date for the full deregulation of crude oil and gasoline prices and the dismantling of the cumbersome allocation regulations and entitlements program associated with price controls.[40] Despite the fanfare, the move was mainly symbolic. The EPCA, passed under Ford, had set the time for deregulation as October 1, 1981, and Carter, once his crude oil equalization tax had been rejected, had affirmed the decision to deregulate and accelerated the process of phased decontrol. Indeed, when Reagan at the end of January decided to advance the date by 8 months, decontrol was already all but complete, with only about 15 percent of the crude processed by American refineries remaining under controls.[41]

The decision to decontrol set off a chorus of criticism from consumer representatives and dire predictions of price increases, but the President was in no danger. The really difficult political ground had been traveled by Carter. Deregulation had proceeded far enough so that prices were, for the most part, undisturbed by presidential action; they continued to soften and then decline.

The new administration approached natural gas decontrol with greater caution, a reflection of the political and economic forces that affected that fuel. Natural gas, like oil, was no longer in shortage, for many of the same reasons. But few in Congress wanted to reopen the debate so soon after the difficult compromises achieved in 1978; they preferred, as in the case of oil, to let time bring deregulation. They could wait until 1985. Furthermore, gas producers themselves were divided about accelerated deregulation; some even opposed it, fearing a drop in prices.

The gas market, in the meantime, became tangled in still another regulatory thicket as the economy plunged into recession and demand for energy weakened. The framers of the 1978 NGPA were worried mainly about price increases, and paid little attention to problems associated with price reductions. When demand began to decline, many utilities found themselves burdened with long-term contracts that required them to "take or pay," that is, to buy the amounts agreed to or pay the sellers as if they had purchased those amounts. Such contracts were important to producers because they guaranteed an income stream that would compensate them for the risks of exploration and development. But to utilities faced with reduced demand and seeking to minimize costs, these arrangements posed a serious challenge. The result was that, as demand declined, prices paid by consumers in many gas markets did not, and in some cases actually increased. These developments did little to ease the fears of consumers about the capacity of the free market to protect their interests.

When the Reagan Administration, after nearly two years, finally got around to proposing gas decontrol, its proposal was carefully qualified. It called for full decontrol in 1986 (rather than new gas decontrol in 1985) but provided that price increases to that year would be held to levels below those agreed to in the 1978 Act. Despite these assurances and a somewhat belated drive by administration officials to push deregulation, however, Congress would have none of it.[42] Gas remained as before, with new gas deregulation beginning in 1985 and everyone involved quite unhappy with the operation of the regulatory system in existence.

Subsidies and the Department of Energy

Consistent with its view that markets should determine both the success or failure of different energy forms (except nuclear) and the distribution of costs and benefits stemming from their development and use, the Reagan Administration tried to abolish the Department of Energy and, in its annual budget proposals, sought to eliminate most incentive programs and research and development subsidies for fossil fuels, conservation, and solar energy. It also requested major cuts in programs to help poor people pay for the increased costs of energy.

The plan to redistribute the functions performed by the DOE made no headway in Congress. Although the Department served no major outside constituency, dismantling it involved no real budgetary savings.[43] The bulk of the agency's budget turned out to be in defense-related nuclear matters anyway. Furthermore, the administration had already eliminated much of the DOE's regulatory authority in oil and was in the process of cutting and reorganizing its international affairs division. The Department did lose a significant percentage of its research and development budget, and nearly 20 percent of its work force, but it survived otherwise intact.

The proposed cuts in subsidies and research and development programs provoked a defensive response from the energy "advice" community that had promoted them and now had a stake in their continuance. The Reagan proposals were based on the premise that only long-term basic research really needed support. Energy systems with a near-term promise should be left to the private sector. In practical terms, this meant the administration would end the government's role in subsidizing, promoting, and "commercializing" fossil fuels, conservation, solar energy, and conventional light-water reactors. It would continue to support the fast-breeder reactor, and would increase its support for long-term basic research in nuclear energy areas such as particle physics.

Congress eventually agreed to cut back subsidy and research programs, but it refused to abandon them entirely. With the crisis atmosphere gone, subsidies seemed less urgent, and problems with the management of price and allocation programs had raised doubts in the minds of many legislators concerning the capacity of the federal government to intervene effectively in the energy markets.[44] But many were nevertheless reluctant to abandon programs so recently brought into existence.

The synfuels program (and the SFC) posed special problems. On the one hand, they represented precisely the kind of commercialization activity Reagan had promised to eliminate; on the other, they benefited large industrial interests that had backed Reagan's election bid. After an intense struggle within the government, Reagan agreed to subsidies for the first three projects, two oil shale ventures in Colorado and a synthetic gas project in North Dakota. These were in the planning stage before the change of administration, and were the only projects ready for support. After this, the administration decided, in effect, to let the synfuels program atrophy. Accordingly, the SFC moved slowly in its deliberations, making no new agreements in Reagan's first term. Nor did it return to Congress for an additional $68 billion in 1984.

Declining oil prices, in the meantime, rapidly eroded private-sector interest in the heavily capital-intensive synfuels projects. It was clear by early 1985 that the targets set in the Energy Security Act of 1980—500,000 barrels per day in 1987 and 2 million in 1992—would not be achieved. In 1985 the most promising of the projects, the coal-gasification project in North Dakota, went bankrupt when the DOE refused to grant a supplementary subsidy of $720 million.[45]

During his first term, Reagan twice tried to halve the low-income energy-assistance program but failed both times. The program began in 1980 with a budget of $1.6 billion. Reagan proposed reductions of about $700 million, but Congress instead increased it to adjust for inflation. By 1984 it had grown to $2 billion.[46]

Production

To promote conventional energy production, the Reagan Administration tried, on the one hand, to remove regulatory and legal obstacles, and, on the other, to enlarge the private sector's access to energy resources themselves. As was the case with its attempts to abolish subsidies, this was only partially successful.

Environmental regulations, including the many directly and indirectly impinging on energy development, were a prominent target of

Reagan's attacks on the role of government in the economy, and his appointees worked hard to implement his views. However, the landmark laws like the National Environmental Policy Act, the Clean Air and Water Acts, and the Surface Mining and Reclamation Act, all proved invulnerable to direct attack. They were, after all, the products of a lengthy process of consensus-building and political compromise about how the nation should approach its mounting environmental problems.

As with all major regulatory legislation, the environmental protection laws did leave a great deal of discretion to the Executive Branch to find the best means of fulfilling the intent of the law. The administration therefore sought to reduce their impact by changing the manner in which they were enforced. Cuts in the budgets of regulatory agencies such as the Environmental Protection Agency, appointment of regulators unsympathetic with the goals of regulation, and reduced enforcement activities by such agencies as the Office of Surface Mining in the Department of the Interior—all helped Reagan's managers achieve their objectives.[47] But these indirect methods also led to a growing backlash that, though not strong enough to prevent the crippling of many regulatory programs, in the end helped thwart the achievement of the larger goal of significantly reducing regulatory obstacles to energy development.

Reagan's experience with the promotion of new production was similar. This was led by Interior Secretary James Watt, who fashioned a controversial new leasing system designed to make nearly one billion acres of public lands—mostly offshore—available for private lease to oil and gas companies. Under the new system, known as "areawide" leasing, the government abandoned the old method of offering limited, well-defined tracts and instead offered vast areas of ocean bottom to private interests.

As might be expected, Watt's plan met fierce resistance from Congress and conservationists. Of the 41 sales planned by the Interior Department, fewer than 30 were actually held because of Congressional moratoria and court-ordered restrictions. Industry, too, proved far less excited about the prospects for new discoveries. Of the 265 million acres that were offered, only 13 million were actually leased. In some cases the government was embarrassed to find no takers at all. One sale in the Atlantic in 1984, for example, attracted no offers from industry; the only bidders were environmentalists trying to protect a lobster-breeding ground.[48] The program did succeed in accelerating the leasing process—in the previous 29 years of leasing on the outer continental shelf, 62 million acres were offered and 24 million were leased—but it did not live up to the administration's expectations.[49]

Security

The energy-security policies of the Reagan Administration attracted persistent criticism from experts in the energy-policy community.[50] This was because, as the world oil glut increased and the country's profile of import dependence shifted to include fewer barrels from insecure sources, Reagan's energy managers demonstrated very little concern about another supply crisis (see Figure 4). What had become the standard measure of the effectiveness of energy policy for three Presidents, displacing imported oil, had now became a secondary concern to the government, and many were nervous about this reorientation.

The first major controversy arose when the EPAA expired in October of 1981, and with it the emergency authority for the United States to impose price controls and allocate supplies of crude oil and products by utilizing the standby rationing plan approved by Congress. Many experts felt the power to intervene in a crisis was necessary if the United States were to fulfill its obligations as a member of the IEA, since that agreement called for each country to have "demand restraint" policies available should they be needed. The Reagan Administration claimed that it did not want such authority, since it planned to allow the market to manage any future emergency, and that in any case existing law covering emergencies contained all the necessary provisions. Congress disagreed with this interpretation, and passed a bill in the spring of 1982 providing new standby authorities, but Reagan quickly vetoed it. The Senate tried to override him but failed.

Critics also complained that the Reagan Administration did not fill the Strategic Petroleum Reserve (SPR) quickly enough. In 1982 Congress reduced the target from 1 billion barrels, the goal under Carter, to 750 million barrels, but mandated a minimal fill rate of 300,000 barrels a day; however, the legislators stipulated that the President could lower this for national security reasons or if the budget required it. In December 1982, Reagan reduced the rate to 220,000 barrels per day; and in 1983 he reduced it again to 186,000. For 1985, the administration proposed a fill rate of only 145,000 barrels per day, announcing that it planned to have the SPR completely filled by 1990, but it actually filled it at a rate of approximately

50,000 barrels per day.[51] Opponents of these actions focused on the seeming incongruity of insisting on budgetary stringency with re- spect to defensive energy measures while paying much larger sums to prepare for military intervention in the Middle East in the case of an energy-related emergency.[52]

The slowdown in the fill rate of the SPR, along with the elimina- tion of the International Affairs section of the Department of Energy and the decision to cut the budget for energy contingency planning by about 40 percent, also raised fears in IEA member countries that the United States had turned against the idea of consumer self- protection in energy. For the most part, however, these fears proved unjustified. Despite the administration's lack of enthusiasm for col- lective demand-restraint measures and its apparent complacency with respect to the possibility of another supply crisis, the United States remained an active member of the IEA. Among other things, the Agency continued to test emergency preparedness in periodic simulations of oil-supply crises. One of the simulations, in fact, re- vealed that the market allocation approach of the Reagan Adminis- tration could result, if simulated conditions were to occur in the real world, in oil prices of as much as $98 a barrel and U.S. domestic gasoline prices of nearly $3 a gallon.[53] This, plus the realization that by mid-1984 the SPR had grown to more than 400 million barrels, led the administration to consider the possibility of using the stored oil as a kind of buffer stock, to be released for sale early in a crisis to reduce market pressures. In July of 1984 IEA members agreed that in a crisis they would form an informal consultation group to coor- dinate the use of IEA stockpiles for this purpose, hoping thereby to avert the need to activate the IEA demand-restraint or allocation mechanisms.[54]

At the end of his first term Reagan could look back on his experi- ence with energy with none of the bitterness and frustration that characterized Carter's reminiscences. The world was awash with oil, even if domestic production had not responded as Reagan claimed it would with deregulation. Prices had come down, helping to curb inflation. OPEC seemed to be weaker than at any time since the embargo of 1973–74. And there had been no disruption severe enough to tighten supply and send prices soaring, despite the drawn- out war between Iran and Iraq and the continuing tensions between Israel and its Arab neighbors. To be sure, in retrospect it is clear that none of these things was the result of Reagan's own policies, except insofar as he and Congress agreed to follow the trend-line of return to "normalcy" set in place by governments that preceded his. But the point remains: "energy" had left the headlines, along with the sense of national impotence and frustration that it represented. The crisis was over.

Summary

The years after 1977 were years of bitter political struggle over energy policy, a struggle intensified by the mounting perception among policymakers that existing policies were not working well. President Carter tried to replace the regulatory system affecting oil and to promote a host of new policies designed to reduce imports, increase the efficiency of energy use within the country, and assure an equitable distribution of the burden of high prices. He found the policy system locked in a stalemate, with producers, consumers, and other stakeholders unwilling to agree on coherent alternatives. Although a number of new measures did survive the gauntlet, key policies continued to reflect this fundamental political paralysis. In the end, the best Carter could do was to accelerate the process of deregulation, a process set in place before he was elected. Reagan completed the dismantling of petroleum price and allocation controls, and sought, albeit with limited success, to reduce still further the government's role in the energy regimes. The next chapter examines in some detail what U.S. policies accomplished—and did not accomplish—in these years.

PART THREE   Assessment

CHAPTER 8

Energy Policy in Perspective

It is time now to return to the broader questions that form the concern of this inquiry. How did we do, as a country, in managing the energy crisis? Did our policies work? Are we better equipped now to cope with similar crises? Can we look back with any sense of satisfaction, or even pride, at the way our capitalist democracy performed?

In this chapter I take the first step in addressing these questions by examining more closely just what happened in the energy system and asking about the role of energy policies in shaping this outcome. Among other things, I am interested in how patterns of energy use changed (and why), how well we prepared for future crises, and how costs and benefits were distributed.

Despite the enormous confusion and conflict that surrounded the embargo and its aftermath, the key political problem created by the crisis was the forced transfer of wealth, on an unprecedented scale, between producers and consumers of petroleum. The political economy had to answer, in short order, several momentous questions. Just how large would the OPEC tax be? And, since price increases for all petroleum products and their substitutes would result, how would the domestic transfers of wealth be handled? Which Americans would benefit, and which would lose?

One approach, of course, would have been for the government to ignore the matter, allowing existing arrangements to handle necessary adjustments. In retrospect, this would have had a number of attractive features. But it was not the approach chosen. OPEC, especially its Arab contingent, appeared to be achieving a degree of influence over U.S. policy that American leaders found intolerable; they viewed it, in effect, as a fundamental threat to the country's security. The domestic transfer of wealth from consumers to producers, in the eyes of American voters, was so unfair that their legislative representatives feared for their jobs if they did not do something to prevent it. Finally, the issue was heavily influenced by the fact that "existing arrangements" already involved the government so extensively that the question of whether or not public policy would influence these transfers was already moot.

Petroleum Imports and the Energy Economy

To someone examining energy statistics for the first time in the mid-1980's it would appear that the United States, after a poor start, eventually did quite well in reducing its dependence on imported oil and its vulnerability to embargo. Petroleum imports declined briefly after the embargo, but then quickly resumed their growth, reaching a historic high in 1977 (see Fig. 4, p. 119). Moreover, much of the new oil came from precisely those Arab members of OPEC that engineered the embargo itself. But after 1977 the trend reversed; imports declined steeply while the profile of import sources changed so that the United States received fewer and fewer barrels from insecure sources. (See Table 5, p. 120.)

What caused this change? To begin with, there was the impact of oil from Alaskan oil fields, which compensated for the continuing decline of production from fields within the lower 48 states. (See Table 7 and Fig. 9.) Most of this oil was discovered before the embargo but became available just in time to help out. And it became available when it did in part because the embargo accelerated the passage of the Alaska Pipeline Act of 1973. Second, there was the recession. Energy use is closely tied to the overall level of economic activity, and the recession that gripped the country after 1980, itself at least partly a product of energy price increases, in turn reduced the nation's appetite for oil. As shops and factories shut down, they stopped using energy. Unemployed workers had less to spend to heat their homes and drive their cars, and demand for electricity, fuel oil, and gasoline declined.[1]

There was also the direct and indirect impact of energy price increases and expectations of future increases. As price controls were phased out in the late 1970's, consumers increasingly had to pay the full world price for their petroleum products. High prices reduced demand when consumers simply could not afford supplies and changed their life-styles and expectations, and when individuals and businesses chose to invest in more efficient cars, buildings, and equipment.[2] High oil prices also promoted investment in different energy sources, conventional and unconventional, thus shifting the mix of fuels used in the country. The impact was thus not limited to petroleum imports, or even to oil itself, but affected the energy

TABLE 7
Crude Oil Production and Oil Well Productivity, 1960–85
(ooo barrels/day)

Year	Production Lower 48 states	Production Alaska	Production Total	Thousand producing wells	Average productivity per well (barrels/day)
1960	7,034	2	7,035	591	12.0
1961	7,166	17	7,183	595	12.1
1962	7,304	.28	7,332	596	12.3
1963	7,512	29	7,542	589	12.7
1964	7,584	30	7,614	588	12.9
1965	7,774	30	7,804	589	13.3
1966	8,256	39	8,295	583	14.2
1967	8,730	80	8,810	565	15.3
1968	8,915	181	9,096	554	16.2
1969	9,035	203	9,238	542	16.9
1970	9,408	229	9,637	531	18.0
1971	9,245	218	9,463	517	18.1
1972	9,242	199	9,441	508	18.4
1973	9,010	198	9,208	497	18.3
1974	8,581	193	8,774	498	17.6
1975	8,183	191	8,375	500	16.8
1976	7,958	173	8,132	499	16.3
1977	7,781	464	8,245	507	16.4
1978	7,478	1,229	8,707	517	17.0
1979	7,151	1,401	8,552	531	16.3
1980	6,980	1,617	8,597	548	15.9
1981	6,962	1,609	8,572	557	15.4
1982	6,953	1,696	8,649	580	14.9
1983	6,974	1,714	8,688	603	14.4
1984	7,157	1,722	8,879	620	14.3
1985	7,121	1,799	8,920	647	13.8

SOURCE: United States [23], 1985:103.
NOTE: Production figures include lease condensate and are rounded to the nearest whole number.

system as a whole. Indeed, the percentage of "premium fuels," oil and natural gas, in the total declined from 78 percent in 1972 to 67 percent in 1983.[3] This was mostly due to the increased use of coal and, to a lesser extent, nuclear energy to generate electricity, but also stemmed from the use of wood and other renewable energy sources.

Sorting out the precise impact of these different variables is a challenge. One way to approach the problem is to look at total energy and imported oil consumed to produce each dollar of Gross National Product (GNP). As Figures 7 and 8 reveal, the overall energy "intensity" of the American economy appears to have declined noticeably after peaking in 1970.[4] Between 1973 and 1983 this occurred at an

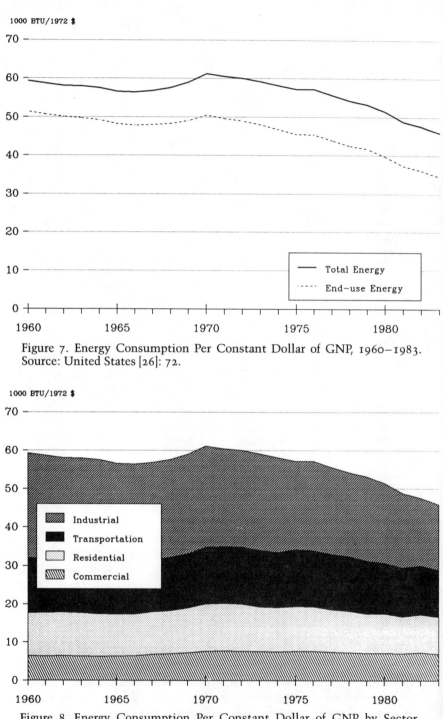

Figure 7. Energy Consumption Per Constant Dollar of GNP, 1960–1983.
Source: United States [26]: 72.

Figure 8. Energy Consumption Per Constant Dollar of GNP by Sector,
1960–1983. Source: United States [26]: 72.

TABLE 8
Consumption of Energy and Oil per Constant Dollar of GNP, 1960–83

Year	GNP (billion 1972 $)	Total U.S. energy use (trillion BTU)	Total U.S. oil use (trillion BTU)	Net oil imports (trillion BTU)	Alaskan oil (trillion BTU)	Net imports (1000 BTU/$)	Net imports plus Alaska (1000 BTU/$)	Total energy use (1000 BTU/$)	Total oil use (1000 BTU/$)	Percentage oil
1960	737.2	43,741	19,673.50	3,232.08	4.02	4.38	4.39	59.33	26.69	45%
1961	756.6	44,405	20,034.85	3,493.05	34.13	4.62	4.66	58.69	26.48	45
1962	800.3	46,481	20,878.00	3,834.33	56.21	4.79	4.86	58.08	26.09	45
1963	832.5	48,274	21,560.55	3,834.33	58.22	4.61	4.68	57.99	25.90	45
1964	876.4	50,436	22,122.65	4,135.45	60.23	4.72	4.79	57.55	25.24	44
1965	929.3	52,619	23,106.33	4,577.10	60.23	4.93	4.99	56.62	24.86	44
1966	984.8	55,592	24,250.60	4,757.78	78.29	4.83	4.91	56.45	24.62	44
1967	1,011.4	57,507	25,214.20	4,476.73	160.60	4.43	4.59	56.86	24.93	44
1968	1,058.1	60,942	26,880.43	5,239.58	363.36	4.95	5.30	57.60	25.40	44
1969	1,087.6	64,127	28,386.05	5,881.98	407.52	5.41	5.78	58.96	26.10	44
1970	1,085.6	66,364	29,510.25	6,343.70	459.72	5.84	6.27	61.13	27.18	44
1971	1,122.4	67,831	30,534.08	7,427.75	437.64	6.62	7.01	60.43	27.20	45
1972	1,185.6	71,195	32,862.78	9,073.90	399.49	7.65	7.99	60.05	27.72	46
1973	1,254.3	74,192	34,749.83	12,085.15	397.49	9.63	9.95	59.15	27.70	47
1974	1,246.3	72,459	33,424.87	11,824.18	387.45	9.49	9.80	58.14	26.82	46
1975	1,231.6	70,478	32,762.40	11,743.88	383.43	9.54	9.85	57.22	26.60	46
1976	1,298.2	74,278	35,050.95	14,233.18	347.30	10.96	11.23	57.22	27.00	47
1977	1,369.7	76,202	36,998.23	17,184.20	931.48	12.55	13.23	55.63	27.01	49
1978	1,438.6	78,038	37,841.38	16,060.00	2,467.22	11.16	12.88	54.25	26.30	48
1979	1,479.4	78,830	37,158.83	16,039.93	2,812.51	10.84	12.74	53.29	25.12	47
1980	1,475.0	75,927	34,247.95	12,767.70	3,246.13	8.66	10.86	51.48	23.22	45
1981	1,513.8	73,977	32,240.45	10,840.50	3,230.07	7.16	9.29	48.87	21.30	44
1982	1,485.4	70,755	30,714.75	8,632.25	3,404.72	5.81	8.10	47.63	20.68	43
1983	1,535.3	70,515	30,574.23	8,652.33	3,440.86	5.64	7.88	45.93	19.91	43

SOURCES: United States [26]:71; [23]:89, 91.

average rate of 2.5 percent per year, for a total of about 22 percent. Here a caveat is in order, however: recession and structural changes in the economy, particularly the decline of large, coal-using heavy industry, as well as changes in the types of goods and services produced, almost certainly account for a portion—perhaps as much as half—of this decline.[5] A decline in this measure, even if only 10–15 percent rather than 22 percent, is particularly important because it signals a fundamental change in the way that goods and services are produced.

With these trends in mind, note the role of oil in this picture. First, the oil-import intensity of the economy grew more quickly and then declined more rapidly than changes in either overall petroleum or energy intensity. A drop in domestic production of more than two million barrels per day between 1973 and 1979 helps account for the increase, and the appearance of Alaskan oil, as noted, helps explain the speed of the decline. Figure 9 and Table 8 depict these changes. As they reveal, consumption of imported oil per dollar of GNP by 1983 had, after rising precipitously, declined to about the level it had reached in 1969–70. This left the economy, per unit of production, about as dependent on imported petroleum as it was before the first oil shock. The overall petroleum intensity of the economy also decreased after 1977, thereafter closely paralleling the changes in the economy as a whole.

A brief look at changes that occurred in the way oil was used in the various sectors of the economy helps clarify what happened. As noted, the energy intensity of the industrial sector declined. However, the use of oil in that sector, per unit of production, remained quite stable while the use of electricity increased and the use of coal actually declined. This was because demand for oil as a feedstock for petrochemicals and as a fuel for industrial equipment remained strong while demand for metallurgical coal declined with the continued stagnation of the steel industry.[6]

Data on energy consumption per household reveal that in the residential sector demand peaked in 1972 and declined rapidly for a period after each of the major price increases (1973 and 1979–80). This was due to a combination of consumer actions, from tolerating colder rooms to caulking, weatherstripping, and installing storm windows and doors.[7] Homeowners also turned increasingly to electricity and away from oil, mainly as a result of the use of heat pumps in new homes. As a result, electricity's share of total residential energy use increased from 17 percent in 1970 to 31 percent in 1983, while oil's share declined in the same period from 29 percent to 16 percent.[8] This meant, in effect, greater reliance on coal and nuclear

1000 BTU/1972 $

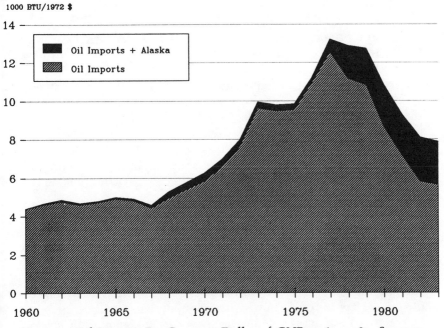

Figure 9. Oil Imports Per Constant Dollar of GNP, 1960–1983. Sources: United States [23], 1984: 89, 91; [26]: 71.

Million BTU per capita

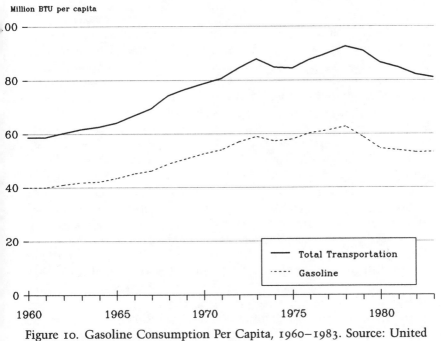

Figure 10. Gasoline Consumption Per Capita, 1960–1983. Source: United States [26]: 117.

energy, the principal sources of new electrical generating capacity after 1970. Homeowners also turned increasingly to wood to heat their homes.

Energy use in commercial buildings responded much more slowly to the oil shocks, but here also it leveled off and began to decline by the late 1970's. Demand for electricity in the commercial sector also increased—from 22 percent of the total in 1970 to 36 percent in 1983—while the demand for oil dropped from 28 percent to 17 percent.[9] Gas use remained about the same. Commercial buildings built after 1973 were far more efficient than the ones built before the crisis and subsequent price increases.[10]

Perhaps the most dramatic changes in energy consumption patterns occurred in the transportation sector, where two-thirds of the nation's petroleum is used as fuel in cars and trucks. As Figure 10 illustrates, each of the oil price shocks was followed by a reduction in gasoline demand as people drove fewer miles. More importantly, the fuel efficiency of the auto fleet improved as new cars replaced old ones. New-car efficiency increased more than 6 percent per year between 1974 and 1983. However, new-car efficiency then leveled off and in 1983 actually declined a fraction, almost certainly a response to the declining real price of gasoline that accompanied the weakening world oil market.[11]

To summarize, it is evident that the energy crisis was associated with significant changes in the energy economy in the United States. However, when these changes are examined to determine which are likely to endure—in the sense that they are basic changes in the way we use energy—the picture becomes both more complex and far less gratifying insofar as an assessment of the national performance in response to the crisis is concerned.

American demand for imported oil did decline dramatically after 1977, as did American reliance on the most insecure sources of oil, Arab OPEC members. However, this decline reflected to a significant extent a combination of new production from Alaska and reduction in demand owing to the slowdown in the economy as a whole. The remainder was the result of two other variables, ones that are more significant for our purposes: a change in the mix of fuels used by Americans, and an overall reduction in the energy intensity of economic activity. The most notable change in fuel mix was a shift in favor of electricity as an end product, and thus away from oil and natural gas and toward coal and nuclear energy as primary fuels. These changes left the economy nearly as dependent on petroleum, as a percentage of total energy used, as it was before the first oil shock.[12] As noted, over the decade the adjusted energy "in-

tensity" of the economy as a whole decreased by some 10–15 percent as a result of crisis-induced changes in life-style, investment in
more efficient buildings and capital equipment, and improvements
in the fuel efficiency of automobiles.

The Role of Policy in Altering Behavior   What, then, about the
role of public policy, and more specifically energy policy, in these
changes? To what extent can either import reduction, changes in
fuel mix, or reductions in overall domestic energy intensity be cred-
ited to the actions of the government?

The answer to these questions has two parts. The first is that the
most striking characteristic of government energy policies during
the crisis years is that they worked against each other. While some
policies acted to reduce the consumption of imported oil and encouraged Americans to conserve, others actually encouraged the importation of petroleum and the consumption of fuels derived from
it. The second is that for most of the crisis decade from 1973 to 1983
the net effect of government policies appears to have been to *increase* the level of import dependence, petroleum consumption,
and energy intensity beyond the levels they would otherwise have
attained.

In other words, insofar as a "solution" to the energy problem
meant reducing the country's imports and, thereby, limiting the
transfer of wealth abroad, government actions were, on balance, an
impediment. The reason for this is that for much of the time price
controls and entitlements encouraged refiners to import oil, and
consumers to use it, and did so to such an extent that they more
than nullified the effects of public actions with the opposite intent.

Before I proceed with an examination of the reasons for these conclusions, a brief caveat is in order. As most policy specialists are
painfully aware, the impact of public policies is difficult to measure
with precision. It is the more difficult when the assignment involves
estimating the interdependent effects of many policies whose impact has been changing over several years as well as trying to sort
out the independent influence of real and expected price increases.

In the case at hand the problem is made somewhat easier because
only a handful of policies appear to have had a very large impact on
energy use and imports. Fortunately, too, the regulations directly affecting petroleum imports—price controls and entitlements—have
been carefully examined by a number of specialists, and a broad consensus has emerged on the overall results of government action.[13]
Conservation and fuel-switching policies are more troublesome, but
here too enough data are available for us to make estimates that,
though rough, are reliable enough for present purposes.[14] The ap-

proach I have adopted in the case of policies where the relative impacts of prices and regulations are difficult to sort out is to credit *all* the plausible savings to the policy when toting up the balance sheet. As we shall see, the results still support the broad conclusions outlined above.

The Role of Conservation and Fuel Switching   Consider first those policies directly affecting the consumption of transportation fuels, especially gasoline. At the height of the crisis, American trucks and cars were consuming directly about one-ninth of all the petroleum produced in the entire world. Nearly 40 percent of this amount was used in automobile transport alone.[15] All who dealt with energy matters were aware of this, and energy-policy debates returned again and again to methods of reducing auto fuel consumption. Noting the European example, decisionmakers repeatedly considered, then rejected, hefty increases in gasoline taxes. The hikes needed to reduce demand were large, and the political costs were considered too high. Instead they legislated regulatory solutions: the 55-mph speed limit and the Corporate Average Fuel Efficiency (CAFE) standards. Interestingly enough, in the long run these will almost certainly turn out to have been the most important pieces of conservation legislation passed during the energy decade—and not solely because of their immediate impact on demand for oil imports.

The speed limit is the clearest case. After a decade in place it had saved an enormous quantity of petroleum—as much as 200,000 barrels per day, or a total of 730 million barrels of oil, extrapolating from estimates made in 1984.[16] Yet though this was a significant reduction, it was only a small percentage of total imports.[17] The 55-mph speed limit survived not because it saved energy but because it saved lives. As many as 30,000 Americans escaped death, and another 365,000 escaped injury, as a truly inadvertent consequence of this energy-saving regulation. Ironically, this great toll of injury and death avoided may, in the end, turn out to have been the single greatest and clearest benefit of a decade's labor in the energy-policy field.[18]

The CAFE standards, which mandated a fleet fuel efficiency of 27.5 miles per gallon by 1985, had no such clear external benefit, and appear equally unlikely to survive for long. As noted above, improvements in auto efficiency were important in reducing petroleum demand, and will continue to have an effect as new cars replace older gas guzzlers. If we assumed that the entire improvement in auto fuel efficiency between 1977—when they began to take effect—and 1982 were due to the operation of the CAFE standards, this would be the equivalent of approximately 405,000 barrels per day of petroleum.[19]

However, the relationship between the CAFE standards themselves and the subsequent improvement in vehicle performance is suspect. Although they vigorously opposed the passage of the standards, automakers have stated that, until as late as 1982, the market for fuel efficiency was probably at least as important as the standards in forcing adaptations in auto and truck technology.[20] The market shift, driven by a combination of price increases and hysteria, was so pronounced that it caught American automakers unprepared. The growth in demand for fuel efficiency was an important reason for the dramatic loss of market share to Japanese cars between 1976 and 1981, a period in which imports grew from 9 to 22 percent of the American market.[21] When the CAFE standards and the market finally did begin to clash, as prices declined and the public appetite for larger, heavier vehicles reasserted itself after 1982, auto companies chose to follow the market and at the same time try to influence the government to revise the standards.[22] Only if the government refuses to do so will the standards begin to exert a major independent influence on fuel consumption patterns—and this appears unlikely to happen.

The point is that though increased fuel efficiency in the transport sector was important—and may continue to be if the standards are kept or tightened—the immediate cause for the improvement was a mix of public expectations about shortages and price increases, not merely government regulation. To be sure, the CAFE standards were part of the overall context within which the automakers and the public operated, and thus contributed to the mood of urgency and concern, but this is true of all government actions during this period. The impact of exhortation or persuasion cannot be denied. But the evidence suggests that more practical concerns—real and expected prices, and availability of gasoline supplies—were at least as important in motivating decisionmakers.

In the industrial sector, changes in energy use were the target of the Power Plant and Industrial Fuel Use Act (PPIFUA) of 1978, which gave the federal government authority to regulate fuel choices by utilities and major fuel-burning installations. In particular, the Act envisioned federal prohibition of the construction of new electric power plants using oil or natural gas. In practice, however, prices were high enough to provide all the incentive that was needed to give coal a competitive advantage; and where this was not the case, the Act contained enough escape clauses to make it possible to avoid enforcement.[23]

As noted above, demand reduction and fuel switching in the residential sector contributed also to the reduction of oil imports. A number of federal programs sought to promote this change, some by providing information and subsidies directly to homeowners, and others by encouraging or requiring utilities and state energy-assistance programs to offer or subsidize energy audits and the installation of insulation, weatherstripping, and solar water heaters.[24] And conservation activity was surprisingly widespread. A survey by the Department of Energy, for example, revealed that fifteen million households made energy conservation investments of some kind in 1978.[25] Of these, nearly six million took advantage of government tax credits.[26]

For purposes of rough calculation, if we assume that petroleum-product use in the residential and commercial sectors had continued to increase after 1973 at the rate of the previous decade (2.2 percent per year), and if we then attribute to policy half the difference between these higher use levels and the actual ones to the year 1982 (when use rates began to increase again), we arrive at an annual savings of approximately 340,000 barrels per day.[27] But here too, prices and the climate of energy anxiety were also at work, and it is very difficult to credit the savings to the independent effect of policy incentives—except for a few cases (such as solar hot water heaters) in which tax credits appear to have been especially decisive.

A review of the changes in fuel mix in the residential sector also suggests that real and expected prices were by far the most important determinant. As Figure 11 reveals, there was a close correlation between changes in price and changes in consumption patterns. Although the quantities used dropped in the case of all fuels, those experiencing the smallest increases in price also experienced the smallest reductions in consumption.[28]

The Role of Price Controls, Entitlements, and the Windfall Profits Tax   Price controls on crude oil, and the regulatory arrangements associated with them, changed the operation of the energy economy in many ways that were clearly unexpected by those responsible for maintaining them. The immediate objective, of course, was to prevent domestic crude oil, and the products derived from it, from rising to OPEC-determined world price levels, thus protecting consumers from harm and blocking producers of oil from reaping "unjust" profits.[29] Insofar as controls did reduce the consumer price of petroleum products, however, they increased demand for those products beyond the levels they would otherwise have reached. In this respect, they increased overall demand for petroleum products and reduced incentives to conserve oil and all forms of energy. But the impact of controls extended also to the mix of domestic and imported petroleum used. By holding down the price received by

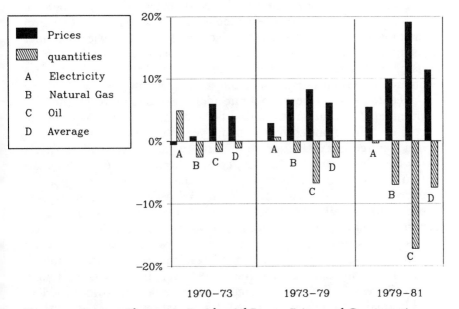

Figure 11. Percent Changes in Residential Energy Prices and Consumption, by Energy Type. Source: United States [26]: 92.

domestic crude oil producers, price controls reduced the amount of domestic petroleum produced and increased the amount of oil imported.

As noted in Chapter 6, the government at first simply tried to freeze existing price and supply arrangements. This proved untenable because it gave refiners with access to controlled domestic production a privileged position compared to those forced to pay for imported feedstocks.[30] Responding to mounting protests, energy administrators then created the entitlements system, in which those using low-priced domestic oil would make a payment to those forced to use higher-cost uncontrolled oil. This arrangement, for all its administrative complexity, was effective in preventing any refiner from profiting at the expense of others as a result of the control system. It was, at heart, a mechanism to assure fairness within the controls regime.

Unfortunately, the entitlements system also created perverse incentives insofar as the larger objective of import reduction was concerned. It made each new barrel of imported oil seem cheaper to the refiner than it was, since the refiner would receive a compensatory payment for that barrel from the entitlements system. As one analyst put it: "the effective cost of incremental crude oil to such a refiner is the uncontrolled price [or world price] *minus* the increase in receipts from the sale of entitlements."[31] It also made each barrel of domestic oil seem more expensive than it was, because the refiner using it would have to make a compensatory payment in return for using it. The result was that refiners expanded their use of imports and reduced their reliance on domestic petroleum.

According to the best economic analysis of this problem, the "entitlements" incentive subsidized between 10 and 20 percent of the cost of each imported barrel in the years between 1975 and 1980, and resulted in extra crude oil imports averaging 1.1 million barrels per day. Price controls, in turn, caused the importation of an additional 900,000 barrels per day. This extra 2 million barrels per day ended up increasing the country's annual import bill by an average of roughly 14 billion dollars.[32] Contrast these figures with the estimates cited above for the savings from the speed limit regulation (200,000 barrels per day). If in addition we were to assume that the entire fuel savings in transportation stemming from automobile efficiency improvements were due to CAFE regulations (and that none was the result of real or expected price increases), this would add an additional 405,000 barrels per day, for a total savings of 605,000 barrels per day. If we also assumed that fully half of all the commercial and residential reduction in the use of petroleum products was attributable to conservation policies, this would add an additional 340,000 barrels per day, for a total of 945,000 barrels per day, or well below the average extra imports resulting from petroleum regulations.

Note that this rough comparison of the most important policies reducing oil demand and imports purposely overstates the case by, in effect, attributing to these policies what most experts feel must be attributed in large part to the effect of prices. Nor does it include all the "lost" oil conservation savings—a kind of opportunity cost—that resulted from the fact that prices were held down by government controls.

The Role of Policy in Reducing Imports   To recapitulate, American energy policies worked at cross-purposes insofar as oil imports were concerned. Price controls and entitlements increased the overall demand for oil, and imported oil in particular, while other policies sought to reduce that demand. Though the relative impact of both sets of policies can be estimated only in very rough terms, available evidence suggests that for the critical years between 1975 and 1980 the overall impact of price controls and entitlement transfers was greater—perhaps much greater—than that of demand-reduction regulations. Over the most critical period of the energy "crisis," in other words, the policy balance—the independent influence of policy on the energy system—favored an increased demand for oil and oil products and, more specifically, for imports.

With respect to the basic problem of wealth transfer overseas, therefore, the country was worse off rather than better: OPEC received more income because the United States imported more than would otherwise have been the case. Over time, of course, this balance shifted. As price controls were phased out, the import subsidy disappeared. Demand-reduction policies then became the more important (and no doubt contributed to the downward pressure on world prices that brought OPEC considerable distress). Although the Windfall Profits Tax (WPT) did add a new disincentive to domestic production, it ceased to have an effect when oil prices dropped below the necessary threshold (about \$19.50) in the mid-1980's.[33] Thus it was not until the energy crisis was receding as a national concern, to be replaced by a world oil glut and downward pressure on international prices, that American energy policies finally began to discourage imports in a real way—and even then not as vigorously as they might have in the absence of an excise tax on domestic production.

The Issue of Security

Dependence on imported oil, of course, is not the same as vulnerability to embargo or price increases.[34] Thus, despite the fact that energy policies tended to increase imports, it is still appropriate to ask whether the government succeeded in reducing the country's actual energy vulnerability. The answer here, unfortunately, is similar to that given above: policies worked at cross-purposes, resulting in a net increase in vulnerability for much of the decade of crisis, and becoming effective only when market conditions had made the threat far less tangible.

As is so often the case with security matters, measures adopted after the Arab embargo heavily emphasized defense against a repetition of the last "enemy" success—another embargo. In doing so, unfortunately, they left the country even more vulnerable to a crisis that was quite different in character. The energy diplomacy that led to the formation of the IEA and its defensive program of stockpiles and oil-sharing arrangements was unquestionably a contribution to the nation's security. It raised the perceived costs of a targeted or general embargo, and thus acted as a deterrent to the use of the "oil weapon" in subsequent years. But the world oil system was undergoing changes that would reduce the likelihood of an embargo anyway. Key oil-exporting countries, most notably Saudi Arabia, were becoming more deeply enmeshed in the Western world economy as they recycled their revenues and mounted massive development programs relying on the purchase of foreign technology.

At the same time, quiet changes had made the world oil market less flexible and had led decisionmakers to adopt defensive attitudes that would magnify the effects of even small fluctuations in supply. As the OPEC countries took control of their resources, long-term contracts and government-to-government deals replaced the more flexible arrangements that had prevailed under the management of oil multinationals. The spot market became increasingly important as the source of contingency purchases. And American oil buyers became increasingly convinced that any change in the market would lead to higher rather than lower prices.[35]

Taken together, these conditions made it possible for the modest shortfall produced by the Iranian events of 1978–79, a shortfall of some 4 to 5 percent, to translate into a major panic and then a serious economic disaster for the world economy. Spot market purchases drove prices upward, and oil dealers quickly began to build stockpiles.

The IEA security arrangements were designed to assure adequate supply to keep economic activity going, but they did not address the possibility that the main danger was economic damage caused by uncontrolled price escalations. Since the shortfall was small, the oil-sharing system could not help. The U.S. stockpile was still quite small and not adequately connected to the crude supply system of the country. Nor had the government prepared plans for its use. Thus it was not used to cushion the shock. Efforts to regulate the spot market proved ineffective. Finally, the price-control regulations tended to exacerbate the impact of the panic by allowing buyers to increase inventories with the assurance that they would be able to pass through the added costs in future sales.[36] In this respect, policies in place had an effect similar to that they had had in the first crisis—that of enlarging the problems associated with shortages. Thus six years after the Arab embargo, just as the world economy was regaining its equilibrium, a smaller shortage of oil caused even greater economic damage. Not only did policies fail to prevent the damage, they tended to worsen it.

The reasons for the disastrous response to the Iranian shortfall have been widely analyzed.[37] Indeed, among energy analysts there has emerged a near consensus on the approach that should have been taken and on the kinds of policies that should be adopted to prevent a recurrence. These involve a combination of taxes to reduce demand and capture rents, recycling arrangements to return rents to consumers, and careful management of stocks to cushion market fluctuations.[38] A detailed analysis by the Office of Technology Assessment, a Congressional research agency, has also recommended a number of regulatory actions that would decrease the damage to the economy in the case of an extended shortfall by encouraging the adoption of oil-displacing technologies.[39] However, many of these measures, to be effective, must be in place before a crisis.

At the time of this writing, only the Strategic Reserve component of this package is in place, and plans for its use have not been firmly set, although, as noted earlier, the United States has agreed to discuss the uses of stockpiled oil with the other members of the IEA in the event of a crisis. Although some progress was achieved on the other steps toward the end of the Carter Administration, advance preparation in these areas has been rejected by the Reagan Administration as too interventionist.

The Distribution of Costs and Benefits

If energy policies actually increased the transfer of wealth from Americans to the nations selling us oil, the reason is to be found partly in the country's overriding concern with how the costs and benefits resulting from that transfer would be allocated within the United States.[40] How, then, were these costs and benefits distributed? Who won, who lost, and who emerged well placed with respect to the future? And what was the role of energy policy, in particular, in producing these results?

It is important to recall again the enormity of the stakes involved. By 1980 Americans were paying more than $75 billion a year for imported oil. Largely as a result of the actions of OPEC, the value of domestic oil reserves increased, between 1973 and 1982, from about $100 billion to over one trillion dollars.[41] Though startling enough in itself, this figure does not include associated increases in the prices of other fuels, especially coal and natural gas, or the many other alterations in the energy system, and the economy as a whole, that changed the relative status of individuals, firms, and whole regions of the country.

Despite considerable effort expended on the measurement of the distributive consequences of energy policies, there remain wide areas of disagreement on this issue among the most technically qualified experts in energy economics. This is partly because of the sheer complexity of the changes wrought by the price shocks and the policies enacted in response to them, and partly because of the technical difficulty of estimating the first- and second-order consequences of new government interventions. Since controlling costs and benefits was so central to energy policy, however, it is worthwhile trying to estimate, in broad terms, what they were.[42]

Before turning to this task, I should stress that the price increases of the 1970's had pervasive redistributive implications independent of the effects of government policies designed to manage the crisis. On this matter experts agree. The general burden of energy price increases has been greatest for the poorer people in society, and for those regions of the country with cold winters or hot summers—or both—and no indigenous energy. Surveys reveal that low-income people spend a much greater proportion of their income on energy, and in many cases have no choice but to continue buying it to heat their homes, cook their food, and get to work. Wealthier people pay a less visible price, because many of the goods and services they consume require energy to produce; but they also have more choice about what they consume, and more money to insulate and purchase new appliances and vehicles.[43]

This is but a special case of a broader tendency, of course, but it becomes particularly visible at times of sudden change, as it did after 1973. Poor people have fewer options, fewer resources, less access to information about how to protect themselves; they are already, by definition, the losers in society's arrangements for distributing wealth. Thus, insofar as the price shocks of the 1970's caused general economic losses, these too were suffered in greater proportion by those least well off.[44]

What applies to individuals also applies to regions of the country. Not only are the poor themselves not distributed evenly—some major cities have large numbers of poor, as do some states—but states differ in their degree of dependence on energy and in the availability of energy resources within their borders. To the extent that they were able to retain it through taxation or regional investment, energy-producing states could and did benefit enormously from the increased value of their natural resources.[45] Those forced to import energy, and those dependent on energy-intensive economic activities, faced a new and unpleasant drain on their incomes.

Finally, a host of individuals and special groups, from middle-class commuters to truck drivers and steel makers, also found themselves paying larger than average portions of the OPEC tax, and in some cases these payments threatened their very livelihood. Others, of course, stood to benefit. Manufacturers of insulation and solar collectors, energy-policy specialists, woodlot owners, drivers of small cars, mechanics working on nuclear power plants—all experienced an "unearned" windfall of one kind or another.

This, more than anything else, was the driving force behind the politics of energy policy, a matter to which I will return in Chapter 9. Since the embargo and subsequent price increases were considered hostile, illegitimate acts, and since many Americans suspected that the energy companies had collaborated in those acts, those who faced economic loss saw no reason to accept it as simply a piece of poor economic luck, a consequence of life in a capitalist society, to be accepted without protest. As individuals, groups, corporations, and regions made it clear that they would hold their elected representatives responsible for unfair burdens associated with energy price increases, the option of relying on existing arrangements (which themselves were heavily shaped by the government) became simply untenable. The government had to "do something," or at least appear to be doing something, about the unfairness of it all.

Oil Price Controls and Regulations   As we have seen, the government "did" a lot; but what effect did government policies, per se, have on the distribution of costs and benefits? The answer to this question is also to be found in large part by examining the consequences of price controls and allocation regulations that affected crude oil, petroleum products and, secondarily, other fuels. It was primarily by means of these policies that Congress sought to control the incidence of the OPEC "tax" within America. And it was these policies that shaped the truly massive transfers of wealth that took place during the crisis decade. When petroleum price controls were finally lifted, the windfall profits tax took over this job, with some of the same results.

The principal objective of price regulations was to protect consumers from paying, and the owners of domestic petroleum from capturing, the rents that would have resulted if prices of domestic crude oil and products had been allowed to rise to world levels. As it turned out, price regulations both succeeded and failed.[46] Because the price of crude oil from domestic wells already in production was controlled, the first-order losers in the price-control system were unquestionably the owners of that crude. They lost the money they would have made if their oil had been allowed, as it would under open market conditions, to rise to world price levels. The fact that producers of domestic crude could not obtain these profits, however, does not mean that no one got them—or that they did not get some of them back. The intent of the price controls, of course, was precisely to assure that consumers "got" these profits in the form of deferred price increases in products. But this is not the way it turned out.

The redistributive impact of oil price controls was heavily dependent on the operation of the entitlements program that was adopted to assure equity in the allocation of benefits within the refining industry itself. Recall that the entitlements were payments made by those with access to cheaper domestic oil to those who relied on more expensive imported oil. In effect, they represented a subsidy received by importers to compensate for the cost of imported oil, a subsidy in size quite similar to the profits that were denied the producers of the crude oil by price controls.[47] As noted earlier, in addition to allowing all refiners to experience reduced costs, the subsidy helped make imported oil more attractive to refiners than it would otherwise have been.

The most important question, for present purposes, concerns the degree to which refiners then passed this subsidy along to consumers in the form of reduced prices for products.[48] If they did, then the controls succeeded in protecting consumers; if they did not, then the refiners, and the larger oil companies of which many were part, captured some or all of the profits after all, negating the intention of the controls.

Unfortunately, there is intense disagreement among energy economists who have studied this question.[49] Some, among them a group at the Rand Corporation, concluded that controls did not succeed in holding down the prices of domestic refined products at all.[50] Others have argued, though with less analytical support, that consumers got most of the benefit.[51] The most exhaustive, and convincing, review of the evidence is that of Joseph Kalt, who has concluded that, overall, approximately 40 percent of the entitlements subsidy was passed through to consumers, whereas approximately 60 percent remained in the hands of refiners.[52] The work of other analysts suggests that, if anything, Kalt's estimate of consumer benefit may be too high. Therefore, we may posit a rough division of benefits that accords 20 to 40 percent to consumers and 60 to 80 percent to refiners.[53] In other words, consumers probably received about a third, and perhaps less, of the entitlements subsidy created by government policy.

Of the benefits passed through to consumers, most went to the users of gasoline and several middle distillates.[54] Consumers of other products received very little benefit, since the prices of these products floated more rapidly to world levels. Of the benefits that went to refiners, small refiners, which received an extra entitlement in the program, received a somewhat larger share as well.

It is important to bear in mind that these losses and gains occurred in a changing pattern over the years between 1974 and early 1981 (when oil prices were deregulated). They were greatest in the years immediately following international price jumps, but the amount of domestic crude affected declined as the portion of domestic oil from uncontrolled sources (e.g. stripper and "new" oil) increased, and as the process of phased decontrol proceeded.[55] By the time Reagan ordered full decontrol, the consumer subsidy had decreased significantly from what it would have been otherwise, as had the rents being collected by refiners from the entitlements program.

Nevertheless, the amounts involved were very large indeed. Kalt estimates that the loss to crude oil producers from 1974 to early 1980 *averaged* approximately $21 billion (in 1980 dollars) per year— for a total of some $127 billion over the six years involved. As of early 1980, following the second "shock," he puts the total at approximately $50 billion per year, of which some $12 billion (24 percent) went to consumers in the form of reduced product prices, and some $32 billion (64 percent) went to refiners.[56] Again, these are benefits that would otherwise have gone as profits directly to the producers of domestic oil.

After 1980, the Windfall Profits Tax (WPT) took up the job of capturing producer rents. As noted earlier, it was expected to garner an average of about $23 billion a year over a decade, with the total eventually reaching $227 billion. In the first three years $52.6 billion were actually collected (an average of $17.5 billion per year), but the amount declined rapidly with oil price decreases. In 1985 the tax yielded $6.4 billion, and in 1986 collections ended because prices dropped below the threshold of approximately $19.50.[57] The amount to be collected in the future depends heavily on the course of world energy prices. The WPT was expected to collect as much as 65–70 percent of crude oil price increases, but fell far short of that goal in practice. Although domestic crude producers remained the losers, the recipients were now the taxpayers.[58]

Oil regulations and taxes had other distributional effects as well, most of them as difficult to measure as those already described. Since the price of oil set the terms for the prices of other energy sources, government success in reducing the price of oil also caused a loss to the owners of those other forms of energy.[59] Natural gas provides a good example. The jump in oil prices intensified the conflict between producers and consumers of this fuel, while increasing demand for it. This contributed to the shortages experienced in the mid-1970's. The FPC responded by allowing significant increases in price, which temporarily alleviated the shortages. But it was not until the passage of the NGPA in 1978, which held out the prospect of further price increases as well as deregulation, that much of the tension in the gas regime began to ease. Suddenly new supplies became available and drilling activity increased. Again, the increases allowed by ratemakers, as well as the compromises of the NGPA, might have been larger without oil price controls; hence owners of gas probably suffered a loss, and consumers a gain, accordingly. The same applies to coal and other primary substitutes for oil.

As noted earlier, these costs and benefits were not distributed equally among the regions of the country, or among companies of different sizes and levels of integration. Indeed, the controls on oil created a direct parallel in the petroleum world to the bitter regional rivalries that festered for decades over the allocation and pricing of natural gas. Meanwhile, price controls on oil exacerbated the rivalries over natural gas. Regional redistribution of income was an important result of the entitlements system, since the shift of profits from producers to refiners meant that income was no longer concentrated so extensively in states with indigenous energy resources but was instead spread about the country much more evenly, reflecting the geographical dispersion of the refinery industry.

Entitlements also created significant rifts in the oil industry itself. Independent producers with no refining interests lost all "OPEC" profits for many years, whereas large, integrated companies were able to capture a large percentage through their ownership of refineries. Small refineries and independent producers did gain some compensation, however, in the form of special benefits within the regulatory and tax arrangements.

The Distributive Effects of Other Policies   Although the most important costs and benefits attributable to public policy decisions were the direct and indirect result of regulations affecting the oil industry, government actions also created a host of other losers and beneficiaries. Low-income households received energy assistance. Owners of homes and businesses investing in energy conservation and efficiency improvements benefited from tax subsidies, as did the manufacturers and distributors of solar collectors, efficient heat pumps, insulation, and wood stoves—to mention but a few of the products affected. Corn and sugar producers and distillery owners collected—and will continue to collect for many years—profits made possible by the gasohol subsidies. Scientists and engineers found new demands for their talents in the research and development projects funded by the government. And last but not least, the energy policy community, which probably experienced the highest rate of growth of any in the decade, benefited from a generous flow of funds for research and analysis. In most of these cases, of course, the burden was borne, and will continue to be borne, by the taxpayers.

Efficiency and Administrative Costs

Energy policies do more than increase or decrease imports, change patterns of energy use, and confer benefits and losses on individuals and groups in society. In order to accomplish these things, they change the way resources are used. Technically speaking, these changes usually result in a loss of efficiency, i.e. a pattern of resource use that is less optimal in an economic sense, that provides fewer services and produces fewer goods, than would otherwise be the case. This does not by itself mean that the distortions in resource allocation are not justified; they may be necessary to attain other goals not encompassed by the narrow economic definition of efficiency, such as security or equity. Even in these instances, however, it is important to be aware of the price paid to attain social objectives.

Clearly, there were significant losses of economic efficiency associated with government efforts to manage the energy crisis.[60] These were scattered throughout the economy. Some can be traced directly to regulations or subsidies, but others are more elusive, encompassing everything from the time lost sitting in gas lines to the distortions resulting from incorrect price signals that led buyers to purchase the wrong equipment or investors to make poor decisions.

Once again the most striking of these losses were associated with petroleum regulation. As noted, price controls in combination with the entitlements program led refiners to import more oil than they otherwise would have, and domestic producers to sell less than they otherwise would have. Because these results were contrary to several stated objectives of energy policy, the efficiency costs have been categorized by economists as deadweight losses, money that did not have to be spent to get the same benefits (because those benefits were available for less in the absence of regulations). Of course they might also be viewed from a different perspective, as costs necessary to secure the benefits to consumers associated with price controls, or even as a contribution to the nation's long-term security in that they slowed the depletion of domestic resources.[61] However they are classified, the point is that they were large costs and should be recognized. Kalt estimates that deadweight losses ranged from $1 billion to $6 billion per year between 1975 and 1979.[62]

There were other important resource reallocations that resulted from energy policies. In the case of the entitlements program, an example is the special subsidy granted small refiners (ones with a capacity of less than 175,000 barrels of crude per day). This promoted a burst of investment in refineries that were smaller than optimal (given the state of refining technology), a poor allocation of resources that would not otherwise have occurred.[63] It also left these entities vulnerable to the impact of deregulation. Another example is the incentive in the Windfall Profits Tax to independent producers, whose first 1,000 barrels per day of output is taxed less and allowed a high price. Presumably this resulted in an uneconomic level of investment in operations at this scale. To be sure, other goals, such as the preservation of small contenders in the business system, might be served by both of these provisions; but this should not obscure the fact that a price has been paid to attain them. Since 1974 these costs, too, have almost certainly averaged several billion dollars per year.

Finally, administering energy regulations proved a costly and cumbersome endeavor, exacting a price all citizens had to pay. As the energy specialist Paul MacAvoy has noted: "More than 300,000 firms were required to respond to controls, ranging from the three dozen major refining companies to a quarter of a million retailers of petroleum products. The respondents had to file more than half a million reports each year, which probably took more than five million man-hours to prepare, at an estimated cost alone of $80 million."[64] To these expenditures must be added the additional costs to the government of collecting and processing these reports, monitoring compliance, and managing the complex process associated with setting forth new regulations and adjudicating disputes. All together, it seems likely that the administrative costs, private and public, directly attributable to the regulatory process also exceeded $1 billion a year from 1974 to 1980.[65]

Summary

During the crisis decade, patterns of energy use in the United States changed significantly. Efficiency of energy use increased, and imports first increased but then suddenly plummeted. Although many things caused these changes, price increases stand out in most cases as fundamental. The effects of government policy, which varied from sector to sector, were less influential than many anticipated, but were most important in the petroleum regime. By holding crude prices down, subsidizing imports, and discouraging domestic production, government actions led to an increase in imports, especially before 1980.

One of the clearest accomplishments of national energy policy during the years of crisis was to move wealth around, across national borders as well as within the United States—although often not in the ways intended by the originators of policy. By increasing oil imports, government policy almost certainly increased the flow of money to OPEC countries by many billions of dollars a year.

The chief goal of legislation was to control the effects of the OPEC price increase, protecting consumers from paying it and preventing domestic producers from benefiting from it. This goal was accomplished only in small part. After accounting for the significant fraction—perhaps as much as 10 percent at any one time—lost to inefficiency, some 20 to 40 percent of these earnings (on a declining fraction of domestic crude production) went to consumers over a period of years in the form of lowered product prices. The rest remained in the hands of refineries, many of which were owned by the larger integrated oil companies. When the Windfall Profits Tax came into force, the funds collected went to the Treasury instead.

Thus the overall effect was to create a small, and temporary, price bridge for consumers, partly cushioning the impact of OPEC action over a decade, while channeling most of the windfall rents into the hands of the integrated companies through the refining industry, and thereafter sending a portion to the Treasury. The cushion was most effective immediately after sudden price increases, but was quietly phased out after 1975. The success of the phaseout is revealed by the fact that, when decontrol was finally ordered by Reagan, nothing happened; the introduction of world prices at the product level was virtually complete by the end of 1980, and those most seriously affected by decontrol were small refiners who faced the loss of their special entitlements subsidy.

Within this larger picture, perhaps the most striking secondary feature was the degree to which policies worked at cross-purposes. Price controls and entitlements counterbalanced demand-reduction policies, resulting in a net increase in imports and greater vulnerability to externally caused petroleum price "shocks." Though oil purchases for the Strategic Petroleum Reserve gradually improved the country's ability to cope with crises, as did continuing cooperation with other members of the IEA, the government weakened the value of these accomplishments by abandoning its commitment to manage the market's response in the case of another shock. Low-income people, despite receiving some direct help, almost certainly ended up net losers as the price shocks jolted the American economy and they lost jobs or took cuts in pay to pave the way for recovery. A host of other winners and losers made good their claims to special protection, diverting national resources in their favor but creating significant losses in efficiency that had little justification in terms of national objectives. Finally, to fulfill its responsibilities, the federal government was forced to create an enormous and intrusive regulatory apparatus that, despite the best of intentions, ended up imposing a costly administrative burden on hundreds of thousands of private businesses.

CHAPTER 9   Patterns of Governance

The last chapter analyzed the effects of policies adopted during the years of energy crisis, asking how they changed the energy economy, who won, who lost, and who ended up well placed with respect to the future. This chapter examines the transformation of governance arrangements that occurred as a result of the crisis, setting the stage for an evaluation of the performance of the political economy as a whole, the subject of Chapter 10.

In many respects, the task of this chapter is no less difficult than that of sorting out the independent effects of energy policies. Even with the passage of time, the term "energy politics" for most Americans still evokes images of confusion and disorder—as well as considerable frustration.[1] The crisis was the occasion for a tremendous mobilization of political interests. Some saw in it a threat of loss or a chance for enrichment; others feared it would damage the nation's security or undermine hard-won progress in protecting the environment; and still others viewed it as an opportunity for a fundamental change in the technical character, and associated values, of industrial society itself.

For a decade, struggles over these issues occupied the attention of the nation's leaders to an extent and with a persistence reserved in recent history for only the most fundamental problems of war and peace. And yet, for all of this, when the dust had settled few came away with a sense of satisfaction or confidence that the matter had been handled well—or, for that matter, handled at all. To a considerable extent this is because the polity dealt with the crisis in conventional ways, within the existing rules of the game of American pluralism. These rules make almost no provision for problems, or solutions, that threaten or involve sudden, highly visible redistributions of wealth or influence.

Governance Arrangements Before the Crisis

The United States had neither energy policy nor energy politics, as these are understood today, before the Arab oil embargo of 1973. Decisions about energy were handled by separate regimes, each of which was the product of a long process of historical evolution. In each, free market forces had been attenuated to some degree: in the coal and petroleum regimes to assure stability and higher profits to private participants, and in the natural gas and electric power regimes to do this and to protect consumers. The government was "involved," but not in a manner that permitted public authorities to treat energy affairs in a unified manner.

Despite appearances, each of the energy regimes was vulnerable by the early 1970's. Oil was the key. The government had been drawn deeply into the affairs of the petroleum regime in order to help manage uncontrolled supply. Layer upon layer of protective administrative arrangements, at the state, interstate, and national levels, protected petroleum companies from the free market. But these at the same time prepared the way for newly assertive public intervention when the crisis struck. Since the other regimes depended heavily on petroleum—that industry, in effect, set the terms for all energy markets by providing the cheapest source of marginal supply to substitutors—the crisis in petroleum quickly affected the other fuels. In natural gas the struggle between consumers and producers had escalated to a dangerous stalemate, and tentative steps toward accommodation were dependent on price stability in the petroleum regime. In coal internal tensions were building within the UMW, a key participant in that regime's market-control arrangements, and the opportunity for higher profits by operators would only increase the chance for conflict. And many of the utilities managing electricity production and distribution, happily prosperous as long as energy prices were stabilized by the petroleum regime, were vulnerable to fuel cost increases and changes in demand for their product.

As luck would have it, national economic policy had also reached a crossroads of sorts in the late 1960's and early 1970's. Unable to understand or control changes in the rates of inflation, employment, and economic growth, the Nixon Administration resorted to economywide wage and price controls. These, applied to the petroleum regime, helped create brief shortages while at the same time enlarging the government's involvement in that industry's affairs. The shortages of petroleum products, along with natural gas shortages provoked by the regulatory stalemate in that regime, in turn led to the widespread belief that the country's energy industries were in disarray—all before October of 1973—and further increased Congressional willingness to extend the scope of public control.

Thus the United States was vulnerable to the Arab embargo not just because the economy required imported oil, but because the governance arrangements affecting energy were vulnerable to a sudden shift in the petroleum market, and because energy affairs had already become conflict-ridden and politicized. The public was upset and suspicious; Congress was nervous about the shortages; the Executive Branch had backed into price controls which it could not remove, and which before long forced it to begin allocating supplies as well.

A New Energy Politics

In the larger political system the embargo and price increases enlarged and made more prominent two great cleavages: one between producers and consumers, and the regions of the country in which they were concentrated; and the other between the executive and legislative branches of government. An understanding of these powerful divisions in the body politic, and the way in which they overlapped, helps make more sense out of what otherwise appears a hopeless tangle of political pressures, interests, and ideologies.

The split between producers and consumers is the easiest to grasp. The embargo and price increases constituted a "crisis" for most Americans precisely because they forced a major involuntary transfer of wealth across the oceans, and because they created the opportunity, by forcing prices for petroleum and other energy sources upward, for enormous transfers of wealth within the United States. The political crisis came when decisions had to be made about who would pay for these transfers, and who would be allowed to benefit from the opportunities they created.

As we have seen, conflict over income distribution had been a chronic problem in the gas regime for decades. Now this became a problem throughout the energy system. In this respect, the crisis had the effect of politicizing the petroleum regime, transforming proprietary to compensatory regulation, by giving consumers some political access to the price of oil (and, indirectly, other fuels) in the same way that the *Phillips* decision of 1954 gave natural gas consumers access to the price paid to producers at the wellhead. Consumers used this access to try and protect themselves from price increases they felt were illegitimate because they had resulted from the illegal collusion of foreign governments and, many suspected, energy companies. A continuation of price regulation appeared to be the only way to do this.

Energy producers had a different view of the matter. The crisis, of course, forced a wide-ranging redefinition of interests in all the regimes. And, taken together with the federal government's regulatory response, it also created the grounds for significant conflicts within and between regimes—a point to which I will return below. At the same time, however, the crisis forged a very powerful, overriding, collective interest that unified owners of energy resources of all kinds: the desire to see prices rise to world levels and stay there.[2] Such a rise, especially as it affected resources for which investments had already been made, would (and eventually did) allow owners to collect hundreds of billions of dollars in unanticipated profits in future years. It would also provide powerful new incentives for exploration and development, new opportunities for management, and the justification and support for exciting new avenues of growth and diversification.

The cleavage between the executive and the legislature was complicated by the conflict between consumers and producers, but the central issue in this area was different. The problem here was that different branches of government asserted different interpretations of the nature of the problem to be addressed. To U.S. presidents and their advisers, especially in the aftermath of the oil "shocks," the energy crisis was first and foremost a problem of national security and demanded prompt action to protect the country and its industrialized allies from hostile conspiracy. Solutions, from Project Independence to Carter's *Plan*, began with this objective and went on to try and set forth a coherent program that would also take into account other objectives, such as overall impact on the economy, efficiency in resource allocation, and equity.[3] Since this meant reduced consumption and reduced imports, price increases were an important part of the *solution*.[4]

Congress, in sharp contrast, insisted that the division of costs and benefits be the overriding concern, and put most of its efforts into deliberations which, at heart, were extensions of the struggle between consumers and producers.[5] Unfortunately, on these matters Congress also found it nearly impossible to act, and this paralysis affected other aspects of policy as well, most notably the legislature's ability to deal consistently with the packaged proposals sent up by the Executive Branch. While producers, with growing Senate support, argued that price increases were desirable, consumers, backed by a majority of the House, insisted again and again that they were the *problem*.

The result was a frustrating stalemate on the key issues of petroleum and natural gas price regulation, a stalemate that was, in effect, never resolved.[6] To be sure, Congress found it possible to pass some important measures, such as the national speed limit and CAFE standards, and to grant an array of subsidies to groups and industries affected by the crisis. But it simply could not address the central policy problem, the one that made the most difference as far as the structure of the energy system was concerned and that involved the highest stakes for participants—at least not while it remained a problem. Instead, the problem was allowed to resolve itself with the passage of time and the *de facto* introduction of world prices in the U.S. energy economy.[7] A closer look at the events that led to this stalemate helps explain its persistence.

The Struggle over Oil and Gas Deregulation

The first year and a half were critical for oil. Nixon signed the EPAA, a bill formulated prior to the embargo, as an emergency measure. There followed two parallel activities, each of which fundamentally shaped the nation's response: Congress tried, and failed, to produce an alternative to the EPAA; and the administration's energy managers, under tremendous pressure from deprived refiners, invented the entitlements program as a means of equitably distributing within the refining industry the benefits created by multitier price controls. And that was it: the pattern was set, the temporary then became permanent. The best that Congress was able to do thereafter was extend the existing arrangement, via the EPCA, and give it an expiration date distant enough to have no political significance and, as it turned out, very little economic significance either.

The reason for this, in a nutshell, is that consumers were able to block price decontrol, oil and gas interests were able to block new measures to redistribute "crisis" rents, and the Executive Branch was unwilling to embrace one without the other. Ford came close to doing this when he nearly opted for decontrol, but the election deterred him and he agreed to extend the EPAA when he signed the EPCA. Both sides made alliances where they could, and these changed frequently. A variety of "spectators" with other, energy-related interests—such as senators and representatives with strong environmental interests—joined one side or the other, seeking concessions in the written law.[8] The result was a great deal of confusion and, occasionally, some strange bedfellows. But the cleavage between producers and consumers dominated the struggle.

Consumers opposed deregulation and clung to price controls as the only means of protecting themselves. They recognized that a windfall profits tax would capture crisis-created rents, but they also knew that the beneficiaries would be taxpayers in general rather than specific end-users of fuels. There is little evidence, incidentally, that consumer representatives were aware of how ineffective existing arrangements were in protecting end-users; in any case, the status quo appeared better than the alternatives under discussion.

The oil industry held out for deregulation, strongly opposing any alternative mechanism for distributing crisis-derived rents. This opposition, championed in the Senate by oil-state representatives, proved critical in derailing the Emergency Act as well as the crude oil equalization tax proposed by Carter. With the entitlements program in place, with prices continuing to rise, and with the prospect of deregulation in the near future—the EPAA was "temporary," and even the EPCA was due to expire—it is easy to see why the status quo appeared more attractive to someone holding an interest in refining than an alternative that contained a more effective mechanism for protecting or repaying consumers.[9]

The resulting paralysis lasted until Carter, deeply frustrated by his failure to gain passage of a "balanced" approach, finally threw down the gauntlet and actually went ahead with phased decontrol of oil prices. This was perhaps the most important single decision taken during the crisis decade. Consumer interests remained powerful enough that oil industry representatives, fearing an extension of controls, concluded that they would have to accept a decade of excise taxes in order to assure the completion of the decontrol process. By this time, of course, world prices had experienced much of their increase from the second "shock" and appeared likely to stabilize in the future, and a significant portion of that increase had already been incorporated in domestic product prices.[10]

A similar quandary can be discerned in the natural gas regime. Producers saw their stake in deregulation (of oil as well as gas), but federal regulatory decisions affecting both oil and gas were favorable enough, in the sense that prices were allowed to rise, that their demands for deregulation were far from hysterical. Prices were high enough, and shortages had created enough anxiety, that producers had little need to compromise their opposition to measures that would benefit consumers, or worse, extend consumer power in gas affairs. In this respect, they were like the beneficiaries of the entitlements arrangements.

Price increases, of course, upset gas consumers. But their political strength, which grew in the first years after the crisis, began to weaken toward the end of the decade. This was due chiefly to the effects of shortages, which convinced many pipeline companies, distributors, and representatives of Southern states that deregulation and price increases were the only way to make new supplies available. The politics of gas deregulation was also complicated by the role of coal interests, which were themselves divided over whether to press for decontrol and higher prices, or to support deregulation of gas in return for forced conversion to coal.[11]

As was the case with oil, Congress found itself paralyzed for years as bill after bill surfaced and then failed, and as the stalemate between producers and consumers, and associated shortages of supply, worsened. As with oil, consumers were strongest in the House, producers in the Senate. In the end, the Congress chose, and the President reluctantly accepted, a compromise that acknowledged but did not resolve the conflict. Like the EPCA in oil, the NGPA provided some protection for consumers in the short run, and an end to compensatory regulation, plus a guarantee of the introduction of prices keyed to world petroleum prices, in the longer run.

Organizational Integration and Interest Mobilization

The most tangible immediate change in governance patterns that resulted from the crisis was the discovery by the Executive Branch that it must accept a continuous, affirmative responsibility for the energy system as a whole. This new role was not acknowledged at first, but the decision to manage the petroleum market directly, forced upon the Executive first by Nixon's price controls and then by soaring international prices, drew the government more and more deeply into a quagmire of administrative responsibilities. And it quickly became evident that the federal bureaucracy was organizationally unprepared to handle the job.

The fact is that no one in government knew much about energy in 1973; responsibility for regulation, data collection, and analysis was scattered about in agencies concerned with helping or regulating specific energy regimes. The overworked Cost of Living Council, charged by Nixon with managing the wage/price freeze, was hardly in a position to take on the job. Nor was the government conceptually equipped to come to grips with its new responsibilities. Decades of sector-specific policy had produced many provisions to protect threatened interests but little competent analysis and no generally accepted principles that might form the basis of policies.

As the crisis worsened and it became clear that the federal government would continue to have a political stake in the operation of the energy system as a whole, a succession of reorganizations resulted in the formation of a full-fledged executive department (the DOE) plus an independent regulatory body (the Federal Energy Regulatory Commission, or FERC, housed within the DOE) with responsibilities that extended across the various energy sectors (and with a formidable will to survive).[12]

Congress eventually followed this lead, although with less success. The scope and complexity of energy issues, intermingled as they so often are with environmental and resource-management problems of other kinds, had resulted in a fragmentation of authority in both legislative houses. The number of committees and subcommittees seeking a role in decisionmaking concerning energy multiplied rapidly.[13] The House, after struggling with the issue, eventually placed the principal responsibility for energy matters in the House Commerce Committee. Some jurisdiction, however, continued in the hands of several dozen other committees and subcommittees. The Senate was somewhat more successful: as part of a broad reorganization in 1977 it gave most responsibility for energy affairs to a newly formed Committee on Energy and Natural Resources.[14] In 1977 the Congress also abolished the Joint Committee on Atomic Energy and distributed its oversight role to separate House and Senate committees. Thus, though authority for energy matters remained more fragmented than it was before the crisis, Congressional reorganization did result in some improvement over the conditions that reigned during the first years after the crisis.

These changes in the executive and the legislature were important for several reasons. They signaled the demise of old-style sectoral energy policymaking, in which regime-specific bureaucratic agencies worked closely with one or two dedicated Congressional committees and industry lobbies to shape legislation, paying little attention to anyone else. Although the degree to which these "iron triangles" were able to dominate policymaking had already begun to decline in the 1950's and 1960's, the organizational realignment that took place in the mid-1970's made it more difficult for them to resume their work after the crisis. These changes were also important because they assured at least some continuity to an integrated policy perspective on energy affairs, especially in the Executive Branch, that would outlast the statutory termination of compensatory market intervention.[15] As we have seen, however, these changes were insufficient to overcome the deep cleavages that held energy

policy in thrall and for years prevented the government from replac-
ing the regulatory arrangements set in place during the first months
after the Arab embargo.

Outside the government, the energy crisis gave rise to a truly remarkable mobilization of interest groups and lobbying organizations. Notable in this process was the formation of a number of new
groups representing (or purporting to represent) consumers, renewable energy enthusiasts, advocates of conservation, opponents of nuclear energy, and other broad "citizen" concerns. A significant number of these, groups like the Solar Lobby and Friends of the Earth,
drew their inspiration from the work of Amory Lovins and others in
the solar energy movement, described below. In a survey of interest
groups active in the energy area, political scientist John Chubb
found that "five of the nine consumer groups in this sample formed
after 1973, and four of those in direct response to the new issues in
the energy field."[16] This process of group formation was a clear example, in most instances, of the use of new technologies of participation by political "entrepreneurs" to foster political action. These
new organizations were joined by many existing "public interest"
groups in the effort to influence national energy decisionmaking.[17]

Business interests also responded to the new circumstances. Energy producers and their industry associations enlarged their Washington staffs and increased their lobbying activities.[18] Several mounted
expensive publicity campaigns to explain their positions and justify
their actions (and profits). The most intense activity focused on the
federal regulatory agencies that had day-to-day responsibility for
price controls and allocation decisions. However, campaign contributions from oil and gas companies, already very large, also increased dramatically during the 1970's. Corporate political action
committees (PACs) carefully targeted critics of the industry who
held key congressional positions and in a number of cases helped
replace them with more acceptable representatives.[19] In a significant
number of cases, energy companies broke the law in their efforts to
influence the newly politicized environment in which they had to
operate, handing out large amounts of cash surreptitiously or making other illegal contributions to decisionmakers.[20]

The mobilization of interests was also accompanied by the appearance of an entire new industry: that of professional energy
analysis and consultation. Recognizing the technical complexity of
energy problems, policymakers and interest groups alike sought advice from research professionals. The major foundations and think
tanks also rose to the occasion. The result was an impressive series

of studies of the energy problem—perhaps the most sophisticated investment of analytical talent ever assembled in so short a time outside of the defense field.[21] The Ford and Rockefeller Foundations, the Trilateral Commission, the Atlantic Council, the Council on Foreign Relations, the American Enterprise Institute, the Rand Corporation, Resources for the Future, the Office of Technology Assessment, the Congressional Budget Office, the Congressional Research Service, the General Accounting Office, Harvard, MIT, and other major universities—the list of sponsors of significant energy policy research goes on and on. The specialists and managers whose interests and expertise spanned all or part of the energy system quickly formed themselves into a prototypical "issue network," to use Hugh Heclo's term,[22] replete with newsletters and meetings at the attractive retreats of the powerful—places like the Aspen Institute in Colorado, Wye Plantation on the Chesapeake, and Airlie House in the Virginia countryside. Participants in this network moved in and out of office as different parties and presidents sought to come to terms with energy policy.

To summarize, the energy crisis caused the consolidation of policy organizations within the Executive Branch; a proliferation of jurisdictional claims followed by partially successful efforts to focus responsibility in the Congress; a rapid expansion of political participation among affected interests; and the formation of a loose issue network of specialists and decisionmakers with an associated mobilization of analytical talents. Although this resulted in a significant improvement in the understanding of energy problems and a much expanded participation in the politics of energy, it did not break the political stalemate that gripped the nation and that assured the continuation of policies that were achieving few of the objectives in behalf of which they had been adopted.

To what extent did, or will, these institutional and political changes outlast the crisis? This question is important because it will heavily influence the character of the nation's response to future problems in the energy sector. With respect to the federal government, two contradictory trends are evident. First, the broad, holistic definition of the "problem" persists. Structural changes in Congress and the Executive assure this, as does the enormous policy literature on "energy." Second, the reduced salience of energy issues has resulted in a tendency for interests to return to regime-specific policy discussions and deliberations. Thus, for example, issues associated with matters such as gas deregulation, the revival of the nuclear industry, carbon dioxide accumulation, or refiners' problems with product imports tend to be viewed in greater isolation than they were in the mid-1970's, and links between the energy bureaucracy and specific industries are growing in importance.[23] These trends can be expected to coexist in the foreseeable future, with the integrative perspective becoming more salient at times of price fluctuations and other major perturbations in the energy system, and with regime-specific discussions tending to become more customary during times of stability.

Outside the government, there has been a reduction in concern about energy and a gradual reduction in the number of groups and interests focusing on specifically energy problems. As John Chubb has noted, a significant percentage of the interest groups that sprang to life after 1973 relied heavily on what incentive theorists call "purposive" incentives; that is, they attracted funds and members by promising to help achieve a goal or purpose—protecting consumers from predatory oil companies, ushering in a benign solar future, and so forth.[24] Such groups could be expected to disappear when the "crisis" that made those purposes salient became less important unless they could also begin to offer other incentives or unless their patrons agreed to "carry" them. Other incentives include such things as solidarity—the pleasure of associating with others with similar goals or world views—or, more importantly, materially useful benefits, such as newsletters and lobbying services.[25]

Although detailed data on the universe of energy groups are not available, these theoretical propositions predict a number of trends which seem, in fact, to have materialized. To begin with, it is clear that the number of groups and the intensity of their activity have declined. The casualties have been greatest among those relying most heavily on nonmaterial incentives, such as those advocating energy conservation and those seeking to represent diffuse "citizen" interests. Many such groups have succeeded in retaining patron support or in providing solidary or material incentives sufficient to continue to survive, but their ranks and support have dwindled. Business groups have also reduced the intensity of their involvement, but have found it easier to survive.[26]

To recapitulate, the crisis left the world of energy politics characterized by (1) greater policy integration (in the sense that both executive and legislative branches treated energy as an interconnected set of problems) but with gradually reemerging regime-focused policy deliberations; (2) a centralization of decisionmaking in the Executive Branch and a continued, albeit somewhat reduced, fragmentation of responsibilities for energy matters in the House and Senate; (3) a level of group participation lower than existed at the height of the crisis, but much higher than was the case before 1973; (4) a tendency, within the group universe, for those (notably business-related groups) offering significant material rewards to remain the most influential; and (5) a permanently enlarged, but latent, capacity for a new and explosive expansion of participation on the part of all interests, including "purposive" ones, should energy issues, especially ones involving the threat of income redistribution, reemerge on the national scene.

The Debates on Technology and Sociopolitics

While the polity remained deadlocked over the central issues of oil and gas price and supply regulation, and interest groups rushed to join the fray, the energy crisis fomented a variety of vigorous intellectual debates. "Energy" quickly became the celebrated issue, one upon which prominent individuals and organizations felt the need to take a stand of one sort or another. Of particular note was the emergence of a penetrating and wide-ranging debate over the possible implications of the newly perceived resource scarcity for the future of industrial society itself. Often called the "soft/hard" debate, it was catalyzed by the work of a number of advocates of renewable energy who used the crisis as a vehicle to challenge the very ethos and organizational basis of the American political economy. The renewable/solar energy movement eventually captured the attention, directly or indirectly, of nearly everyone involved with energy affairs. It did so partly because its leaders appeared to offer an alternative set of technical solutions to the nation's energy problems. But its appeal was also deeper; it touched basic anxieties felt by many Americans about the evolution of the political economy itself.

The most articulate spokesman of the solar movement was Amory Lovins, author of *Soft Energy Paths: Toward a Durable Peace,* who argued that there was a connection between energy technology and the structure and values of society. He asserted that the energy problems experienced by America and the rest of the world were partly the result of the excessive power of large corporations and heavy-handed bureaucracies bent on using massive, expensive, centralized technologies (epitomized by nuclear power plants). The solution he suggested was to choose "soft-path" technologies, ones that were renewable, small-scale, dispersed, and "congenial" to those who depended on them (epitomized by solar collectors). He asserted that "hard" technologies required a "hard" society, prone to authoritarianism, militarism, and nuclear war; whereas "soft" technologies left open the possibility of a society that was more diverse, decentralized, peaceful, independent of foreign influence, and that nurtured classical American values such as "self-reliance," frugality, conviviality.[27]

These were powerful ideas, and they enlarged the intellectual commitment in America to the development of renewable energy, the promotion of conservation, and the prevention of further government support for nuclear power development. As noted in Chapter 8, this resulted in relatively little concrete policy. But it motivated the formation of a surprising number of interest groups and, most importantly, forced many policy discussions into a broader framework, one in which the connection between technology, institutions, and basic values was the chief concern. At a time when American intellectual life found itself lacking coherent and idealistic visions of the future, when the country still suffered the nihilism of the antiwar movement, the political alienation of Watergate, and the despair created by the growing specter of nuclear war, the appeal of a technically elegant, freer, more diverse, peaceful, and nonnuclear "soft" society was extraordinary.

Interestingly enough, though the hard/soft debate generated a great deal of controversy, it subsided as quickly as it arose, taking many of its organizations and leaders with it. The end of crisis, in fact, quickly swept the solar energy movement back into the shadows of the counterculture. Part of this may have been because solar advocates turned out to be mistaken in many of their assertions about the low cost of renewable technologies. It may also have been a result of their overplaying the degree to which benign sociopolitics would follow the adoption of these technologies.[28] The main reason, however, is almost certainly that Americans dislike debates about the fundamentals of political and economic life, and found it more comfortable to avoid such matters when the end of distributional conflicts, the demise of nuclear energy, and the return of low-priced energy made that possible. Nonetheless, the anxieties and yearnings awakened by the "soft-path" advocates can be expected to command attention again should another crisis of scarcity provide the opportunity, for they retain a potent, if now dormant, appeal.

The Crisis and the Energy Regimes

The energy crisis forced widespread changes in the energy regimes. In each case, the regime's adaptive response was heavily influenced by government policies as well as by crisis-induced alterations in the economic conditions it faced.

Coal   The energy crisis represented an important opportunity for the coal industry, and many experts predicted a rosy future for the nation's most abundant, if least convenient, fossil fuel as the price of its substitutes, oil and natural gas, skyrocketed. Nixon called for large increases in coal production as a means of curbing OPEC power, and this commitment was echoed by Ford and Carter in subsequent years. For a variety of reasons, however, the bonanza for coal turned out to be much more modest than expected. Coal production did increase (See Figure 1), but the expansion was constrained by a number of serious problems, many of which would continue to trouble the industry after the crisis had passed.

Before the crisis the coal industry had experienced nearly two decades of relative market stability and labor peace. An alliance between union leaders and the managers of the large coal companies had, in a sometimes brutal (and illegal) fashion, controlled the chronic tendency to overproduction and destructive competition and succeeded in increasing productivity by promoting mechanization of mining operations. However, these accomplishments masked growing problems within the industry and the emergence of new obstacles to the production and utilization of coal.

To start with, the stabilizing alliance began to crumble as rank-and-file dissatisfaction with union leaders mounted. Miners had many complaints. The mechanization of the underground mines, though it increased productivity, also increased the danger to workers. Black Lung Disease, the result of breathing coal particles, became more common as the work force grew older and as machines filled the mines. In 1969 Congress passed the Coal Mine Health and Safety Act, which set standards for mine safety, but miners felt the bill did not go far enough. Miners also complained that wage increases were not adequate, that pension funds were misused and replenished too slowly, and that union bosses were no longer accountable.

The upshot of this was the breakdown of union control, which in turn led to increasing numbers of wildcat strikes and bitter and violent internal struggles over control of the UMW.[29] The eventual triumph of leaders determined to improve the lot of the miners led to open conflict with mine operators. This culminated in the reappearance of major industrywide strikes, first in the winter of 1977–78 (110 days, the longest in history) and then again in 1981 (72 days). Although stockpiling by major users prevented serious dislocation during stoppages, these strikes did little to convince prospective users that the coal regime had overcome the troubles that had plagued it for half a century.

Then, too, there was the growing power of the environmental

movement. As was the case with the other energy regimes, coal affairs became deeply politicized as the changing technology of participation created new opportunities for those concerned about the environmental consequences of coal mining and combustion. Partly by chance—the pressure for action had been building for many years—and partly because the prospect of major commitments to coal development activated groups, the growth of demands for regulation coincided with the energy crisis itself. The National Environmental Policy Act (1969), the Clean Air Act (1970), the Federal Water Pollution Control Act (1972), and the bitterly contested Surface Mining Control and Reclamation Act (vetoed by Ford and signed by Carter in 1977) all imposed new constraints on the coal industry as it sought to expand. Its lobby group, the National Coal Association, fought hard to counter the growing power of environmental interests, but with limited success.[30]

These changes decreased coal's price advantage over rival fuels. Compliance with environmental regulations imposed new costs, and worker productivity in the mines dropped precipitously from more than 19 tons per worker per day to less than 14 tons.[31] The drop had many causes, including strikes, the influx of new and less experienced workers, and the restrictions imposed by health and safety regulations. But the result was more expensive coal.

Nixon, Ford, and Carter all sought to promote coal use, but they were often frustrated in their attempts to use federal leverage to do so. The 1974 Energy Supply and Coordination Act required that utilities capable of switching to coal do so, but the bill was so full of exemptions that it had little effect.[32] Carter made coal central to his energy plan, hoping to double use by 1985. The Fuel Use Act of 1978 prohibited the use of oil or natural gas in new power plants and industrial boilers and ordered the phaseout of natural gas in existing facilities by 1990. This law, though forcefully worded, had only a limited effect in practice since few new plants were built in the decade after its passage.

The coal industry also underwent structural changes during the crisis era, but these too were a continuation of trends visible in earlier years. Western coal grew in importance as strip-mining became more attractive. Output from west of the Mississippi represented about 15 percent of production in 1973; by 1983 it had grown to 36 percent. And utility companies continued to dominate the market: by the early 1980's utilities consumed fully 85 percent of the nation's coal output, up from 69 percent in 1973.[33] Oil companies, utilities, and steel companies also continued to acquire coal interests—to the point, in fact, that one specialist concluded in the early 1980's that the industry could no longer be considered independent.[34] In 1980 most of the large companies were owned by outside interests, and they accounted for at least half of all production. One of the consequences of coal's increasing association with utilities in terms of market and ownership has been that its fate has become more and more tied to the fate of that industry, itself caught in near paralysis due to changes in regime governance brought on by the energy crisis.

The upshot of these developments is that coal, though it benefited from the crisis, has been unable to take advantage of the new conditions. Production did expand, but excess capacity remained a problem. The export market, which seemed promising in the early 1980's, collapsed as oil prices leveled and then began to erode. The industry also became increasingly captive to other industries, making governance processes as well as ownership more and more dependent in character. Despite its many problems, the coal industry could look forward to more stable demand because new nonnuclear power plants had to burn it (partly as a result of crisis-related regulations). But price competition remained a threat, especially for the "noncaptive" suppliers.

Oil   The exercise of cartel power by OPEC turned the world upside down for the U.S. petroleum industry. Decades of exploration and production made it unlikely that existing or newly discovered fields would again produce enough oil to require restriction of domestic supply. World prices were now higher than domestic prices, and imports no longer posed a threat to the domestic price structure. Many in the industry felt that OPEC would continue to govern world petroleum trade, making domestic proprietary regulation permanently obsolete. For the industry to adjust to these conditions, however, the U.S. market had to be allowed to respond to world price signals. The best way to accomplish this, of course, was price deregulation. Unfortunately for the owners of domestic oil, the government's habit of protective intervention, cultivated by the industry itself for so many years, proved a serious obstacle to the immediate accomplishment of this objective. The entitlements program, a natural outgrowth of the old import "ticket" system the industry had relied upon to distribute access to imports, proved a second-best solution when accompanied by weakening product price regulation. But deregulation was still the goal. Eventually, of course, the industry had to accept an excise tax on crude oil (the WPT) as a price for achieving deregulation.

The advent of compensatory regulation in oil heightened existing divisions within the petroleum regime and added some new ones. The first of these new divisions arose during periods of actual shortage, when independent retailers lost access to gasoline supplies as integrated companies favored their own outlets. Then, with price controls and a freeze on buyer-supplier relationships, access to lower-cost domestic crude supplies became a major source of conflict within the refining industry.

The entitlements program helped manage the tensions between companies that arose from their differing degrees of integration and import dependence, but these flared again when the Congress decided to replace price regulation and entitlements with the WPT. In the resulting struggle, small refiners (favored in entitlements arrangements) lost out, but small independent producers won an exemption for a portion of their production.

The end of market regulation in 1981 effectively depoliticized many intra-industry conflicts, leaving them to private resolution. In practice, of course, this meant that the large integrated majors would have a greater influence, since small independent producers and refiners would have less recourse to regulatory protection.

Government efforts to manage petroleum markets, along with changes in the organization of Congress, also forced representatives of the industry to take politics even more seriously. Petroleum affairs were no longer handled quietly by experienced and sympathetic advocates in separate, fuel-specific federal agencies or Congressional committees; they were now the focus of major, and often bitter, debates involving the nation's most prominent political leaders. Consumers now had "access," and sought actively to shape the rules of the game. Day-to-day decisions of enormous significance fell to inexperienced regulators who were closely attuned to the changing political climate.[35] Accordingly, representatives of the industry as a whole and of its several components stepped up their efforts to influence decisionmakers and the public.

These activities, as might be expected, provoked an angry response from critics of petroleum companies—the most prominent of whom, of course, was President Carter himself—and led to new efforts to dismantle or restructure the industry. Hefty profits, especially in the years immediately following the oil shocks, only increased political hostility toward the industry. Neither divestiture legislation nor antitrust suits acquired the support needed, however, and the end of the crisis made it possible for the Reagan Administration to abandon these direct attacks on the structure of the industry.[36] But public suspicions of "big oil" remained a latent but powerful ingredient of the nation's political culture, and the crisis clearly served to embed it more firmly. The revelations, in subsequent years, that the oil companies had taken advantage of the crisis—and the complexity of the regulatory system—to make many billions of dollars illegally through overcharges only worsened this problem.[37] In 1985 an appeals court upheld charges by the Department of Energy that Exxon had improperly interpreted federal oil price regulations and ordered the company to pay damages of $2 billion. This was the largest single damage judgment in history.[38]

The structure of the petroleum industry changed during and immediately after the period of crisis. The most notable alterations occurred at the international level, where the great integrated majors lost direct control of oil reserves to producer governments. Though many companies retained special ties with countries, the companies became, in essence, offshore buyers of oil, dependent on the decisions of foreign governments for access to crude supplies. This rigidified and politicized world oil markets. Oil was sold increasingly by governments to governments or to bidders on the spot market, which in turn affected the kinds of actions that could be expected in the event of another crisis.[39]

The crisis also brought changes to the domestic petroleum industry, but these represented for the most part a continuation and acceleration of broad trends that were evident in industry affairs well before the Arab embargo of 1973. During the 1970's oil corporations increased their investments in other energy sources, in non-energy minerals, and to a lesser extent in unrelated economic activities. By the early 1980's, oil companies owned about 40 percent of nongovernment coal reserves and between a third and a half of U.S. proved reserves of uranium oxide.[40] Nearly three-quarters of domestic copper production, following the acquisition of Anaconda by Arco, was in the hands of five petroleum companies.[41] Petroleum companies also owned department stores (Montgomery Ward, purchased by Mobil), an electric motor company (Reliance Electric, purchased by Exxon), and many hundreds of other unrelated businesses. They also consummated a series of celebrated intra-industry mergers, increasing somewhat the degree of concentration of the industry as a whole. By early 1985, Texaco had acquired Getty Oil, Mobil had taken Superior Oil, Royal Dutch Shell had purchased the portion of Shell Oil Company that it did not already own, and Socal had acquired Gulf Oil Corporation.[42]

Some of these changes, immediately after price increases, were motivated by the need to dispose of large sums of cash, or were the result of an anomalous undervaluation of oil reserves on the stock market. But they were also a response to a realization that the petroleum industry faces an epoch of gradual decline as domestic reserves dwindle. The option chosen by many oil companies, under these circumstances, has been to become "energy" companies and, to an increasing degree, more generalized natural resource firms.

To repeat, these changes reflect trends that were in process before the crisis began. As noted in Chapter 3, concentration levels in the petroleum industry had been increasing for decades, and the acquisition of coal, uranium, and nonfuel minerals had already begun to accelerate in the 1960's.[43] Nor did these changes result in a major alteration in the basic structure of the domestic industry—indeed, if anything, the degree of stability and continuity in that industry over the crisis years is perhaps the most surprising outcome.[44] The crisis did result in a deepening of the industry's ties to the other energy regimes, with the result that the objectives of the industry as a whole have become much more diverse and complex, encompassing a much larger domain of energy-related activities and reflecting calculations of self-interest that are increasingly difficult to penetrate.[45]

Natural Gas   In the gas regime the embargo halted the movement toward compromise between producers and consumers that had begun in the early 1970's. As oil prices increased, gas, at regulated prices, automatically became even scarcer as demand for it grew. Supply did not increase partly because low prices did not stimulate greater production, partly because that production associated with oil declined owing to depletion, and partly because increases in oil prices created a new intransigence on the part of producers, who knew that gas prices would also have to rise rapidly in the near future. This, in turn, increased pressure on the FPC to allow new price hikes, which, when granted, then aroused anew the ire of consumers.

In sum, the process of accommodation between producers and consumers of natural gas—a process that before the crisis seemed to be leading to modest price increases and new supplies—was quickly replaced by another round of even more hostile conflict. The twenty-year war began again with still greater intensity. This time, however, events strengthened the hand of producers and they were able, after long and complex political struggles, to make important gains. These gains included significant price increases, granted by the FPC after oil prices skyrocketed, as well as the commitment to phased deregulation of new production after 1985. In a nutshell, the crisis created the political conditions for an eventual end to compensatory regulation. For the gas regime, this was an even more fundamental transformation—because it had been regulated for so long—than was the case with oil.

As with oil, there were important divisions in the gas regime that can be traced to the crisis and government responses to it. When the shortages of gas increased, some consumer regions broke ranks and supported deregulation in the belief that this was the only way that new supplies would become available. And the decision to unify markets—i.e. to end the deregulated status of intrastate gas trade—damaged the interests of some owners of gas reserves. Indeed the struggle over the enactment of the NGPA compromise was marked by bitter disagreement between independent producers and other segments of the gas regime, including large producers, distributors, and pipelines, many of which eventually concluded that the compromise was better than the status quo.

Electricity   Real and prospective price increases in primary fuels caught utilities off guard. A cohort of conservative managers, used to incremental change and expecting to be able to pass price increases along to customers, found themselves facing regulatory commissions deeply suspicious of the fairness of price increases. They also found themselves forced to lead the country in the search for least-cost, environmentally safe fuels on terms that were set increasingly by regulators and policymakers outside of the industry.

Although the symptoms of trouble were slow to appear, the electric utility industry proved extraordinarily vulnerable to the energy crisis and the changes in the economy that accompanied it. Indeed, the losses suffered by many utilities (and their investors and customers) will, over the long term, represent a significant part of the total loss imposed by the crisis on the national economy. As noted in Chapter 5, firmly established institutional practices, which in turn reflected technical changes and economic and regulatory incentives that had prevailed for more than half a century, made it difficult for the industry to adjust to crisis-induced changes in fuel prices, demand patterns, construction costs, interest rates, and regulatory requirements.

For as long as they could remember, utility executives had been able to count on steady, predictable increases in demand for electricity. And they had been able to meet those increases with electricity that was less expensive because fuel costs were stable or declining and because technical innovations and economies of scale made new and larger plants more efficient. Government subsidies and promotional regulatory policies supported them in their efforts to borrow funds and bring on line new facilities.

The energy crisis changed these terms of reference fundamentally. Price increases for fuels and, therefore, electricity reduced demand. For some utilities higher prices cut back total demand for long periods and for others they slowed the growth in new demand. In 1974, average electricity usage per customer declined for the first time in nearly thirty years. Reduced or unpredictable demand meant, in many cases, reduced sales and, thereby, lower revenues to pay back loans, reward investors, and cover large fixed costs. Price increases to cover deficits would only serve to make matters worse by further cutting demand. Finally, the industry gradually discovered that economies of scale in generation had reached their limits, and still larger plants could no longer promise significant savings to be passed on to consumers.

The industry was very slow to adjust to these new conditions. Many companies continued to invest in new plants, basing their decisions on estimates of demand growth that were becoming progressively more unrealistic. Inflation, spurred in part by energy price increases, raised the costs of these facilities, as did increases in the rates of interest that borrowers were forced to pay. Unexpected delays, many of them the results of poor planning, also hurt.[46]

The nuclear construction programs upon which many utilities had embarked were particularly troublesome, since cost overruns and delays made them unsupportable under new financial circumstances—even with continued subsidies and the skyrocketing costs of alternative fuels. The near-meltdown at Three Mile Island in 1979 struck a profound blow to the industry partly because it dramatically altered public attitudes toward the safety of nuclear plants, and partly because it revealed, to investors and regulators both, that the uninsured costs associated with even a "minor" on-site accident could be truly catastrophic.[47] In the decade after the embargo of 1973, more than 100 nuclear power plants, representing over 100,000 megawatts of capacity, had to be canceled at a loss of billions of dollars.[48]

When utility managers finally recognized the full implications of the crisis-induced changes, many companies were well down the road to insolvency. Indicators of financial troubles became increasingly alarming by the mid-1970's: earnings on equity deteriorated, stock values declined, bond ratings dropped, and indebtedness increased. When utilities finally began to abandon unrealistic plans for future expansion, many once again faced the unpleasant task of asking consumers to pay higher prices—but this time to pay for facilities that could not be used at planned capacity or that would never be built at all.[49]

As might be expected, these problems provoked fundamental changes in the regulatory processes affecting utility decisions. Quiet, cooperative, proprietary regulation gave way in state after state to compensatory conflict as consumer groups demanded access to decisions about higher rates and construction programs.[50] The simultaneous awakening of environmental activism and antinuclear protest only served to complicate matters. Unlike compensatory regulation in the petroleum and natural gas regimes, however, there was no prospect in electricity for significant deregulation brought on by political stalemate. Indeed, the activation of voter and interest-group concern for utility decisionmaking can be expected to influence the course of regime affairs for the foreseeable future.[51]

The policies adopted by the federal government were inconsistent in their impact. Oil price regulations and refiner entitlements made oil cheaper for a while and thus made nuclear power seem less attractive. Regulations aimed at reducing oil imports for the utility industry—chiefly the fuel-switching provisions of the Fuel Use Act—would have worsened the financial troubles of the industry had they been effective. The continuation of tax subsidies and promotional programs made the addition of new nuclear power plants seem more attractive than they would otherwise have been, but, later on, the decision to abandon work on the Clinch River Breeder Reactor project had the opposite effect. Primary responsibility for coping with the crisis, however, remained at the state level.

The new pattern of regime governance had several consequences. To begin with, it made it more difficult for utilities to raise rates, complicating their struggle to compensate for fuel price increases and poor management by passing costs on to consumers. It also made it increasingly difficult to add new, large-scale generating capacity of any kind, anywhere. Regulators and utility executives, facing a political process marked by greater participation and concern for consumer protection, were simply unwilling to accept the risks involved in light of uncertainties concerning oil prices, inflation, interest rates, and costs of energy from new facilities. As one industry leader put it: "A major supply project may take ten to fifteen years from conception to operation and have an operating life of thirty-five to forty years. These time periods . . . are substantially longer than the two- to six-year periods that dominate political decisionmaking or the one-year or even quarterly earnings periods that apply to business decisions."[52]

The inability to build new large facilities threatened eventually to create a serious dilemma for publicly franchised monopolies charged with satisfying the electricity needs of their districts. This became more worrisome as, by the mid-1980's, economic recovery and the reduction of world oil prices resulted in a resumption of growth in demand for electricity.[53] (See Fig. 3.) A number of utility companies responded by promoting conservation and the installation of small-scale cogeneration facilities instead of large power plants.[54] Though the evidence suggests that the industry has indeed been forced to discover effective (and often cheaper) means of managing demand in the near term, the prospect of a utility industry more or less permanently unable to add new large-scale capacity was a source of growing alarm to industry observers in the 1980's.

Summary

The energy crisis was first and foremost a crisis of wealth distribution. As such, it was the occasion for a tremendous mobilization of interests seeking to avoid losses—and preserve gains—as national policy addressed the consequences of the OPEC tax. But the result was paralysis more than anything else. The key legislative measures that would form the basis for policy had already been introduced in response to problems stemming from Nixon's economywide price control program—a program that antedated the crisis—as it affected a petroleum regime whose affairs were already deeply entangled in regulatory relationships with the government. Once these measures had been passed, two great cleavages quickly formed in the body politic, one between producers and consumers, and the other between the executive and the legislature. As a result, an approach chosen temporarily in the first few months of the crisis became locked in, and could only be changed when the distributional issues it addressed had resolved themselves. This deadlock in the polity, more than anything else, explains the character of national energy policies.

By the mid-1980's the energy political economy had settled into a new pattern. The federal government's assertive, crisis-related involvement in markets had been largely dismantled, along with much of the bureaucracy that was responsible for it. To be sure, the government continued to manage the SPR, enforce a variety of demand-reduction regulations, and hand out a dwindling collection of special subsidies and tax incentives. And federal regulators continued to oversee "old" gas and pipeline prices and collect the WPT. But direct intervention in energy markets themselves had been dramatically reduced.[55] Intervention was cut, in fact, to a level that had not been experienced for many, many decades—since the 1940's for gas and the 1920's for petroleum. Both proprietary and compensatory federal regulations had, in effect, become obsolete, and most of them had been dismantled.[56] Only at the state and local level did the adversarial process stemming from compensatory regulation persist.

What made all this possible was the disappearance of the political necessity to intervene in behalf of equity objectives, on the one hand, and the apparent stability of the protective umbrella of public regulation provided by OPEC, on the other. To the extent OPEC could maintain high and stable world oil prices, it replaced the proprietary supply prorationing and import controls that had set the terms for energy markets in the United States for many years before the crisis. The recurrent threat of price fluctuations induced by competition and associated "oversupply" no longer appeared to require the industry to seek federal assistance. This, of course, placed a heavy burden on OPEC, especially insofar as it necessitated the management of world supply. It also created an important source of potential instability in energy governance, a point to which I will return in the next chapter.

However—and this is important—the decision to terminate regulation was the result neither of "principled" choices by decisionmakers nor of political consensus, but of a persistent stalemate in the body politic that made this the only possible outcome. It was, if you will, deregulation by default.

Despite the end of compensatory regulation at the federal level, a number of the changes in governance patterns wrought by the crisis persisted. More cross-regime integration of executive and, to a lesser degree, legislative institutions, the emergence of an "issue network" of analytical and policy specialists, and corporate mergers and acquisitions—all assured that "energy" would continue to be treated as an interrelated set of problems by analysts and policymakers. This occurred despite the tendency for regime- and industry-specific problems to occupy more of the attention of those handling day-to-day problems.

The various energy regimes thus emerged from the crisis decade structurally altered and with different future prospects. Coal emerged even more captive to utilities and steel mills. The oil and gas industry emerged more concentrated and with firmer connections to other energy and mineral industries. And utilities emerged in financial distress and heavily burdened by nuclear commitments made during and before the crisis. All these trends were in evidence before 1973, but the crisis added impetus to them.

Crisis politics was also marked by a dramatic mobilization of interest groups, a process that reflected important new terms of reference in American politics generally and that contributed to the persistence of both regulation and stalemate. Although producer interests were unable to prevent the advent of compensatory regulation, they were able to exercise considerable influence on the operation of the regulatory system itself and were able to veto efforts to make those regulations permanent or establish new ones with greater redistributional impact. Consumer and "citizen" interest groups, many of which relied heavily on the sponsorship of political patrons and the use of new technologies of participation, were able to win price concessions and delay deregulation as well as force decisionmakers to engage in a wide-ranging, if temporary, debate about the broader sociopolitical implications of technical alternatives in energy. The end of crisis saw a decline in the strength and survival rate of those consumer and "citizen" interest groups that focused solely on energy issues and relied heavily on "purposive" incentives. This left business interests in a better position overall, but the level of group activity remained greater than before the crisis, and consumer and "purposive" groups remained a potent, if now more latent, political force, able to mobilize again with even greater ease should another redistributive threat arise in the energy system.

PART FOUR   Conclusion

CHAPTER 10   The Cycle of Failure

It is time now to put the pieces together. The chapters of Part Two chronicled the government's response to the energy crisis. This was followed in Part Three by an analysis of the impact of those policies and by an examination of the political and institutional changes that were associated with the crisis. My objective now is to draw conclusions and, where possible, lessons from this experience.

It should already be evident to the reader that the political economy of energy offers little gratification to those who seek confirmation of one or another conventional worldview, whether "liberal" or "conservative," as those labels are used today. Indeed, if there is a central conclusion to this chapter, it is that, to the extent that our response to the energy crisis can be a guide, we are very much adrift when it comes to basic principles of political economy.

I should add that by "principles" I mean lawlike generalizations about how individuals and institutions behave, not normative preferences, although I recognize that the two are always found in association. Indeed, here is part of the problem: ideologies bind science and values together, but if ideologies are mistaken about how things work, i.e. if their science is wrong, they doom true believers to frustration in their efforts to shape the world.

This, I suggest, is one of our major problems: our prescriptions fail because, even if we have a clear sense of our values, we rely upon increasingly mistaken conceptions about how the world works. This may be the fault of academic disciplines—the tendency to apotheosize "free" markets and "pluralist" politics persists, despite articulate and persuasive attacks. But I think it is deeper, extending to our country's very heritage of ideas and institutions. I will return to these matters in the next chapter, where I explore alternatives, but I raise them here because I feel that an appreciation of the argument in this chapter requires at least a temporary suspension of the habit we all share of rejecting conclusions that appear to contradict our preferred ideological formulae.

A Balance Sheet

Specialists in government agencies, universities, and private research organizations have carefully scrutinized American energy policies over the last decade.[1] They have employed analytical techniques that range from elaborate formal modeling exercises to detailed chronological accounts and historical interpretations based on careful scrutiny of documents and interviews with decisionmakers.[2] As might be expected under these circumstances, the standards they used to measure success or failure varied greatly.[3]

Many of the most vocal critics of policies during the years of crisis were advocates of strong government action. Confident about the effectiveness of government intervention, they called for a decisive "plan" and were often willing to see the American people pay a significant price to change consumption habits and reduce the country's vulnerability to embargo or economic blackmail. These "energy technocrats" often disagreed among themselves: some advocated nuclear energy and a crash program to develop fossil and synthetic fuels; others preferred a strategy based on regulations to promote conservation and renewable energy sources. But all were deeply disappointed with energy policy. They watched in growing dismay as the Congress rejected strong, effective measures and dismembered the most carefully designed presidential "plans" to achieve energy independence.

Another group—call them "marketeers"—blamed the government itself for the crisis and all the troubles associated with it.[4] More theoretically sophisticated—many of them economists by profession—the marketeers focused their attention on efficiency in resource allocation and the economywide effects of distortions in energy prices.[5] They were equally critical of energy policy. In most cases what they "learned" from their research was what they already believed: that the government is hopelessly incompetent at promoting the efficient use of resources, and that therefore its involvement has been a burden on every American.

Unfortunately, very few serious analysts adopted a broad enough perspective to allow a balanced evaluation of what was done in relation to the political and institutional imperatives of the democratic polity. This made it difficult, on the one hand, to see where the system performed well and, on the other, to probe beyond policy failures to the deeper, systemic problems of which the failures were but symptoms.[6] If pluralist politics had any redeeming value, or fatal flaws, it was not evident in the work of those debating or analyzing energy policy.

Few of the technocrats, for example, paused and asked in retrospect whether the sacrifices they proposed during the crisis later appeared wiser than the more modest price the society proved willing to pay for energy security. And few of the marketeers carefully considered the value of any "goods" purchased at the price of economic efficiency—such as equity—or sought to compare the costs of crisis regulations with the costs of the proprietary arrangements they replaced. And neither group made significant efforts to join political and economic analysis in search of insights about the institutional basis for their disappointments.

I raise these matters not because energy policy studies have not accomplished a great deal, for they have. Few problems have received such intensive and technically sophisticated scrutiny in such a short period of time. Rather, I raise them because it is important, before itemizing our failures, to acknowledge what we accomplished and understand why we were able to avoid even greater disasters.

How, then, did we do? What did we accomplish, what mistakes did we avoid, and how well did we prepare ourselves for the future? The first observation to make is that if we judge the American pluralist system as one for managing conflicts and responding to the demands of injured claimants according to their wealth and power, then the system performed very much as we might have expected. The energy crisis raised, after all, an extraordinarily difficult set of problems. And it caught us unprepared. Not only were the stakes high, but society was deeply divided. There was no consensus about the appropriate response, and there was enormous, continuing uncertainty among specialists as well as the general public about the character (and causes) of the problem itself and about the consequences of different government actions. Too, the political system was caught at a juncture when leadership was weakened and the structure of legislative decisionmaking was in transition. As the crisis worsened, those affected quickly mobilized to protect themselves, virtually swamping decisionmakers with demands for protection and support, whereas others sought refuge in cherished ideological principles about the market or the power of monopolists.

In light of these observations, consider the overall outcome: a foreign cartel imposed a series of very large price increases on us. At the international level, the government brought the developed consuming nations together in a loose defensive alliance that made another "targeted" embargo less likely. Domestically, the government reacted by trying to prevent the price increases from forcing sudden, dramatic losses and gains on U.S. citizens, who in turn quickly mobilized to try and influence the resulting policies. The means decisionmakers chose was a complex system of compensatory intervention that distributed burdens and benefits within the petroleum industry as well as within the larger society.

The outcome was a ten-year transition period in which the economy adjusted to the new conditions while the government delayed the inevitable accommodation to world prices and cushioned the impact on consumers by distributing to them (by protecting them from paying) some 20–40 percent of the new rents on domestic petroleum made available by the actions of the cartel.[7] Integrated oil companies received most of the rest, and a variety of other interests also received compensation of one kind or another. In the absence of consensus on how to proceed, or on whether the rents should go to the owners of petroleum reserves, the "decision," in effect, was to split the difference, favoring corporate interests in the process.

While America struggled with equity issues, "crash" solutions, though widely advocated, never gained more than tentative support. It is instructive, in fact, as we judge the performance of our democracy, to ask ourselves how well we might have done if one or another of the grand schemes proposed by American presidents at times of energy "emergency" (1973–74 or 1979–80) had actually been approved by Congress. Would the country be better off if we had actually achieved energy "independence" by 1980 or even 1985? What price would consumers today be paying for fuel if that price had to be high enough to accelerate domestic production to the point where it displaced imports or dampened demand enough to make them unwanted, or both? Would we be better off if a massive, heavily subsidized synfuels industry were close to achieving the 1992 production goal (set in 1980) of two million barrels a day? And what if we had significantly relaxed environmental and safety standards in a crash program to promote domestic production of fossil fuels and nuclear energy?[8]

With respect to the governance of energy, the ultimate "decision" was to allow federal government involvement to lapse in energy markets, except in the roles of tax collector and pipeline regulator, once that involvement was no longer necessary to distribute income. This was possible not because of agreement on the application of principles for the management of economic affairs but because (1) producers felt they no longer needed assistance to manage the market; (2) many consumers, as prices increased, accepted the conclusion that they would be as well off without regulatory intervention; and (3) the political stalemate was so persistent that no other solution—or definition of the problem—could gain acceptance.[9]

Taken together, these elements do in fact constitute a set of "solutions" to the immediate problems posed by the energy crisis. To recapitulate, the pluralist system produced a weak defensive alliance, divided the spoils, rejected costly "crash" solutions, and, after a transition period, permitted the introduction of world prices into the U.S. economy. America weathered a tremendous economic shock with relatively little domestic disorder and resisted the temptation to pay a very high price for an "independence" that would soon prove to be of little value. Whether or not we like them, these were "real" answers to very difficult problems. We might have been considerably worse off.

This is not to say that the energy crisis did not reveal deep and serious difficulties in the U.S. political economy—it did, and I will examine these more closely in the pages that follow. It is to assert, rather, that the first step to wisdom is recognizing—and, where appropriate, appreciating—the achievements of our democratic institutions and rules of the game. The kinds of solutions we chose during the crisis are very much the product of our pluralist political and organizational inheritance.[10] This is important because it means that, other things being equal, it is precisely these kinds of solutions that we can expect in the future as our country confronts new crises of this sort.[11]

Unfortunately, as we have seen, not only was the price paid for these accomplishments high, but the public policies chosen worked so poorly, and contradicted each other so consistently, that, as a set, they can only be judged a costly failure. The direct and indirect economic costs of regulatory policies, summarized in Chapter 8, ran to many billions of dollars. The price controls and entitlements increased imports from the most insecure foreign suppliers, enlarged the payments made to those countries that mounted an embargo against us, made the country more vulnerable to the second "shock" that followed the Iranian revolution, nullified the value of demand-reduction policies, and forced widespread and costly distortions in the allocation of economic resources. Energy policies also hurt our allies by further tightening the world market, thus increasing their vulnerability and the sums they were forced to pay to OPEC. Furthermore, although the major justification for these costs, in the minds of those who set up the regulatory mechanisms, was the assurance of some distributional equity, that objective was achieved to a large extent only within the petroleum regime (via entitlements), not in the society at large.

Perhaps the most telling criticism, however, is that the decision-making process was so turgid, confused, and prone to immobility and stalemate, that it could not produce or permit other solutions, solutions that were simpler and better, and would have accomplished the same (or greater) distributional results while avoiding many of the inefficiencies that actual policies exacted. The reasons for this, summarized in Chapter 9, were complex, but of critical importance. The regulatory regime, established in emergency, became increasingly complex, cumbersome, and counterproductive, yet Congress and the Executive Branch found it impossible to replace that regime with broad, "national" solutions. Instead the government was forced to respond to the demands of particularistic interests, especially those that were well organized and had a large economic stake in the outcome. These interests, with a clearer sense of what was at stake, quickly adapted to the new conditions, vetoing proposals that might have proved better national policy but that did not promise a clear improvement in their circumstances and prospects.[12] The result was a frustrating stalemate that was never broken, but that quietly became irrelevant as the price transition became complete and the petroleum industry agreed to an excise tax to smooth the way.

All of this damaged the standing of the government and the political process, both of which lost legitimacy, authority, and respect. Indeed, if there was consensus that arose from the energy crisis, it was that U.S. public institutions are incapable of handling problems of this kind with any degree of success. The policies proposed by the Reagan Administration reflect this loss of standing. The decisions to embrace the deregulation of oil and gas that Ford and Carter initiated, to dismantle the Department of Energy, to cut research and development activities, even to veto a bill granting the President the right to allocate fuels in the event of emergency—all confirm this outcome.

To recapitulate, it is impossible to avoid the conclusion that the United States simply did not perform well in responding to the energy crisis, whether that performance is judged narrowly, by the standards set by the policies themselves, or more broadly, in terms of reasonable expectations concerning how a modern industrial society should perform under circumstances of this kind.[13] Although we avoided political instability and crash commitments to poor technical options, the net results of our government interventions were not satisfactory or even acceptable. Policies did not work, or worked against each other. Even the clearest objectives, such as distributional equity or reduced import dependence, were beyond our reach. By our own actions we paid a larger OPEC tax than we need have paid, increasing our energy vulnerability in the process, and we failed to protect the disadvantaged in distributing the burden of that tax. A principal remaining question to be addressed in the pages that follow is, How well did we prepare ourselves for future problems?

The Prospects for Unregulated Markets in Energy

The predominant image of the future in the energy sector in the mid-1980's was that of a return to a largely fictional past in which the private sector controlled decisions about investments and alternatives, and in which effective competition in turn guided these decisions so as to conform with the needs and demands of consumers. In this image, the government was again distant and ignorant, neither willing nor able to intrude and disrupt.

Can we live with this kind of arrangement in the future, in energy as well as, perhaps, other areas of economic life? Is it viable?

In terms of distributional justice, the answer is probably "yes, we can live with it"—although many will strenuously object to the degree of inequality implied in this answer. If there is a widely noted consequence of the operation of pluralist democratic decisionmaking, it is that it overwhelmingly favors the status quo. As many careful observers have pointed out, there is also a bias in favor of large and well organized economic interests.[14] This bias is normally even more pronounced in governance arrangements that rely heavily on markets to allocate wealth and resources. This is borne out in the case of energy policy, where the impulse to prevent a major shift of wealth was powerful in shaping policy, and where well organized economic interests were able, despite this impulse, to capture a significant portion of newly available rents anyway, and ended up well-placed with respect to future opportunities. The very poor, as might be expected, did badly in the competition. Although I am not particularly happy about these results, it nevertheless appears that outcomes of this kind may well be tolerated by U.S. citizens for many years to come.

In terms of the workability of the post-crisis "solution"—government withdrawal and free markets for energy—the answer is different. For a variety of reasons, it is almost certain to fail. More importantly, the failure itself will contribute to what is already a deepening quandary in the nation's approach to economic governance. A look at the prospects for stability in the energy regimes, a review of the historical record, and an analysis of the patterns of market and regulatory evolution revealed by the record will help explain why this is the case.

The reasons why current arrangements are not likely to prove acceptable in coming years can be summarized quickly: (1) instability in energy markets, already significant by 1986–87, will almost certainly become a chronic problem, affecting all regimes; (2) U.S. dependence on imported oil, already increasing rapidly, will soon match and exceed the levels of the early 1970's, resulting in greater vulnerability to international economic and political events; (3) price fluctuations and supply interruptions are economically costly and force significant and visible redistributions in wealth; and (4), however reluctantly, the government can be expected to respond to demands to control these costs, manage security threats, and mediate the process of wealth redistribution in some manner.

Consider the problem of market instability. When the Reagan Administration dismantled the remaining regulatory controls on petroleum, it was widely assumed by energy decisionmakers that international prices would remain high and relatively stable—increasing, perhaps, by an average of two percent per year, but not fluctuating wildly. In effect, most specialists had concluded that OPEC had, for practical purposes, replaced the old proprietary prorationing/price support mechanism that had worked so well before the crisis to stabilize the market.

By the mid-1980's, it was already becoming clear that OPEC's ability to provide a framework of stability and high prices was collapsing and could no longer be counted on. At the height of its power in the early 1970's, OPEC members controlled nearly 80 percent of world oil supplies, and demand for those supplies was so strong that there was little need to control production levels in individual countries. By 1986 this was no longer the case. OPEC controlled only about 40 percent of the oil entering international trade, the dominant position of its members eroded by new supplies coming from places like the North Sea and the Gulf of Mexico. A combination of factors, prominent among them the high prices set by OPEC decisions, had weakened demand to the point where nearly all producers had excess production capacity and could not sell all the crude they wanted to at existing prices. OPEC countries were producing at 80 percent of capacity when the price increases of the 1970's occurred; by 1986 they were producing at less than 60 percent of capacity.[15]

OPEC made serious attempts to sustain high prices by prorationing supply. In the first years, Saudi Arabia, which for years had earned several times more for its oil than it needed for domestic purposes, made most of the sacrifice in the form of unilateral cutbacks. Later the organization sought agreement on formal quotas, meeting twice a year to seek consensus on its market control measures, eventually even hiring an accounting firm to audit the production levels of member countries. There was always some cheating, but there was also some very real sacrifice. By the mid-1980's, however, OPEC's discipline had begun to weaken, and prices began to erode sharply.[16]

The collapse of OPEC control of the world oil supply means a return to instability in world and U.S. petroleum markets.[17] Ironically, it is the possibility that prices may move still further downward that is the source of immediate concern for the energy regimes and therefore the most likely cause of demands for intervention in the near term. High prices become embedded in economic decisions. The fluctuations experienced in the early and mid-1980's caused deepening worry among financial experts who feared that a price slump could worsen the international banking crisis by eroding the ability of debtors such as Venezuela and Mexico to repay money borrowed in expectation of high export earnings. Within the energy industries, investments in new crude production in places like the North Sea and Alaska and in more expensive energy sources such as deep natural gas deposits all required high prices as a condition of profitability.

The price collapse also devastated the economies of those U.S. states that had become dependent on oil revenues. The worst-hit were Oklahoma, Texas, and Louisiana, but Alaska, New Mexico, and Colorado suffered as well. Not only did their economies slump, but state governments found themselves forced to cut back on basic public services just when they were most needed. Early in 1986, for example, Oklahoma forecast a budget deficit of $467 million (in a budget of $2 billion) for the next fiscal year.[18] Oklahoma in 1986 lost $15-$20 million for each dollar that the price of oil fell.[19] The American Petroleum Institute predicted in the spring of 1986 that if oil prices remained below $15 per barrel for the next five years, U.S. crude oil production would drop 31 percent and gas production would drop 22 percent, while 300,000 workers would lose their jobs in the oil industry.[20]

Instability also implies upward fluctuations in prices, and it is these that are likely to be the more serious threat in the longer run. Several trends will contribute to this. Most observers agree that economic recovery plus the expected growth in demand from developing countries will soon close the gap between demand and production capacity without new price increases. This will likely occur by the end of the decade or shortly thereafter. The United States will be able to do little about this, since its own production capacity will continue to decline—indeed, U.S. markets will become increasingly tied to world oil markets as imports grow.[21] The U.S. Energy Information Administration forecast that OPEC will once again be producing at 80 percent of capacity by the end of the 1980's.[22] This means that world petroleum (and thereby energy) markets will once again be tied to the turbulent politics of the Middle East, suffused as those politics are with hatred and bitter religious and ideological rivalry.

If there is a single point of agreement among critics of current energy policies, it is that the Reagan Administration acted irresponsibly in failing to make contingency plans—beyond the possible auctioning of Reserve oil—for the possibility of another crisis. Reagan's decision in 1982 to veto a bill giving the President standby authority to allocate supplies in case of emergency reflects the orientation of the administration in this matter; it was a decision, in effect, to allow market forces to manage any emergencies. Energy analysts have pointed out repeatedly that markets cannot be expected to give the most efficient signals under crisis conditions, but the Reagan policymakers have apparently concluded that the incompetence of the government during the crisis years was so great that it is better to avoid any intervention.[23] This commitment extends even to advance planning.

A little noticed study by the Congressional Office of Technology Assessment concluded in 1984 that careful planning for an emergency, involving chiefly the identification of temporary means of accelerating the introduction of oil displacement technologies, could significantly reduce the economic costs of an unexpected, but long-lasting, supply shortfall (or price increase) crisis. The study estimated that emergency measures could reduce GNP losses by as much as 40 percent and employment losses by as much as 30 percent, over a scenario marked by less intervention. This could be accomplished primarily by the use of incentives (i.e., without government-mandated conversion to new technologies) and would, though costly, be more than compensated by a tax designed to collect half or more of the increased profits on domestic production such a crisis would generate.[24] The unwillingness of the government to consider contingencies of this kind seriously represents still another instance of our learning the wrong lessons from the crisis years.[25]

Beyond the very serious immediate problem of instability and strategic insecurity stemming from the world petroleum market and renewed U.S. vulnerability to OPEC and events in the Middle East, there is the additional, and more profound, problem of chronic instability in uncontrolled fuel markets generally. I refer now to structural tendencies rather than the result of specific trends or events. Although this instability would take different forms for each of the energy regimes, it can be expected to afflict each of them in time. Indeed, since the end of petroleum regulation there have been signs of instability in the form of excess supply in natural gas and coal, as well as oil.[26]

If there is one great lesson to be drawn from the history of energy regimes, it is that supply and price instability will recur in unmanaged markets for resources of this kind. The reasons for these attributes are discussed at length in Part One. It is true that a number of recent changes (e.g., the control of coal by utilities, steelmakers, and petroleum companies; new mergers; the decreasing likelihood of major new giant field discoveries) have changed the outlook somewhat, but the basic problem remains. Indeed, the freer the markets, the more serious that problem is likely to be, especially if OPEC also fails to regain any control of world petroleum.

Over the longer run, as depletion increases the prices for fossil fuels, another source of instability can also be expected to come into play. Liquid and gaseous hydrocarbons can be produced from organic matter (biomass) at costs that probably do not exceed double the current price for refined petroleum fuels and natural gas. When the two markets interact, price and supply of energy can be expected to be influenced by the same unpredictable forces that have made food, feed, and fiber markets so unstable. A trend in this direction is already visible in the market for ethyl alcohol to be used as a gasoline additive (gasohol), and can be expected to become much more prominent as the percentage of alcohol in American fuels increases owing to existing subsidies and the decision to remove lead from commercial fuel.

If there is a second important lesson to be drawn from the history of the energy regimes, it is that those forced to live with unstable markets will seek to manage them, privately if possible, but with public assistance when private efforts fail—as they almost always do. We saw this most clearly in the cases of the coal, petroleum, and gas industries in the decades before the crisis. In the case of coal, private market management, mostly on a regional basis, gave way to federal price controls. These failed to stabilize the industry because they were not accompanied by control of supply. Only when private collusion between management and union leadership was able to limit coal supply was it possible for the industry to experience a degree of market stability. And this, of course, began to crumble when labor leaders ceased to represent the interests of miners effectively. The oil industry was more successful because industry leaders recognized very early that control of supply, rather than price, was the key to taming the market, and harnessed state and national government support in achieving this objective.[27] Natural gas producers, once private control by means of holding companies failed, proved too weak and fragmented to duplicate the stabilization arrangements pioneered by oil producers, and succumbed to compensatory regulation after 1954.

Thus, even though domestic fuel markets may experience less structural instability than they did in the days when the energy industries were younger, some instability is certain, especially if markets are able to adjust freely to changing conditions. It is just as certain that those subject to this instability will find it intolerable and seek private recourse—and, when that fails, public support.[28]

The other side of the coin, of course, is that public authorities will find it expedient to assist in the taming of the market. Whether it be as a result of international events—a price drop, an interruption of supply, a sudden price hike—or domestic market instability, the government will find it necessary to act as it has in the past. There are many reasons for this, but the clearest is simple political accountability, as the events surrounding the energy crisis illustrate. Voters and influential interests hold the government responsible for economic damage they suffer, even if that damage happens to be the result of "market" action. The most ubiquitous and binding rule of the game in American politics is this: "There shall be no costly, visible redistributions." The enlargement of political participation in general, and the mobilization of stakeholder groups in particular, has only made this rule more sovereign over the last two decades. No one familiar with the political economy of energy or the basic attributes of American politics really believes that another "shock" will be ignored by the U.S. government, with economic circumstance determining winners and losers. And no one familiar with the world energy market, and oil politics in the Middle East in particular, believes we will fail to have another crisis.

A Theory of Regulatory Evolution

The form that regulation takes, of course, makes a great deal of difference. With respect to this, the experience of the energy regimes in the years before and during the crisis suggests the appropriateness of a loose model of the evolution of market regulation in the modern American political economy. It is a model that, especially if generalizable beyond energy, holds important implications for how we understand, and respond to, problems of resource management.[29] At the heart of this model is what might be called the problem of "degenerative instability in progressively politicized pluralist market management." (The phrase is a difficult one, admittedly, but it covers the basic elements of the problem.) It refers to the tendency of forms of regulation to fail, for a number of reasons, only to be replaced with new forms that are themselves unstable, a cycle that leads to ever-greater economic waste and loss of political legitimacy.

The process begins with that hypothetical condition, similar to Hobbes' "state of nature," of free and unregulated markets in a sector of economic activity—the kind that might be found, for example, in the first years after the birth of a new industry. The pattern suggested by the history of the energy regimes is that participants in such markets, especially if they are subject to price and supply instability, first seek to tame them through private efforts. The Rockefeller monopoly and the international cartel in oil, the holding companies in natural gas and electricity, the regional monopolies and the legal cartel embodied in Appalachian Coals—all are examples of this. As Sam Peltzman has demonstrated, this kind of market management is theoretically the most attractive to participants because it produces a more optimal solution by bringing larger shares of available rents.[30]

For reasons that are equally understandable in theoretical terms, such arrangements do not last. If they take the form of pure monopoly they will be politically vulnerable, as was the case with the Rockefeller empire and the holding companies in gas and electricity. But even if they are not, they create an attractive field for new entrants willing to break the rules to share in the high profits and rapid growth available there. And they encourage cheating by "free riders" among the existing, privileged membership. The examples cited above owe their eventual demise to one or another of these causes. OPEC's current troubles can also be understood within this theoretical framework.

The failure of purely private means of controlling competition normally leads market participants to seek public assistance in the form of some kind of proprietary regulation. The multi-tiered regulatory system that worked so well in the petroleum business after the New Deal is an excellent illustration of a "successful" arrangement of this kind.[31] Proprietary regulation is unlikely to work, however, unless it involves control of supply rather than price. The difficulties involved in administering price regulation are illustrated clearly by the fate of the system set up under the Guffey Act of 1937 (described in Chapter 2), in the natural gas regime after the 1954 *Phillips* decision (described in Chapter 4), and, of course, in the price-control system in oil after 1973. The economic costs of supply prorationing may be quite high, as they were in the case of the oil industry before the crisis, but even if they are—indeed, even if they are higher than the costs associated with price regulation—they generate far less opposition from economic analysts because they do not create a shortage and thereby lead to government allocation, as price regulation nearly always does.[32]

Even where supply is brought under control, proprietary regulation imposes a cost on consumers. Therefore, to endure it usually requires either invisibility or political autonomy. Its participants must be able to avoid or deflect attempts to reimpose competition or redistribute benefits. This is the key to the demise of past arrangements and the reason why proprietary regulation is likely to be more difficult to establish and maintain in the future. The expansion of political participation, the mobilization of groups promoting the interests of consumers and the general public, the availability of new technologies of participation, increasing public and professional attention to the consequences of government economic management— all have made proprietary regulation more vulnerable in the American pluralist system, forcing regulators, the courts, and elected officials to dismantle, or grant some form of consumer access to, market-control arrangements.[33] The *Phillips* decision in 1954 plus the defeat of subsequent efforts to override that Court dictum in the gas regime, and steps leading to the EPAA and EPCA in petroleum, are examples of these trends at work. Price or supply "crises" (such as those provoked by OAPEC) can be expected to trigger this process by raising the stakes and promoting the mobilization of consumers.

The circumstances that surround the demise of proprietary regulation are important determinants of the kind of arrangements that will replace it. If enough consumer representatives conclude that a return to freer markets will eliminate the problem, they may successfully demand deregulation. If there is a widespread belief that competition is not likely to help, they will demand, instead, the right to participate in regulatory decisions. The latter is the more likely result in industries that are considered "natural" monopolies (oil and gas pipelines, transmission and local distribution of electricity), in industries that are widely suspected of monopolistic practices (conventional and nuclear electricity production; natural gas production; petroleum production, refining, and retail marketing; and, to a lesser extent, coal production), and where market instability or international events create price and supply fluctuations that threaten significant redistribution of wealth from consumers to producers.

As this list suggests, the conditions that lead to compensatory regulation, as the sequel to proprietary regulation, are clearly predominant in the energy industries and are likely to remain so, despite the current deregulation of oil and gas. As noted earlier, the likelihood of consumer success in demanding such arrangements has also increased as a result of changes in the political process itself.

Unfortunately, compensatory regulation also contains the seeds of its own degeneration (if not necessarily destruction). At heart it is an adversarial process in which producers and consumers compete to influence the price decisions of regulators. Price is always the principal focus because (as consumers view it) supply restriction can only benefit producers. As we have seen in each of the energy regimes, price controls inevitably lead to some degree of shortage, and thus to some state control of the disposition of supplies. More importantly, arrangements of this kind are themselves extraordinarily vulnerable to any change, whether it stem from market instability, technological adjustment, international shock, or even resource depletion.

The reasons for this vulnerability are complicated but worth reviewing. Because compensatory regulation is an adversarial process, it is suffused with mistrust. When producers demand price increases, consumers expect them to overstate the degree of increase that is needed and react by refusing to grant the full increases demanded. Knowing this, producers overstate their needs. And so it goes. Where levels of mistrust are especially high, or where the price changes demanded are large, mistrust feeds on itself. The process can be expected to result in regulatory paralysis and, eventually, the deterioration of the industry itself. This is because the only real proof that consumers will accept regarding the need for price increases may be actual shortages or a decline in the quality of service.

Thus, depending on the dynamics of the adversarial process and the degree of technical and market instability, compensatory regulation is prone to degenerate into episodes of conflict over needed changes in which the soundness of the economic enterprise is always eventually at stake. In this way a cumbersome and often de-structive form of political adjustment replaces market adjustments. In the process everyone suffers a loss of economic welfare, and both government and the private sector lose status and legitimacy in the eyes of the public.

These tendencies can be seen in all the examples of compensatory regulation in the energy sectors as the instability triggered by the OAPEC embargo cascaded through the economy. Natural gas, of course, is the clearest, since the crisis caught that regime in the throes of a difficult episode of adjustment in its long-standing sys-tem of compensatory regulation. The gas case is especially interest-ing because the confluence of economic troubles and political stale-mate actually led to deregulation, albeit not before the industry had suffered considerably. Shortages resulting from the adversarial pro-cess had already eroded consumer strength, and the political mobi-lization associated with adjustment was so extensive and polarized that structural change was possible instead of simply another ad-justment of regulations.

The same tendencies can be seen in the system of compensatory regulation set up to govern the oil industry. Here, too, political stale-mate led to deregulation as the issue of wealth distribution became moot. The oil industry was fortunate that its political influence, though clearly declining, was sufficient to assure stalemate and thereby prevent compensatory regulation from becoming more in-stitutionalized. Since the EPCA included a date for its own demise, this strategy proved successful. It was, as noted earlier, deregulation by default.

The fact that deregulation of gas and oil came about as a result of the degeneration of regulation (gas) and political stalemate (oil) is important because it reveals that these choices were not based on the emergence of a broad consensus about the role of government or, more to the point, on the discovery of more serviceable guiding prin-ciples of political economy.

While political and economic changes led to the dismantling of oil and gas regulation at the federal level, economic destabilization was working its way down to the state and local regulatory mecha-nisms of the nation—most of which had become compensatory in character—causing serious adjustment problems for utilities as they struggled to increase prices and as the levels of mistrust and tension soared to unprecedented levels. In these cases, the extraordinary conditions that made deregulation possible at the national level were absent, and those involved, on both sides, had to live with their predicament.

The loose model of regulatory evolution suggested in the preceding paragraphs has important implications. The future it depicts is one of a political economy containing considerable diversity but with a powerful and continuing propensity for unmanaged markets to revert to some form of regulation. This stems from the economic structure of markets for the major fuels as well as the imperatives of the political process itself. The form of regulation chosen may be proprietary at first, if the conditions are propitious—if, for example, international supply remains ample and problems of "excess" competition and falling prices remain the principal concern to affected corporations. The further horizontal integration of the major petroleum companies may in fact make strictly private collusion for supply management easier across regimes. But the energy regimes remain diverse and competitive enough that government support will almost certainly be necessary for this to succeed for very long. The superior ability of business interests to organize in pursuit of common goals also may lead to renewed proprietary controls, even in the more open, group-filled politics that has emerged and will continue to hold sway.

Sooner or later, however, this is likely to devolve into some form of compensatory market management. Economic instability or international crisis might trigger this change, bringing sudden increases in prices that in turn will create demands for control and protection. And political leaders and regulatory officials, fearing loss of office, will respond to them. The resulting arrangements might last a while, but eventually they, too, will encounter the problems described above. At this point, depending on the circumstances, they might simply persist, despite the damage to the economic activity involved, or, if that damage is too great or the political conflicts are too severe, they might again give way to deregulation. The cycle will then begin again. The costs of this pattern of failure go beyond economic losses; they include mounting damage to the authority and legitimacy of the democratic system itself.

This model of the cycle of failure in politicized pluralist market management differs in important ways from those of such prominent regulatory theorists as Theodore Lowi and Mancur Olson, although it leads to the same broad judgment about the inadequacy of the mixture of pluralist democracy and capitalist economics that we have inherited. It differs by proposing, at least for the energy sector, a greater degree of disorder and adversarial conflict, and by stressing the importance of the degenerative process that results as the government seeks to cope with the demands of stakeholders for security and protection. In this respect, it contrasts sharply with the picture of overwhelming domination by government-industry collusive associations—one version of the corporatist image, to be discussed in the next chapter—that emerges from the work of Olson especially. It fits more comfortably with the findings of Wilson and others who have observed much more diversity and variety in the world of regulation than was suggested by the earlier "capture" theorists.[34] If there is a key reason for this change, it is to be found in the transformation of the political process, a transformation that has made quiet, proprietary market management more vulnerable to political challenge, especially at times of crises of inefficiency or redistribution.

Although the model outlined here does suggest more "openness" in the political economy, it is in many respects even more alarming. This is because it predicts that efforts to manage the economy will tend to become increasingly more incoherent, economically costly, and damaging to the body politic. In a ratchetlike fashion, crises lead to mobilization, compensatory intervention, economic and political damage, stalemate, and drift, until the cycle repeats itself. In this process wealthy and well-organized interests continue to win a disproportionate share of available benefits, but society as a whole loses. The model thus paints a picture of a society not with hardened arteries, as Olson and other critics of corporatism warn, but without alternatives in its efforts to handle one of the most critical governance challenges of the industrial era.

The Cycle of Failure

To recapitulate, a review of the actions taken by the United States in response to the energy crisis provides little basis for satisfaction or optimism. Although we avoided political instability and the lure of crash programs to promote expensive new technologies, energy policies proved both ineffective and contradictory. Because of this we paid more to OPEC, increased our energy vulnerability, and failed to protect the disadvantaged from bearing a disproportionate share of the burden of higher prices. Furthermore, it seems certain that the governance "solution" that emerged from the years of energy crisis will not work and will not last. The solution was possible in the first place not because of the emergence of a political consensus regarding the need to return to markets in energy (or anywhere else), but because the distributional problems sustaining demands for market management had resolved themselves, and decontrol was a way of avoiding further conflict over an issue that had become moot. It will eventually be replaced, in all likelihood, by still another set of ad hoc arrangements designed to prevent costly, visible redistributions of wealth and status, and to provide security and continuity to those affected by economic adjustment and change. This may or may not follow the failure of private efforts to tame the market, and may take the form of proprietary regulation, depending on the circumstances.[35] In either case, it is likely to degenerate into another episode of unstable and costly compensatory intervention, which will also almost certainly fail, perhaps once again to be followed by disillusionment, forced government withdrawal, and another futile attempt to return to "free" energy markets.

This dismal projection of the future of energy affairs, although a hypothetical abstraction, is useful because it helps signal the key elements of the self-reinforcing quandary that is visible in the governance of economic affairs in the United States. Increasingly familiar, it has to do with the fact that markets like those for energy resources must and will be managed, but that the American polity is structurally and doctrinally unequipped for this task. What is worse, the unsuccessful struggle to do so anyway has begun to damage the legitimacy and authority of the democratic system.

The lesson learned from the cycle of failure in regulation is that the government is incompetent, the private sector untrustworthy. Contributions made by the democratic process, among them the provision of a modicum of distributional equity and protection against overreaction at times of emergency, tend to be ignored; and the polity loses legitimacy, weakening its capacity to intervene effectively the next time around. Those with a stake in this process, perceiving all of this, intensify their efforts to protect their interests, making it more likely that future interventions will lead to still more cumbersome and costly compensatory regulation and political stalemate. This only reinforces the process by which built-in mechanisms in our pluralist system create a downward spiral of mismanagement and gradual derangement.

CHAPTER 11   Markets by Design

The difficulties we have experienced with the governance of energy appear to be part of a larger pattern in the management of economic affairs. They seem to reflect, in fact, a syndrome that has been growing more pervasive as our pluralist polity has struggled with the increased demands for a larger government role in economic life and with the expanded political participation that has come with those demands. Where will this all lead? And can we do anything about it? To address these questions it is necessary to step back for a moment and take a broader look at the evolution of the American political economy.

That evolution has been one of increasing government involvement in economic life, a process punctuated by episodes of quite sudden enlargement of federal regulatory responsibility, mostly associated with wars and economic crises. The reasons for this in the various energy regimes are clear enough. They center on the growing demands of those affected by an increasingly complex and dense economic system for protection and security: demands by owners and managers for security from seemingly irrational or vicarious change and, increasingly, from the harsh necessities of fully competitive markets; and demands by consumers and citizens for protection from the exercise of economic power by larger and larger corporate bureaucracies. These demands grew with the economy, but were asserted through the faculties of a political system whose powers to govern were carefully circumscribed and fragmented at its founding.[1]

The expansion of political participation to encompass a widening range of groups and interests within this framework has made it increasingly difficult for the government to avoid responding to demands for security. The result has been what we now experience: a large and fragmented government, responsive to claims for compensation from interests of many kinds, passive or immobilized with respect to the definition of broad national objectives, and suffering

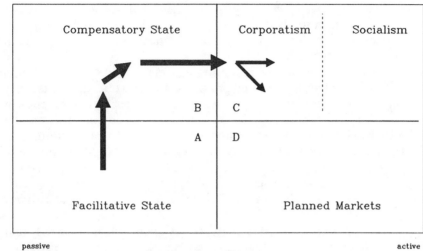

Figure 12. Energy Policy and Political Economy. This figure depicts a number of alternative arrangements in the governance of economic affairs. Quadrants A to D are hypothetical combinations of two key variables: (1) the scope of government involvement in the economy; and (2) the degree to which that orientation is affirmative, providing strong and independent guidance to private decisions. The heavy dark arrows suggest the trajectory that the United States has followed over the last century or so; the smaller arrows indicate possible future directions. Source: Tugwell 1980: 103–18.

from eroding legitimacy as its inability to manage economic affairs becomes more evident and less tolerable. For this condition, labeled here the Compensatory State, no one has provided a better description than Theodore Lowi, who called it the political equivalent of "permanent receivership," analogous to a bankrupt firm that cannot become viable but cannot be allowed to fail.[2]

Dissatisfaction with this state of affairs has grown rapidly in recent years. It has stimulated a number of broad diagnoses, sometimes accompanied by comprehensive reform proposals, by scholars and practitioners of political economy. Perhaps the dominant approach today is that promoted by ideological conservatives and by many economists.[3] The solution they propose, in essence, is a return to the Facilitative State (see Fig. 12), a condition in which the government is both small and weak, and power over economic affairs returns to the hands of private decisionmakers operating with few constraints in free markets.[4] This is the "solution" embodied in current government energy policies.

The problem with this approach, as the analysis presented in earlier pages suggests, is that it is based on a faulty theoretical understanding of the forces at work in the modern American political economy. Free markets in economic sectors like the energy-resource sector (and many others) in a pluralist, fragmented polity with high and growing levels of participation and a weak state, do not last. As they are replaced, the state grows in size but not in competence or authority. Attempts to rely on markets without changes in the structural and ideological framework of the political economy are therefore doomed. The result, as suggested by the likely future of energy deregulation, is almost certainly a return to the Compensatory State, but with the government progressively weakened and the pathology of immobilism, inefficiency, and the erosion of legitimacy further worsened.

A number of thoughtful analysts have concluded, as have I, that movement to another quadrant (see Fig. 12) is necessary, if not inevitable. The cycle of failure is simply too destructive to our institutions. Indeed, much of the current debate over the future of industrial society and over the desirability of a formal industrial policy concerns whether, and how, such a move might take place.

Socialism

Consider socialism first. Like corporatism, it is a planning system, but it is distinguished by the assertion of state control via the direct ownership of key industrial sectors. Writers ranging from John Kenneth Galbraith and Robert Heilbroner (for the economy as a whole) to Barry Commoner and Robert Engler (for the energy industries) have concluded that socialism of some kind is in order, especially insofar as the very large integrated firms are concerned. Robert Engler is the most persuasive of these, especially as far as the petroleum industry is concerned.[5] In his *Politics of Oil* and its more recent sequel, *The Brotherhood of Oil*, he argues on the basis of an impressive amount of descriptive evidence that the economic power of the oil companies is so vast that it exerts a pervasive undemocratic, even antidemocratic, influence on American society. He then suggests the formation of a national committee to discover the best way to assert direct public control over the industry.[6]

The idea of nationalization of the energy industries plays to a powerful American tradition of anger and hostility toward large-scale enterprises and their undeniable political influence. As we have seen, this tradition is perhaps most persistent and deeply felt in the case of oil, an industry that for nearly a century has symbolized for many the evils of distant, secret, unassailable power. But it also extends to natural gas, by association, and more recently to electric utilities.

In many respects, the accuracy of this image of industrial abuse of power is less important than its persistence. As we have seen, the picture of corporate political activity and influence that emerges from a close look at energy politics and policy during the crisis years is quite complex. There is no question that the political hold of the oil industry declined in the years after 1970. This was due partly to divisions within the industry and partly to changes in the Congress that reduced the influence of key representatives of energy-producing states. It was also due to the mobilization of a wide range of groups critical of "big oil" and its role in the U.S. economy. The industry, in consequence, was unable to prevent the loss of some cherished subsidies, among them the depletion allowance; nor was it able to prevent the advent of compensatory regulation and the resulting loss of some of the rents that stemmed from OPEC's actions and the tightening international market. This occurred despite a dramatic enlargement of its lobbying activities and the expenditure of impressive sums of money to influence the electoral process.

On the other hand, the industry did retain most of those rents, successfully vetoing legislative efforts to further redistribute income. And it emerged wealthier, more integrated, and free of the regulatory apparatus that gave consumers political access to the prices of petroleum and natural gas. (As noted, however, the new governance arrangements may turn out to be very much of a mixed blessing; some important companies have already been brought to their knees by the new, more open market.)

Did the political role of the energy industries, and of oil in particular, damage the democratic system? Phrased this way, the query is too simple. An impartial observer, holding tightly to American beliefs about the dangers of economic giantism, might well conclude that the country and its democracy would be better off if the energy majors had a less privileged place in the political marketplace. This is a theme to which I will return. What I argue here, rather, is that the damage to our society and institutions stems from our inability to decide how to manage energy markets—and other markets as well. This inability to decide leads instead to ad hoc interventions which, because they do not satisfy, and because we ignore even their positive accomplishments, leave us increasingly debilitated. Although the energy industries certainly contributed to this situation, so did many other groups and interests. The problem, in other words, is much wider, having to do with our ideology and basic rules of political practice.

These observations point to several basic difficulties with the socialist "solution" to our problems of political economy, especially as it applies to the energy sectors. To begin with, it may not address the basic issue of excessive political influence. To be sure, a publicly owned industry may be less likely to engage in illegal or corrupt political practices involving political parties and elections—depending on the restrictions placed on it. But political influence may be exercised in other ways. The Defense Department is publicly "owned," but its ability to shape public policy is extensive; indeed, incorporation within the public sector, depending on how it is accomplished, may increase rather than diminish political leverage, and even make that leverage less "accessible" to elected leaders.

The fact is that public ownership, per se, is no guarantee that an industry will be either politically weak or responsive to broader public directives. Many of the largest oil companies are publicly owned, wholly or in part, but behave very much as their private counterparts do. The "American" oil company holding the largest domestic reserves, Standard Oil of Ohio (Sohio), is actually a subsidiary of British Petroleum, which in turn is controlled by the British government—in other words, it is a part of a foreign state enterprise.[7] Few Americans are aware of this, and in any case Sohio's political role in energy governance does not seem to have been noticeably altered.

There are other reasons why partial or complete public ownership might be attractive, even within the context of continued competition. As Duane Chapman has pointed out, owning, rather than taxing, large energy companies might be an attractive means of collecting, for the country as a whole, some of the profits earned by them. But this does not imply control of management decisions. Adolf Berle and Gardener Means pointed out many years ago that the direction of the modern corporate economy had passed from the hands of owners to those of independent managers.[8] Legal ownership, in the meantime, has to a surprising extent passed to the hands of U.S. workers through their participation in the pension and insurance programs that have become a principal source of investment capital.[9]

If by socialism we mean not just ownership but comprehensive and detailed centralized direction of the economy as well, other, more familiar objections arise. Even if we leave aside the question of the connection between such extensive central control and possible threats to the political freedoms American cherish—as Charles

Lindblom has pointed out, the two are unrelated in theory but often found together in practice—there are serious questions about the technical feasibility and desirability of such arrangements on economic grounds. Although it is true that modern technology may help overcome some of these difficulties, the examples presented by most command economies provide little basis for optimism. More to the point, if we can imagine circumstances in which we may choose to appropriate large portions of the private economy and enlarge the government in this way, we can more easily envision circumstances in which we invent a novel arrangement that is more attuned to American values and assures a continued capacity for openness and experimental vitality, things so notably missing in most socialist societies today.

Corporatism

Corporatism is economic governance carried on by means of elaborate arrangements for bargaining and cooperative decisionmaking among highly organized private economic interests and government technocratic elites, often with the participation of labor organizations and political parties.[10] Corporatist systems are characterized by (1) a broad national consensus on the need for elite cooperation and, in many instances, on the key objectives of that cooperation; (2) carefully cultivated formal and informal mechanisms of conflict resolution involving private and public elites, mechanisms that are normally insulated from electoral competition; and (3) a willingness to forgo market-based allocation of goods and services where this conflicts with broader national objectives, including political stability (especially labor "peace") and the adaptation of the economy as a whole to changing international conditions.[11] In political terms, corporatism differs from the Compensatory State (see Fig. 12) in that participation in decisions about economic policy is carefully limited, with a predominant role reserved for the functional interest organizations that enjoy a representational monopoly.

Corporatism in the advanced industrial countries—often today called "neo-corporatism" to distinguish it from the more authoritarian experiments of the interwar period—has attracted the interest of political economists in the last decade and a half because those countries governed in this manner have done so well in achieving and sustaining economic growth despite significant vulnerability to international events beyond their control. And they have done this, by and large, while maintaining a high degree of domestic political stability.[12]

In analyzing corporatism it is useful to distinguish between the pattern that has emerged in the small European countries—among them Austria, Switzerland, Sweden, and the Low Countries (and to a lesser extent Germany)—and the more state-dominated variant exemplified by Japan. The former, called "democratic corporatism" by Peter Katzenstein, has been characterized by successful bargaining among elites and "an ideology of social partnership" that has made it possible for the countries involved to attain high levels of economic welfare despite their dependence on the world market and their vulnerability to the actions of more powerful economies.[13] The latter, called the "developmental state" model by Chalmers Johnson, has been characterized by a much more assertive programmatic control by the public sector in behalf of key national objectives—such as growth led by designated economic sectors—and by a much weaker role at the national level of organized labor.[14]

The key question, of course, is whether one or another variant of the corporatist model contains lessons useful in the search for solutions to problems of economic governance in the United States. A growing cadre of American admirers of corporatist arrangements is attracted by the ability of these systems to isolate economic decisions from the fragmenting effects of partisan and interest-group politics, on the one hand, and to accommodate the challenge of international economic competition, on the other. Many feel, as the economist Lester Thurow has put it in his influential book *The Zero-Sum Society*, "Japan Inc. needs to be met with U.S.A. Inc."[15]

Unfortunately, it seems clear that differences in size, historical experience, institutional endowment, and political culture make European and Asian corporatist systems of little direct value as templates for reform in the United States. Indeed, there may be considerable danger in attempts at imitation, depending on the system involved.[16] As Katzenstein has convincingly demonstrated, the emergence and consolidation of "democratic" corporatism in Europe can be explained as the result of distinctive historical crises—the Great Depression, fascism, the Second World War—plus the necessity of the smaller European democracies to operate as specialized, dependent economies in a rapidly changing international market.[17] Similarly, the Japanese corporatist "miracle," including the very distinctive pattern of ideologically sanctioned state-led collaboration between public and private sectors, as well as specific practices such as lifetime employment, enterprise unionism, and the personal savings system, are also the product of a very specific history of political and economic development.[18]

In the abstract, it is possible to imagine the emergence of a corporatist alternative to the Compensatory State in energy in the United States. It would be an outgrowth of recent trends toward vertical and horizontal integration, and would be dominated by a handful of large companies which, properly assisted, would stabilize prices and plan the development of key resources and technologies. They would form cooperative relationships with utilities purchasing resources at the state and local levels. The domestic petroleum market would be protected from price decreases associated with the erosion of OPEC power, and the production of natural gas and coal would come under some form of prorationing to prevent destabilizing competition among producers within and between these regimes. Independent producers of oil and gas might continue to exist, but their role would be carefully circumscribed in accordance with industrywide plans for supply. Coordinated control of pipelines and marketing opportunities would make this easy to do. The nuclear industry might even enjoy a revival, probably with very large government subsidies.

None of this would be possible, of course, without active government support and encouragement. Public authority and regulation would be necessary to enforce decisions arrived at as a result of centralized bargaining among the major corporate contenders and to prevent competition from "breaking out." The arrangements, in fact, would approximate a unified program of proprietary regulation affecting all energy sources. Antitrust laws, obviously, would have to be waived to make these things possible.

Even to list these characteristics—and to note the contrast with the last decade of turmoil in energy affairs—is to understand why such an arrangement would be attractive to many, especially within the energy industries.[19] Indeed, private efforts to accomplish something of this kind are almost certain to intensify in the years to come.

But this description of a hypothetical corporatist future in energy also helps clarify why such an arrangement is difficult to imagine working in the United States. As Peter Katzenstein has put it, referring to the European pattern, "In many ways corporatism is antithetical to the core of American politics."[20] Corporatist economic governance, to begin with, consciously seeks to circumvent the two mechanisms of political accountability and resource allocation upon which the American system has always counted heavily: elections and markets. The concentration and centralization of authority in the hands of a private elite with attenuated and indirect means of accountability would in itself be difficult to legitimize. Historical crises and international pressures have not forged an "ideology of social partnership" or overarching consensus on national economic goals that might legitimize or guide such decisionmaking methods. Nor does the United States have functional confederations powerful or inclusive enough to pretend to represent, at the corporatist bargaining table, the interests of workers, consumers, environmentalists, or other business sectors in decisions concerning energy.[21] The experience of the private corporatist control of the coal regime after 1950, recounted in Chapter 2, is instructive in this regard. Where such confederations have arisen in particular sectors, as in organized labor, they have often proved too willing to abandon the interests of those they claimed to represent.

In the absence of such external controls, a corporatist system could be expected to be slow to adapt to change, hostile to innovation and diversity, and prone to large, economically costly mistakes for which society, and the working men and women in particular, would have to pay—it would, in effect, duplicate the evils Americans have always associated with unrestrained monopoly.[22] The experience of the coal industry after 1950 is instructive in this respect, also.

In the sector of the U.S. political economy that in recent years has most closely approximated the corporatist ideal—the defense establishment—the proclivity of both public and private decisionmakers (sometimes this distinction is unclear) to set aside competitive relationships in favor of "cooperation" in matters of procurement has evoked harsh criticism.[23] Similar problems have arisen with respect to government dealings with the nuclear power industry, another sector where, partly because of the early connection with national security, quasi-corporatist arrangements obtained and the market was partially ignored.[24]

Some examples drawn from American and European experience help clarify these difficulties. During the "energy wars" of the 1970's, analysts and political leaders in the United States often expressed envy of the ability of European governments to make hard choices in energy matters quickly and back them up with effective policies. Among the objects of admiration were high gasoline taxes, more effective residential and commercial conservation regulations, and consistent support for nuclear energy programs in the face of strong opposition from environmentalists and others.

But a closer look at European and Japanese energy planning presents a much more complex picture. Though many countries did move much more rapidly than the United States to reduce petroleum consumption, and did not face the intense and immobilizing domestic conflicts we did, they also made a number of very large, capital-consuming commitments, most notably to nuclear energy, before technological innovations and alternatives had been fully evaluated and before public attitudes had had a chance to mature. In some instances, as in Sweden and Austria, choices made by technocratic elites had to be reversed at great cost when public attitudes did coalesce. In Austria a fully completed nuclear power plant was sealed, never to be used—a kind of monument to poor centralized planning. In other instances, as in Japan and France, the corporatist government was strong enough to continue resisting change, instead imposing enormous costs on taxpayers and consumers by force-feeding nuclear electricity.

In the United States, by contrast, vigorous political conflict and the influence of market forces made possible the abandonment of nuclear power sources as too costly. There were losses associated with this process, and some of them were very large indeed, as noted in Chapter 8, but a major portion must be charged, in fairness, to the quasi-corporatist character of the nuclear regime that led to the original massive subsidization of this industry in the first place. Another illustration of this problem can be drawn from the fate of the synthetic fuels industry. A more centralized, corporatist decision-making system would almost certainly have led the United States to embrace this option more vigorously, ignoring market signals and political opposition and sustaining the effort with multi-billion-dollar subsidies.[25] Certainly many critics feared that this would happen, but with a few exceptions (e.g. the Great Plains coal gasification experiment) it did not.

In all of these instances, the pluralist decisionmaking of the Compensatory State probably provided better—if messier and more piecemeal—solutions to difficult problems. Although clumsy, and clearly less decisive in energy policy, it facilitated and promoted greater adaptability and selectiveness with respect to the choice of alternatives at a time of rapid technical and economic change than did more corporatist contemporaries.

All of this is not to say that broad guidance of the economy is unnecessary or impossible in the United States, for it is neither. Rather, it is to say that corporatist solutions of the European or Japanese varieties are not likely to emerge or be accepted in the American setting. Nor would a more home-grown variety, one dominated by formal or informal consortia of large companies operating without the countervailing controls of a strong state or interests organized in functionally powerful national confederations.

Planned Markets

The most radical model of political economy, in the sense that it appears to run against structural trends that have been dominant for a century or more, is that represented by quadrant "D" of Figure 12, "planned markets."[26] It is also the most interesting, and, it would appear, the most attractive—albeit politically difficult to achieve— for the United States. It is an arrangement in which the government accepts responsibility for the operation of the economic system and the values it promotes, but wherever possible eschews detailed regulation or micromanagement, instead relying on competitive, or marketlike, processes. It does so by consciously and continuously setting the terms for competition—laying out frameworks, or "rules of the game"—and enforcing them, while at the same time carefully attending to the needs of those who are hurt as a result. The image is of a public sector that is more authoritative and active, but not necessarily larger—and certainly not as large as that implied by socialist or corporatist arrangements. It is more appropriate to a society that values diversity, experimentation, decentralization, shared power, and resilience, but that recognizes these must be achieved in a cooperative fashion.

To many, the very label "planned markets" would seem to signal a contradiction, but it need not. The fact that it appears to, however, reveals much about American ideological attitudes toward the role of government—a theme to which I will return. For if we are to have markets, if the economic system is going to be one that promotes diversity, experimentation, efficiency, and participation, it will do so only if these things are carefully nurtured by a legitimate government—they must be planned.

"Planned markets" does, however, suggest a new synthesis of the two broad orientations toward political economy that characterize the grand ideological adversaries of the contemporary world: Marxists and liberal democrats. As Charles Lindblom has pointed out so insightfully in his *Politics and Markets*, these represent two entirely different and opposing views of the proper role of intellect in social organization. The first, characteristic of socialist perspective and practice, is a profoundly optimistic view about the capacity of the human mind—and therefore properly trained technical elites—to comprehend and guide the operation of a society. It is an outlook shared by planners and technocratic elites generally.[27]

The second conception is more pessimistic, but, I believe, more realistic. It holds that we cannot accurately grasp and articulate in "scientific" and applicable theory the complex and changing nature of society. Instead, we must rely on some form of social interaction—intellectual and scientific debates, elections, markets—to make choices, set goals, and allocate resources. Interaction replaces definitive analysis because society cannot be really understood and guided with enough comprehensiveness and accuracy.[28] This is the perspective of most critics of central planning and socialist practice, and of sophisticated admirers of pluralist politics and free enterprise. They point out, quite correctly, that in practice political domination tarnishes the idealism of Marxism, since the inadequacy of theory and the failure of persuasion lead elites to rely on coercion. Socialist theorists understand the operation of capitalist society accurately enough to reveal many of its serious symptoms of disorder—persistent inequality, for example—but insufficiently to replace "automatic" arrangements with acceptable centrally determined alternatives.

In practice, of course, all societies represent to some degree a synthesis of these two "models." Even the most monolithic communist states select their leaders and choose among contending ideological "interpretations" by competitive means (we often call these "internecine power struggles"), and marketlike operations often obtain in the most successful, although often officially illegal, sectors of their economies. Likewise the democratic "process" in the United States operates within a framework that was set forth by founders who relied not on divine inspiration but on their analytical understanding of how society operated. Their genius, of course, was to understand precisely the need for a synthesis that would set boundaries on the competitive processes they felt would permit effective, if limited, government, while protecting their own status as propertied landholders and merchants. Unfortunately, they were a preindustrial elite and not prescient enough to anticipate a time when corporate organization would dominate the landscape of the political economy and when the government would, simultaneously, be swamped by interests demanding access and security and be held responsible for the performance of the economy in detail.

The socialist "solution" to this evolution is to replace the framework entirely with comprehensive public ownership directed by a doctrinally "enlightened" elite. The corporatist answer is to establish a new framework that quietly and gradually replaces markets and elections with bargaining among the elites of corporate, labor, and government bureaucracies.

A better solution, one both more workable and able to protect the diversity and freedom so highly valued by Americans, is to establish and institutionalize a new synthesis in which intellect is applied to the shaping of better frameworks for competitive choice that retain and protect both markets and elections.

Planned Markets in Energy?

All of this sounds fine in the abstract, but how would it apply in practice? A glance at the energy regimes reveals quickly that it is easier to delineate broad theoretical alternatives than it is to devise arrangements for specific industries. Precisely because economic activities differ so much, general principles, though of some help, do not eliminate the need to make very hard choices about which values and objectives to seek first. This, in the end, is a political process, not a technical one. Nevertheless, it is useful to consider what a system of planned markets for energy in the United States might involve. Such an exercise, though necessarily brief, may help clarify the meaning of the concept while signaling the kinds of difficult political choices that would have to be made to move in this direction.

In theoretical terms, a system of planned markets must embody "solutions" to a whole range of recurring problems of political economy. Many of these can be characterized as stemming from the need to make trade-offs between a model of pure market competition and a series of legitimate public goals that may require state intervention. A discussion of several of these provides a convenient framework within which to consider how a new arrangement might operate and what problems it might encounter.

Efficiency, Competition, and Accountability   To begin with, the idea of planned markets implies a strong commitment to diversity, flexibility, and innovation. It suggests a desire for freedom and openness in the economy, ease of entry and exit, opportunities for risk-takers, and the absence of day-to-day government intrusion into private choices about resource allocation. It also implies a commitment to efficiency in the allocation of resources, the kind of efficiency theoretically attainable only under competitive conditions. But here we run into our first stumbling block: it turns out that, even without considering such additional goals as personal and institutional security or societywide equity, there are important conflicts among these objectives.

Take, for example, the matter of efficiency in the oil and gas industry. As noted in Chapter 3, the evidence suggests strongly that the large, vertically integrated corporation is the most efficient organizational configuration in the oil and gas industry. It suggests, further, that extensive cooperation (rather than competition) among a few very large firms in exploration, transport, refining, and marketing may also be the most efficient way of doing business. Although the evidence is less convincing, it is possible that even extensive horizontal integration (oil with coal, for example) may be a good idea on these grounds. A highly concentrated and integrated energy oligopoly may also be capable of some kinds of technical innovation that would be difficult for smaller firms in a much more competitive setting.[29] For a variety of reasons, harsh competition and the associated chronic oversupply that characterized the coal industry made it difficult for that industry to introduce technical improvements.[30] And the research and development investments needed for the more promising synthetic fuel technologies, such as oil-shale retorting and the conversion of coal to gas and liquids, may be within the capability of only the very largest companies.

These ideas are reflected in the conclusion that the oil and gas industry, even after the mergers of the 1980's, is characterized by "workable competition," meaning, technically, that even though it displays some serious departures from the competitive norm, there is probably no other configuration that would produce greater economic efficiency. This means that if we choose to break up the industry, forcing horizontal and even vertical divestiture upon the companies involved, we may achieve increased competition, greater ease of entry, and more diversity, but only at the cost of decreased efficiency (i.e. more expensive goods and services) and reduced innovation in some important, capital-intensive areas of technology.[31]

There is also the more profound problem of the political objectives that are, by necessity, also affected in choices about market configuration and the size and character of the organizations involved. If there is a single, ringing message in recent inquiries into the relationship between the government and the economy in the United States, and in the American energy sector in particular, it is that the growing imbalance between the power of private corporate organizations and that of other interests, including the electorate at large, is something we must worry about seriously. It is what Charles

Lindblom is concerned about when he decries the "privileged place of business," what Galbraith points to when he concludes that we must "emancipate the state," and what Robert Dahl has in mind when he calls for an enlargement of democratic control within the private organizations that constitute the economic order. It is the main concern of critics of the oil industry such as Robert Engler and John Blair.[32] And, as noted above, it must also be a principal consideration in any discussion of the feasibility of a political economy based on planned markets.

The historical evidence reviewed in this study suggests strongly that the integrated energy corporations, if not powerful enough to prevent consumers from demanding and achieving political access and partial compensation during time of crisis, are nevertheless quite capable of preventing the government from imposing a market design upon them—or, if it should be imposed, of undermining its intent over time.

In this sense, the most important trade-off Americans would face, should they seek an arrangement based on planned markets, is one between efficiency and the capacity of the government to achieve the political independence and authority to set forth and maintain such an arrangement. Should we choose a form of divestiture, we would, in effect, pay a tax in lost economic welfare for an energy economy that embodies more diversity, flexibility, and openness, and is maintained in that condition by a government more accountable to the electorate in these (and other) matters.

There are other problems relating to the trade-off between efficiency and market design in the other energy sectors. The coal industry, as noted in Chapter 9, has for practical purposes ceased to exist as a separate regime because such a significant percentage of production is owned and managed by steel companies, oil companies, and electric utilities. Should coal be liberated from these connections in order to reestablish independent firms in a competitive market? The special character of the coal industry suggests that this might be a mistake. Even setting aside social costs, the harsh demands of competition in coal may result in a loss of efficiency, whereas integration with other activities may make capital for technical innovation easier to obtain, especially if a significant degree of competition can be assured in the various regimes that have "captured" coal.

Natural monopolies pose still a different problem. Pipelines cannot compete; the economic price would be too high. They must be regulated, preferably as common carriers. Electricity, similarly, cannot be distributed in a competitive fashion. It may be possible, however, to deregulate small-scale power production as well as the conservation services that make that production unnecessary.[33] As noted earlier, the energy crisis, by making it difficult or impossible for utilities to build new, large power plants, forced managers to consider alternatives of this kind as the demand for electricity resumed its growth in the mid-1980's. Two of the goals of the Public Utilities Regulatory Policy Act (PURPA) were to promote cogeneration by forcing utilities to pay small-scale producers "avoided cost" for contributions to the grid, and to "encourage" utilities to provide such conservation services as energy audits and insulation loans. Whether the approaches adopted by utilities will encourage competition in the provision of cheap electricity and conservation remains to be seen. The point, however, is that the turn to smaller scale, distributed power and conservation services does present an opportunity for those states that want to encourage marketlike processes even within the ambit of "natural monopolies."

This, too, may entail a reduction of efficiency, but at the same time it may help resolve the tension that has become chronic in this industry since the energy crisis activated compensatory struggles between producers and consumers. Consumers might have greater confidence in market-based pricing decisions (insofar as the acquisition of power is concerned) on the part of distributors than they do in decisions made by utility executives on the basis of their own operating costs and plans. It would also, presumably, increase the technical diversity and resilience of the industry as a whole.[34]

In the end, of course, this does not resolve the basic problem: natural monopolies of the kind represented by electric utilities will continue to be governed by public commissions, and those commissions, as long as energy markets are open and prices fluctuate, will be stuck with compensatory regulation. The introduction of elements of competition, as described above, may help; but the built-in problems of such regulation can be expected to keep causing trouble. The best to be hoped for, in such a situation, is that the process of conflict can be structured so that adjustments can occur before the industry suffers, service quality declines, equipment deteriorates, and everyone involved is worse off.[35] Overall stabilization of energy markets, of course, would help tremendously in reducing the damage caused by compensatory regulation in the electricity regime.

These observations point to a related problem that is certain to attract a great deal of attention in years to come if energy markets remain free to fluctuate and adjust and if they exhibit the kind of instability most experts expect. All capital-intensive, large-scale projects require many years to plan and construct. This means that the accuracy of the assumptions upon which investment decisions are made is vitally important for such projects. Changes in fuel prices, inflation rates, costs of construction, or interest rates can be devastating when lead times extend, as they often do in the case of large generating plants, beyond a decade. Not only do cost calculations become obsolete, demand patterns can be expected to change as well.

This quandary, plus accumulating political risks associated with large power plants, may make it literally impossible to build facilities that take advantage of the available economies of scale.[36] Unmanaged free markets and large-scale facilities may be, in a fundamental sense, incompatible. This may mean that efficiencies of scale may have to be sacrificed and that new technical opportunities requiring very large-scale, complex facilities may never be tried unless the government itself undertakes the task. There is an irony here: government unwillingness to stabilize markets may force the public sector to take a larger role in technical innovation.

Market Stability and Security   A commitment to planning markets in behalf of greater diversity, flexibility, efficiency, and technical progress is unlikely to be accepted in modern society unless it is accompanied by a willingness to shape and influence those markets so as to (1) avoid fluctuations that damage the economy as a whole and (2) protect individuals who become caught in the gears of economic adjustment. Here again, however, difficult choices arise, this time involving trade-offs between the extent of government intervention, the speed and ease of economic adjustment, and the degree of security provided.

As we have seen, instability has been a chronic problem in energy resource markets and is likely to become a problem again despite changes that may moderate supply and price fluctuations. When it strikes, it can cause both economic waste and personal suffering. The petroleum market provides a good example. A temporary decline in prices benefits consumers, but may promote a variety of adjustments that make little long-term sense: a return to inefficient equipment, a decline in investment in alternative energy resources, and an across-the-board increase in petroleum dependency. These, in turn, may leave the country more vulnerable to a disruption. As noted earlier, such a price decline would also cause serious dislocations in international financial markets while at the same time forcing companies that had invested in more expensive sources, such as deposits in the North Sea and Alaska, to go out of business or seek government subsidies.

Upward fluctuations can also be a problem. A sudden increase in the price of imported oil can be managed by a free market—this, in fact, is the declared policy of the current administration in Washington. But it, too, may result in a range of economic changes that make little sense in efficiency terms. To be sure, there will be no shortages, since price will rise to allocate available supply. But investment decisions of many kinds will be influenced, only to turn out to have been incorrect, resulting in a reduction in welfare.[37] Those who succeed in forcing the price change will reap a very large profit, and those who own energy resources will once again enjoy windfall gains. Perhaps even more important, instability of this kind arouses powerful demands for immediate compensatory regulation, which entails, as we have seen, significant costs of its own.

A number of actions have been proposed to address these problems in ways that still rely heavily on market processes and that make it much less likely that compensatory regulation would be politically irresistible. To cope with price erosion the government might place a variable duty on imported oil to keep the price at a level that appears appropriate in terms of long-term domestic replacement costs—today this might be $20–$25 a barrel—with the difference between that level and world prices going to the Treasury.[38] The Treasury might then use the funds to purchase oil for the Strategic Reserve—that could in turn be sold when prices rise above the chosen threshold.[39] Edward Morse argues persuasively that an agreement setting a price floor among all members of the International Energy Agency (IEA) would avert many of the problems of a protectionist policy of this kind.[40] The objective is both stability and continuity—preventing users from abandoning the more thrifty habits acquired during periods of high prices—as well as the protection of investments in resource development and technology. Such an arrangement, of course, would also require an effective excess profits tax to capture and recycle rents on domestic production created by market protection.[41]

To address the problem of price increases and cartel power, Professor M. A. Adelman of M.I.T. very early during the energy crisis suggested that the government form a purchasing agency that would buy all imported oil through a system of sealed bids taken from international suppliers. It would then resell supplies to domestic purchasers. The goal was to encourage "cheating" (in the form of price cuts) on the part of cartel members, driving down average prices and weakening the hold of OPEC.[42] If successful—and it appears in retrospect that it might have been—it would have stabilized the market to the extent of bringing prices down closer to the cost of production, though it would still have left the domestic energy system vulnerable to market-induced world price fluctuations.

To manage the domestic impact of sudden price increases themselves, the government might take a number of steps. The Strategic Petroleum Reserve is now large enough to help in moderating the impact of temporary shortages, especially as they affect the spot market. Its effectiveness would be enlarged if its use were coordinated with the drawdown of stockpiles by other members of the IEA. Within the United States, the government in a crisis might place a special tax on domestic oil to bring it to world price levels, and set up a recycling mechanism to return the funds thus obtained to consumers of petroleum products.[43] These interventions "at the border," suggested here for heuristic purposes, involve departures from "free" markets and an enlargement of the government's role in shaping the framework within which competition among energy companies would occur. But the international market for oil is hardly "free" in any case. These possible interventions also provide the kind of stabilization that might, at the same time, prevent waste and illegitimate wealth transfer and deflect demands for price controls or other forms of compensatory intervention. They may, in fact, be the only way markets can be preserved in an open, responsive, democratic polity.

By influencing the entry of marginal supplies of petroleum and products, the government can provide the functional equivalent of the proprietary supply-management arrangements that obtained before the crisis. The difference, in this ideal case, is that the control is exercised not by the industry (directly or indirectly) in its own behalf, but by a public authority independent enough to be pursuing broad national goals.

The stabilization of domestic markets for petroleum and products would be helpful to the other regimes, but might not be sufficient to prevent some significant instability in their markets if they are completely unregulated and if competition is enhanced as a result of horizontal and vertical divestiture. Market stabilization in the case of natural gas and coal, however, presents more serious difficulties, and the best solution would probably be to leave them untouched. If the cost of this should prove too high—resulting in severe disruptions, economic loss, and waste of resources in times of recession, for example—the best alternative, at least in the case of coal, might be a modified price-support system like that used to stabilize farm commodity markets. In this instance, the support prices could be pegged at the top to the BTU equivalent of stabilized petroleum products, and at the bottom at a level low enough to permit a healthy range for competition, but not so low that widespread collapse of efficient operations would result with each downward cycle. The government could buy at the bottom and sell at the top, with any income helping to pay for the stockpiling system.

Security and Equity   If a political economy based on planned markets requires a realization that the preservation of liberty rests upon a strong and legitimate state capable of providing broad guidance to the economy as a whole, it also requires an understanding that competition and personal security need not be viewed as incompatible goals. On the contrary, it is difficult to imagine widespread reliance on competitive processes without a major, parallel commitment on the part of the government to cushion the damage that such arrangements inevitably impose on the individuals, towns, and regions of the country. Put bluntly, the stabilization and compensation that regulatory intervention now seeks (and often fails) to provide must still be provided—indeed, must be enlarged— if an affluent, democratic citizenry is to be expected to put up with markets.[44]

The manner in which security is provided, however, is important; it must be tailored to reinforce competitive adjustment rather than to counter it. The government must allow companies (even very large ones) to fail and whole industries to decline and disappear. It cannot reward poor management with bailouts (Lowi's permanent receivership), and it cannot postpone technological innovation.[45] These are the instruments of corporatist political economy, ones that flourish where the government is too weak to protect efficiency and facilitate adjustment.

This means that security must be provided to individuals, not to organizations, and it must be provided to individuals directly, not through businesses, as it is in Japan and many other countries. And this in turn means that a critical part of the system of planned markets must be agreement on acceptable levels of equity, and on fair mechanisms to provide it, that do not interfere with economic adjustment.[46] Coal miners, nuclear construction workers, gasohol producers, and oil executives who are laid off—all must have enough economic security to find new work or enjoy a reasonable, if minimal, standard of living if they are too old to do something else. Otherwise, they will seek different ways to guarantee their security, and an open, democratic polity will eventually allow them to succeed—at the price of everyone's economic welfare and, eventually, the viability of the political economy itself. Just as markets require public planning, so the flexibility and innovation they promote require mechanisms to protect people from harm. In an affluent society, this is as binding a law of behavior as any that has been identified.

To recapitulate, a system of planned markets in the energy sector in the United States might produce some or all of the following: (1) an oil and gas industry characterized by greater competition achieved by both horizontal and vertical divestiture; (2) a coal industry still competitive but insured against sudden, wide swings in price; (3) electric utilities charged with encouraging competition in the provision of small-scale power and conservation services; (4) domestic energy markets protected against internationally induced fluctuations by (a) a variable import duty and (b) careful standby plans for a reserve drawdown and recycled taxes, plus auction purchase arrangements, in case of a supply or price "crisis;" (5) an energy system with very few subsidies to distort the decisions of producers and consumers; and (6) personal guarantees of security and an equitable claim to a portion of the nation's product for individuals employed in the energy regimes.

What this list illustrates is not a set of necessary results of a system of planned markets. Indeed, the list of another advocate of this approach might easily differ. It illustrates instead the general character of market arrangements that might be expected to result from a disposition to nurture competition and diversity, when that disposition is backed by an authoritative government that eschews wherever possible direct control and micro-management of economic decisions. It is this orientation, and the set of doctrinal and political circumstances that will permit it to predominate, that are at the heart of the approach advocated here.

From Here to There

As these observations suggest, a major obstacle to the achievement of a political economy based on the principle of planned markets is the growing inadequacy of our political process and institutions in the field of economic management.[47] The nature and evolution of this inadequacy in the energy sector has been analyzed elsewhere in these pages, and requires no recapitulation. It is serious. To make matters worse, the same attributes that are responsible for this inadequacy will make it difficult to face the problem directly and seek reforms.

The remedies upon which American policymakers have relied in the past, when confronted by problems of market design, illustrate these difficulties quite well. Antitrust law was successfully applied once in the energy sector with the breakup of the Standard Oil monopoly. Not only did the industry subsequently reconstitute itself as a highly integrated oligopoly, but antitrust law grew more cumbersome and helpless as the decades passed. As John Blair has noted, each time government lawyers have sought to curb monopoly power in oil by invoking provisions of the Sherman Act, their work has been abandoned by political leaders.[48]

The one great success in market redesign was accomplished not under antitrust laws but as a result of the Public Utility Holding Company Act of 1935. This provided the statutory basis under which the Securities and Exchange Commission successfully dismantled monopolistic control structures in the natural gas and electric utility industries over a period of twenty-five years. In many respects, this action stands alone as an example of affirmative market redesign on a large scale. However, it is an exception that proves the rule. The dismantling of holding companies was possible because the abuses associated with them, most of which became evident in the economic collapse during the 1930's, were so profound that they led to a powerful consensus among investors, consumers, and political leaders, all of whom agreed that something had to be done. Like the Standard Oil monopoly, pyramidal holding companies of the kind that emerged in the first decades of the century are no longer features of the corporate landscape; and the forms of corporate behavior that have replaced them are unlikely to provoke such unified and decisive action.[49]

The second major remedy favored by American leaders, regulation by independent commission, has also failed. As we have seen, every form of market regulation in energy has proven unsatisfactory on technical grounds and has become increasingly vulnerable as the political system itself has changed.

The fact is that both antitrust and regulation have been attempts to set aside the political problem of market design, letting "the courts" or "independent specialists" take the responsibility because the political process itself was incapable of responding in a constructive way. We now know that these attempts have failed—worse, they have inflicted serious damage on the legal system and the democratic polity. Courts cannot be expected to find, in statutes, solutions to broad, essentially political, problems. Nor can regulatory agencies find such solutions in their reservoirs of technical expertise. As many scholars have stressed, these responsibilities belong back in the hands of accountable elected authorities.[50]

Unfortunately, it has become evident that the political process, as it currently works, simply cannot accomplish these things. Incentive structures, rules of the game, ingrained habits—all make it unlikely that politics "as usual" can lead to anything but a continued paralysis insofar as broad decisions about the economy are concerned. This means, to be blunt, that the growing incompetence of the government in economic affairs is not just a policy crisis, it is a constitutional crisis as well. Basic institutional relationships and rules of the game have become dangerously inadequate as our society has become affluent and technologically sophisticated, and as citizens have come to expect security and the right to participate in decisions that affect their lives.

What kinds of changes appear to be necessary to permit a system of planned markets to emerge in the United States? Although this is not the place for a lengthy analysis of needed reforms, the broad direction in which we must move is clear enough to be summarized succinctly. The requirements are both doctrinal and institutional in character. Put differently, we must have a vision of what an acceptable future arrangement might be like—this is what the proposal for "planned markets" represents—and what political and administrative instruments we will require to work toward that future.

Doctrinal Adaptation   Ideas come first. Consider the problem of our mythology about political economy—that cluster of beliefs deeply ingrained in the American culture about the government, about the economy, and about how the two should relate. The political attitudes involved are traceable in good measure to ideas that took root in the independence and immediate post-independence era, as articulated by James Madison and others, and they accurately reflect the political conditions that obtained at that time.[51] They assert that the major threat to individual freedom is the state, which, accordingly, must be kept small, divided, weak, and accountable.[52]

The economic ideas that parallel these political views have an intellectual heritage traceable to Adam Smith and many who followed him, but were heavily influenced in America by popular, small-town notions about the benefits of laissez-faire capitalism that arose during the rapid growth of the economy after the Civil War. For our purposes, the critical conception here is that markets are associated with freedom (as government is not), and that they are natural, automatic in operation, and self-sustaining.[53] That is, markets will form and flourish spontaneously unless interfered with by the state— at which time the result is both inefficiency and unwarranted interference with personal liberty.[54] The slogan promoted by President Reagan, "get the government off the backs of the American people," is an accurate representation of this influential tradition.

The problem with these ideas is that they are both incorrect and debilitating. They are anachronistic, pre-industrial conceptions carried forward in time despite their empirical invalidity.[55] As Wallace Mendelson put it in his analysis of this problem: "We live in a Hamiltonian world and dream Jeffersonian dreams."[56] Dreams are important, but they can be dangerous if confused with reality. As the experience of the energy regimes makes clear, markets are diverse, tenuous, and often troublesome. In many cases, they last for only a short time before they wither, to be replaced by cartels, monopolies, or other stabilizing arrangements.

The reason for this is not just greed—although it is that, too—but because markets, when they are uncontrolled and unstabilized, make life miserable and insecure. And when people are miserable and insecure, they try and do something about it. Witness the plight of coal miners and their communities, and, more recently, of those states that have grown dependent on oil revenues. Especially when they are subject to fluctuations, markets can also result in inefficient distortions of economic activity and waste of resources. This was the case, for example, in the oil regime in the first two decades of the century.[57]

A government that is weak, divided, and easily penetrated by interests able to employ the sophisticated new technologies of participation can do little to remedy these things. It cannot prevent markets from disappearing; on the contrary, it readily becomes an accomplice to the creation of proprietary regulation when private efforts to manage competition fail. As we have seen, this can give way—and more and more often does give way—to compensatory regulation that tends, if it lasts, to seriously damage the economic activity involved and further weaken the legitimacy of the state, while adding new inefficiencies.

Nor can such a government successfully remedy the other problems that afflict markets; it cannot provide stability or security to those who participate in them or depend on their success or failure. Its interventions are ad hoc, temporary, and based on no lasting or consistent doctrine or objective other than the immediate compensation of influential injured claimants. All of these things are coming to represent the most serious threats to freedom, diversity, innovation, and economic progress in advanced industrial society. And yet our beliefs about the economy make it difficult for us to imagine alternatives.

Institutional Reform   Even assuming we could agree on the kind of political economy we would like to have, there remains the problem of fashioning one. It is evident, to begin with, that we must have a system of national planning capable of (1) setting broad goals for the key sectors of the economy, (2) determining the relationship between the structure of competition and other valued goals—among them efficiency, stability, security, and equity—and (3) wielding enough control over those sectors to assure that the competitive process achieves the goals set. It must be able, in other words, to design coherent frameworks within which marketlike processes can operate. Many of the necessary instruments for such planning will be new ones, since shaping the broad character of market relationships is well beyond the ability of existing legal or organizational arrangements in the United States—although some of the "post-deregulation" regulatory agencies have a mandate that increasingly requires such shaping.

Even to say this is to open a debate that cannot be pursued in these pages. Suffice it to say that "planned markets" does not refer to the kind of centralized planning familiar to students of the "command" socialist economies. Indeed, one of the most exciting developments in the field of political economy in recent years has been the growing experimentation, on the part of those afflicted with such command systems, to devise means to reintroduce competition into their moribund economies.

A planning process able to protect diversity and competition must be structured and operated in such a way as to avoid the creation of a large, bureaucratic state actively seeking to micromanage the details of business life for thousands of companies.[58] However, control of such things as monopoly practices, entry barriers, anticompetitive mergers, commodity market instability, and restraint of trade do not require public ownership and management, or a massive bureaucracy. Nor does the abandonment of a vast array of subsidies that stifle innovation and adaptation. But these do require a different relationship between the government and the economy as well as a state with the authority and competence to act. As I stressed earlier, this means a new compromise between control and freedom, one that will be difficult to embody in institutional mechanisms.[59] The original compromise, the one from which our constitutional system has evolved over two centuries, simply must be adapted to allow us to manage the affairs of a modern corporate economy.

The problem posed by the fragmentation of authority has been widely acknowledged by those concerned with the American polity, and the list of reforms already suggested to remedy this problem is a long one.[60] Many recommend that electoral procedures be modified to assure that public officials have an incentive to address problems important to the country as a whole. This means reform of the electoral and party systems so that coherent legislative programs can survive. It also means that the polity must be liberated from its growing subordination to particularistic interests, especially those drawing on corporate, group, and personal wealth. In a nutshell, we need a government that is smaller, stronger, and more considerate. To achieve this we need elected representatives free to address national problems; strong parties able to propose and pass coherent programs; a national planning mechanism that is responsible to elected authorities; administrative instruments that permit the government to shape the character of market arrangements without daily intervention in the affairs of participants; and basic guarantees of security and equity that operate independently of markets.

Again, none of these conclusions is new; the need for change in the U.S. political process to allow planning—often called "industrial policy" today—has been signaled by many respected analysts as the full dimensions of our crisis in economic governance has become evident.[61] Nor is it possible in these brief observations to do more than indicate that the findings of this study affirm the need for fundamental change in our political institutions and the beliefs that support them, and to note the general character of changes that appear to make sense.

Simply to list needed innovations, unfortunately, is to highlight the problem that all serious studies of reform eventually acknowledge: the nature of the political process is such that reconstruction is difficult to imagine under normal circumstances. Analytical diagnoses, such as this one, though perhaps helpful in weakening deeply ingrained unwillingness to consider reform proposals, cannot be expected to cultivate the kind of consensus needed for political transformation. A sober assessment of the prospects suggests that this transformation is likely to occur only if a major crisis seriously undermines American ideological beliefs about the political economy and creates the conditions for a new "founding" of our institutional system.

The analysis presented here—derived, to be sure, from the experience with energy, a vitally important, albeit limited, domain of the political economy—suggests both a greater degree of unpredictability and diversity and a greater propensity to degenerative instability than is the case with many widely acclaimed diagnoses of our nation's governance problems. Theodore Lowi's persuasive characterization of what he calls "the state of permanent receivership" calls forth the image of a society that, for all its lack of justice and consistency, nevertheless succeeds admirably in preserving the security of all interests capable of organizing. The same is true, broadly speaking, of Mancur Olson's society of "distributional associations" that clog the arteries of economic life and lead to slow decline as newer, more vital competitors quietly assume the leadership of growth and innovation in the world.[62]

Our experience with the energy crisis reveals a greater potential for what can only be called destructive "disorder" in the management of economic affairs than many others have identified. It is true that the wealthy and well-organized were able to protect themselves from major redistributive demands, emerging free to consolidate their gains and further integrate the bases of their organizational influence; but it is also true that, when the dust had settled, they were unable to move back into the kind of comfortable, behind-the-scenes, proprietary governance arrangements they had enjoyed before.

These arrangements, though they may well re-emerge in future years, are likely to be increasingly vulnerable, especially at times of economic adjustment, thanks to changes in the technology and practice of political participation and mobilization. In the meantime, arrangements based on deregulation "by default" in oil and gas have left the country vulnerable to international events and certain to suffer further struggles to overcome the consequences of market instability. And at the state and local levels the persistence of tension-filled compensatory regulation in the electricity regime has left many regions incapable of adding new generating capacity of any kind.

All of this suggests a future different from the technocratic corporatism that many have come to fear; it suggests rather a political economy suffused with destructive adversarial conflict—conflict poorly managed by integrating institutions—that undermines the health of economic activity, erodes confidence in the private sector, and undermines the legitimacy of the government itself. Should this pathology come to dominate our affairs, as seems increasingly likely, the easiest future to imagine is of a painful, long-term, downward spiral of economic and political decay in which the country's vitality is gradually sapped.

Reference Matter

Notes

Full forms of all works cited in the Notes can be found in the Bibliography, pp. 277–88. Works published by agencies of the federal government are listed under "United States" there, and for ease of finding are identified by bracketed numbers.

CHAPTER I

1. *OMNI*, Jan. 1985, p. 57.
2. Among the most recent are Glasner 1985 and Kash and Rycroft 1984.
3. See for example Rosenbaum 1981, Davis 1978, Schurr et al. 1979, Goodwin 1981, Chubb 1983, Greenberger et al. 1983, and United States [9], [10], [11], and [12], the last four being studies completed by the Office of Technology Assessment (OTA).
4. One of the best introductions to this new field is Abrams 1980. See also Olson 1965, 1982, and Frohlich and Oppenheimer 1978.
5. A modern restatement of the need for this perspective is Bell 1976. The perspective is gaining popularity especially among younger social scientists, some neo-Marxist and some liberal, but all unhappy with the constraints imposed by their disciplines. As Stone and Harpham eds. 1982 put it in a recent assessment of this new work: "by breaking down the artificial divisions between fields of intellectual inquiry, by recognizing that the problem of values is ever present, and by focusing on the real and practical problems of the world, the new political economy tradition will likely yield far greater insights into fundamental questions than the approaches with which it competes."
6. The term "regime" has become popular as an analytical tool in the field of international relations because it highlights the importance of procedures and rules of the game that operate outside the boundaries of sovereign states but that nevertheless regulate behavior. As the authors who are responsible for the term's popularity put it, regimes are "networks of rules, norms and procedures that regularize behavior and control its effects." Nye and Keohane 1977: 19. Hoberg 1980 applies it usefully to the electricity industry.
7. For more on this concept, see Davis 1983, Kash and Rycroft 1984, and Chubb 1983.

8. An excellent review of recent thinking about these trends can be found in Cigler and Loomis eds. 1983.

9. This estimate is based on an interpretation of data and "circumstantial" evidence presented in Walker 1983 and Salisbury 1983.

10. See Walker 1983 and Cigler and Loomis eds. 1983. Changes in federal law that gave such groups standing to sue federal agencies on a variety of public issues contributed to the proliferation of these groups.

11. On these themes, see Hirsch 1976 and Thurow 1980.

12. The phenomenon of competitive mobilization of groups was noted in David Truman 1958.

13. For some of the most important writing in this area, see Olson 1965, Salisbury 1969, Stigler 1971, Peltzman 1976, Clark and Wilson 1961, and Moe 1980a and 1980b.

14. Olson 1965.

15. Salisbury 1969; Walker 1983.

16. In this study I use the categorization of incentives suggested in Clark and Wilson 1961. These include "material" incentives, which are economic benefits; "solidary" incentives, which are those derived from associating with other persons and groups; and "purposive" incentives, which are those that stem from the achievement of broad ideals and social values, such as security. For further discussion, see Salisbury 1969 and Chubb 1983.

17. Walker 1983: 398.

18. Hayes 1983: 113; data from Jeffrey Berry 1977.

19. See Downs 1972.

20. Schattschneider 1960.

21. For more on this point, see Salisbury 1983.

22. See for example Truman 1958 and Walker 1983.

23. Heclo 1978.

24. See Abrams 1980 for a clear statement of this approach.

25. For a readable account of the emergence of these agencies, see Kohlmeier 1969. As Kohlmeier notes, a significant number of the areas of private activity that were subject to federal regulation also received some degree of exemption from antitrust law. By the 1960's, he estimates, fully one fourth of the nation's commerce had received some such exemption (p. 104).

26. For this distinction and an analysis of the impact of newer forms of regulation, which typically cut across industries, see Weidenbaum 1982; and Bardach and Kagan eds. 1982.

27. For a comprehensive taxonomy of regulatory forms, see Mitnick 1980.

28. See Olson 1965 and Stigler 1971.

29. Stigler 1971: 5.

30. Olson 1982.

31. Peltzman 1976. Among other things, Peltzman has suggested that consumers will tend to benefit during conditions of economic expansion, producers during depressions (p. 227) and that in a "growing, technologically progressive industry, producer protection ought to yield to consumer

protection over time . . ." (p. 228). He also suggested, as his "first principle" of regulation: "even if a single economic interest gets all the benefits of regulation, these must be less than a perfect broker for the group would obtain. The best organized cartel will yield less to the membership if the government organizes it than if it were (could be) organized privately" (p. 217).

32. Wilson 1980: chap. 10. See also Anderson 1981.

33. Stigler 1971: 3.

34. For an analysis of the rise of compensatory regulation in the utility industry, see William Berry 1979.

35. See Lindblom 1977.

36. At the state and local level the crisis left the electricity regime, which is in many ways more vulnerable than the others, facing a future clouded by the prospect of continuing conflict between producers and consumers.

CHAPTER 2

1. Adams ed. 1961: 87. In the years between the Civil War and the end of the First World War, roughly the epoch of coal ascendency, per-capita consumption grew to more than six tons, and total production grew to 568 million tons produced in more than 8,000 mines in 23 states. Data from Adams ed. 1961: 78; Schurr et al. 1960: 74; Carman et al. 1961: 69–70.

2. Carman et al. 1961: 68–70.

3. The energy transitions to coal and then to oil and gas have a number of elements in common. Each involved a shift to a fuel that was cheaper, easier to handle and transport, and (especially in the case of oil and gas) less polluting. The availability of abundant energy sources, with new forms coming on line in an almost miraculous fashion to sustain another upward surge in the curve of economic growth, contributed enormously to the success of the American economy.

4. Metallurgical coal remained important in the production of steel, but demand from this sector dropped off as the industry lost its competitive advantage to foreign producers.

5. Stobaugh and Yergin eds. 1979: chap. 4.

6. Davis 1978: 19.

7. To be sure, at the local and regional levels there have been places and times when monopoly conditions have prevailed; moreover, in recent years the movement toward private conglomeration and concentration has been striking, for reasons I will discuss later. But the point remains: from a national perspective the industry for much of its history has been fragmented and dispersed enough that private efforts to impose order and stability on the market encountered serious impediments.

8. This remains true despite significant advances in mechanization.

9. Adams ed. 1961: 86. Labor costs are not as significant in surface mining, which has become increasingly important since the 1960's.

10. Adams ed. 1961: 82.

11. *Ibid.*: 78, 99.

12. *Ibid.*: 80. Income data from Fisher and James 1955: 328.

13. The first efforts to stabilize labor relations, which in some cases led to the formation of regional collective bargaining compacts in areas of union strength, were eventually undermined by competition from nonunion mines, especially in Appalachia and the South. Adams ed. 1961: 80–89.

14. *Ibid.*

15. For an excellent historical sketch of these events, see Davis 1978. A more detailed analysis of the industry after the First World War is James Johnson 1979.

16. Fisher 1948 and Adams ed. 1961: 90–91.

17. Adams ed. 1961: 89; Fisher 1948.

18. The federal government intervened in the coal industry during the First World War when the U.S. Fuel Administration set price ceilings and allocated supplies to remedy shortages. These controls were removed with the end of the war. Fainsod et al. 1959: 625.

19. Fisher and James 1955: 21.

20. *Appalachian Coals, Inc., et al.* v. *United States*, 288 U.S. 344, at 360 (1933).

21. Fisher and James 1955: 27–28.

22. Fisher and James 1955: 28. See James Johnson 1979 for details on this era.

23. Fisher and James 1955: 29–31.

24. See *Carter* v. *Carter Coals*, 298 US 238 (1936).

25. The most detailed study, from which the following conclusions have been drawn, is Fisher and James 1955; see also the excellent summary in Fainsod et al. 1959: 629–35.

26. Fainsod et al. 1959: 631.

27. Fisher and James 1955: 308–9.

28. Fainsod et al. 1959: 635.

29. These changes also brought a sudden decline in employment in the industry as well as serious new health problems for the underground miners. United States [9]: 130.

30. The UMW on several occasions resorted to unilateral, coordinated slowdowns in order to protect prices. This was accomplished by orchestrating "work-sharing" actions in which the union ordered miners to work a reduced number of days per week, in effect reducing output in the industry as a whole. Fainsod et al. 1955: 637; United States [9]: 131–33. For greater detail, see Baratz 1955.

31. Goodwin 1981: 139–42.

32. *Ibid.*: 144.

33. United States [9]: 129. For more detail on this theme, see Seltzer 1970.

34. United States [9]: 130.

35. *Ibid.*: 131.

36. *Ibid.*: 132. Some of the activities of the alliance were illegal forms

of conspiracy, and were formally identified as such in Supreme Court decisions.

37. Adams ed. 1961: 92.
38. United States [9]: 111–20, 133.
39. *Ibid.:* 133.
40. Gimlin ed. 1982: 187 (data from U.S. Bureau of Mines).
41. United States [9]: 132.
42. *Ibid.*
43. *Ibid.:* 129.

CHAPTER 3

1. Pratt 1981: 22.
2. *Fortune,* Aug. 1987.
3. For an excellent review of the structure and operation of the petroleum industry in the United States, see Measday 1977.
4. United States [23], 1985: 117.
5. Measday 1977: 137.
6. For a description of the technical complexity of the petroleum industry, with particular emphasis on transport, see Lovins and Lovins 1982a.
7. Measday 1977: 135.
8. On this point see Mead 1967.
9. The problem of analyzing patterns of competition and cooperation within an oligopolistic industry has concerned economists for many years. Generalizations are difficult, because in a concentrated industry, especially one marked by extensive functional cooperation, the members are usually acutely aware of one another's actions and adjust their behavior accordingly. Patterns of interdependent decision, often called "oligopolistic interdependence," can produce price and supply patterns that closely approximate those of a pure growth or profit monopoly. On this distinction, see Chapman 1983. Then, too, there is the problem of goals. Firms pursue different goals—e.g. profits, growth, consolidation of various stages of integration—with varying degrees of commitment over time. A central goal, of course, is market stability—the proverbial "quiet life" that Alfred Marshall identified as the first benefit of monopoly power. In the oil business the costs of uncontrolled competition are high for established firms, so it is reasonable to expect that some means to provide the collective "good" of market control will be found. And in fact such means have been found. By contrast, with coal the group was too numerous and leadership was too weak.
10. Chapman 1983: 128.
11. Measday 1977: 135.
12. *Ibid.:* 147–48.
13. *Ibid.:* 138; Blair 1976: 131.
14. Blair 1976: 136.
15. Measday 1977: 149–50.

16. Sampson 1975: 31.

17. *Ibid.*: 26–27. The first of the attacks, of course, came from Ida Tarbell, whose muckraking classic *The History of the Standard Oil Company* was published in 1904. The most recent is Sherrill 1983.

18. Sampson 1975: 22–25.

19. Williamson et al. 1963: 466.

20. Pratt 1980, argues convincingly that state policies were influential in shaping the early growth of the industry.

21. Blair 1976: 127; Sampson 1975: 34.

22. Williamson et al. 1963: chap. 8; and Davis 1978: 52–53.

23. Nash 1968 and Williamson et al. 1963 both deal with this topic.

24. Ironically, this followed a period in which the principal concern was the possibility of an oil "famine."

25. Williamson et al. 1963: 540–51; Nash 1968: 123–24.

26. As Williamson et al. put it (1963: 542): "The essential features of the objectives of industry members and the government became intertwined and confused in a sea of conflict over 'waste,' price control, monopoly and property rights."

27. Blair 1976: 160.

28. The East Texas field was producing nearly one million barrels per day in 1932, close to a third of the total for the whole country. Blair 1976: 160.

29. John Blair, one of the most careful analysts of the interconnections between the international and domestic petroleum industries, concluded that the majors were the principal force behind the Texas decision to prorate production to support price. He even suggested that the price reductions in 1932 and 1933 were postings set by the majors precisely to bring pressure to bear on the legislature to pass a law they—the majors—had connived to bring before that body. Although the evidence he assembled for this assertion is circumstantial, the companies involved had both the means and opportunity for such actions. See Blair 1976: 160–61.

30. The American Petroleum Institute, after studying these problems, emerged with a proposal for a formal, worldwide production cartel that the United States might join. (As it turns out, this fit quite neatly with the broad plan for managing world production hatched behind the scenes by the integrated majors.) But it was quickly ruled out by the U.S. Attorney General, who noted that participation of American companies in such a scheme was hardly compatible with antitrust laws. Williamson et al. 1963: 541; Blair 1976: 157.

31. Williamson et al. 1963: 548–49.

32. Fainsod et al. 1959: 650–51; also Williamson et al. 1963: 558.

33. For details, see Williamson et al. 1963: 558–60. The parallel between the role of Oklahoma and Texas as the "balance wheels" of domestic oil control and that of Saudi Arabia in the OPEC arrangements is both accurate and instructive—as is the parallel between Illinois and Nigeria, Mexico, or Great Britain as sources of disruption. Noncompulsory cartel arrangements

are always vulnerable to uncooperative suppliers determined to carve out a market for themselves, and the existence of a very large producer willing to provide the "collective good" of price stabilization is critically important. For an analysis of the theoretical issues involved, see Olson 1965.

34. For a discussion of the problems of waste, see Mead 1976: 136–39.

35. During the Second World War the industry again came under the administrative jurisdiction of the federal government.

36. According to Jacoby 1974: 295: "In 1953 only twenty-eight U.S. firms and fifteen foreign firms—other than the seven largest—had oil exploration rights outside their own countries, and they held no more than 35 percent of concession areas. By the end of 1972, more than 330 other firms had exploration rights in 122 areas of the world and held 69 percent of concession areas." On these changes, see also Adelman 1972.

37. Williamson et al. 1963: 815.

38. *Ibid.*: 552; see also Nash 1968: 202–3.

39. Mead 1976: 144, documents the effectiveness of demand management by the Texas Railroad Commission.

40. Goodwin 1981: 227–51.

41. United States [23], 1984: 126.

42. Goodwin 1981: 251–52.

43. For more on demands for special treatment, and the diplomatic entanglements they created in U.S.-Venezuelan relations, see Tugwell 1975.

44. Blair 1976: 178–80.

45. *Ibid.*: 182, using the data of M. A. Adelman.

46. Battelle Memorial Institute 1978: 226. Data in 1977 dollars.

47. Blair 1976: 394.

48. The most important of these attacks, a 1975 bill to force companies to choose one stage of activity and divest themselves of interests in the rest, failed in the Senate by only five votes.

49. Engler 1961 and 1977 document this phenomenon in detail.

50. Davis 1978: 72.

51. Engler 1977: chap. 3.

CHAPTER 4

1. United States [23]: 5. This figure includes dry natural gas and natural gas plant liquids. The United States produced 18.59 quads of crude petroleum and lease condensate in the same year.

2. Gas pressure is important in the production of oil. The perception of this relationship, which did not become widespread until the 1930's, led to control of the uses of gas in the name of conservation in many states. See Williamson et al. 1963: 329.

3. Sanders 1981: 71. This is the best available work on the politics of natural gas regulation, and in this chapter I draw heavily on its excellent research.

4. Fainsod et al. 1959: 665.

5. United States [23]: 145.

6. See *Cities Service Co.* v. *Peerless Oil and Gas. Co.*, 340 U.S. 179 (1950); also Fainsod et al. 1959: 666.

7. For more on this era, see Troxel 1937; Sanders 1981: 25–38; and Davis 1978: 114.

8. Sanders 1981: 26–27.

9. *Ibid.*: 38.

10. Chapman 1983: 160, 171.

11. *Ibid.*: 159.

12. See, among others, MacAvoy 1962; MacAvoy and Pindyck 1975; Duchesneau 1975; and various essays in Brown ed. 1972. A more technical controversy among specialists has also arisen concerning the degree to which, even given workable competition, the structure of the gas industry, especially given the long production periods and the linkages to oil markets, leads to the earning of unjustified rents and windfalls by owners of gas reserves. The issues are ably discussed by Hawkins in Brown ed. 1972: 161. The key questions, of course, are (1) the degree to which these rents and windfalls are real; and (2) whether the inefficiencies and other costs associated with price control to manage them are large enough to suggest other means (such as taxation) as a remedy. For discussion of these matters, see Dirlam 1958.

13. Sanders 1981: 12–15, highlights the importance of regional conflicts, noting that studies of regulation have underestimated their importance.

14. For a careful analysis of the origins of the Natural Gas Act, see Sanders 1981: chap. 2.

15. Sanders 1981: 143. As common carriers, pipelines would have to accept, for a fixed fee, gas owned by anyone seeking transport services. They could no longer purchase and sell all the gas transported, losing the leverage stemming from their positions as regional or local monopolists.

16. Davis 1978: 117.

17. Spritzer in Brown ed. 1972: 116.

18. These disagreements were resolved in the 1944 Supreme Court case of *FPC* v. *Hope Natural Gas*, in which the Court upheld the right of the FPC to determine rates of return on utility investments by means of formulas of its own design, provided these resulted in rates that met the broad standard of being just and reasonable. This decision was important for the electricity regime as well.

19. The most notorious episode was the one involving the reappointment of Leland Olds. For a description of this, see Davis 1982.

20. See *Colorado Interstate Gas Company* v. *FPC*, 324 U.S. 581 (1945).

21. Sanders 1981: 88.

22. Fainsod et al. 1959: 676.

23. See MacAvoy in Brown ed. 1972: 170.

24. *Ibid.*

25. Spritzer in Brown ed. 1972: 118.

26. Sanders 1981: 113. As it happened, Kennedy was able to appoint five

new commissioners in his first year in office. Normally this is impossible, since commissioners are appointed for staggered five-year terms. See Spritzer in Brown ed. 1972: 113.

27. Sanders 1981: 106–14.

28. Spritzer in Brown ed. 1972: 121.

29. *Ibid.*

30. MacAvoy in Brown ed. 1972: 170–72.

31. Sanders 1981: 125.

32. Spritzer in Brown ed. 1972: 123.

33. Sanders 1981: 129–30; Spritzer in Brown ed. 1972: 120–21.

CHAPTER 5

1. The early history is recounted in Rudolph and Ridley 1986: chap. 2.

2. However, they do compete with each other for access to capital. Messing et al. 1979: 48.

3. United States [24], 1983: 141.

4. Messing et al. 1979: 48. For details on the method of calculating returns, as well as an estimate of the impact of tax regulation, see Chapman 1983: chap. 12.

5. Chapman 1983: 26. Declining real prices for fuels, of course, also contributed to this accomplishment.

6. *Ibid.*: 221.

7. This optimism was nurtured by the Atomic Energy Commission and the vendors of nuclear power plant equipment.

8. For data on the growth of demand for electricity, see United States [23], 1985: 193.

9. United States [10]: 55.

10. Chapman 1983: 223.

11. Messing et al. 1979: 45–46.

12. As one analysis put it: "Financial groups profited not only through security transactions and manipulations but also through control of the operating companies. They forced the operating companies to pay them inflated fees for financial services, for construction and development work, and for management advice. Operating companies could be 'milked' through upstream loans on terms advantageous to the holding-company groups. Such profits of the financial control groups were reflected, first, in inflated operating expenses and unnecessary overhead of the operating companies and, ultimately, in excessive rates extracted from the consumers." Fainsod et al. 1959: 319.

13. As quoted in Fainsod et al. 1959: 349–50.

14. Only two of the six largest private utilities are now holding companies, but their activities as such are regulated by the SEC. Chapman 1983: 223.

15. For background on this, see Davis 1982: chap. 5. Greater detail can be found in, among other sources, Hellman 1972.

16. Messing et al. 1979: 29.

17. See Funigiello 1973: chap. 5.

18. On this issue see Lovins and Lovins 1982a.

19. Although small, it operated safely for two and a half decades before it was decommissioned, and, in 1986, disassembled (at a price of just under $100 million).

20. Bupp in Stobaugh and Yergin eds. 1979: 115.

21. For an excellent analysis of nuclear technology and the problems the industry has faced in recent years, see United States [11]; see also Bupp and Derian 1978.

22. Chapman 1983: 213.

23. *Ibid.*: 216.

24. *Ibid.*, citing Rothwell 1980.

25. Bupp in Stobaugh and Yergin eds. 1979: 114–15.

26. The first of these were established in 1907 in New York and Wisconsin. Fainsod et al. 1959: 323–25.

27. Gormley 1983: 6–7.

28. Fainsod et al. 1959: 336.

29. The FPC was originally a cabinet-level committee established under the 1920 Federal Water Power Act. In 1935 it was reconstituted as a full-fledged, independent regulatory commission.

30. Chapman 1983: 241–42.

31. Fainsod et al. 1959: 681–86.

32. Indeed, several other countries in the earlier years placed a much higher priority on the generation of electricity from nuclear energy, once the knowledge became available, than did the United States. These included Great Britain and the Soviet Union. Fainsod et al. 1959: 693.

33. This was in fact the case with many of the state regulatory agencies overseeing conventional power plants, but it became a serious issue in later years when political and economic conditions created demands for more independent supervision.

34. Fainsod et al. 1959: 694.

35. The Price-Anderson Act, passed in 1957, limited liability for offsite damage to $560 million, of which the government agreed to pay $500 million if necessary. In 1975 this subsidy was renewed and extended to 1987. For details, see Pelham 1981: 149, 157.

36. See Bupp in Stobaugh and Yergin eds. 1979. See also the more extensive analysis in Bupp and Derian 1978.

37. Nuclear facilities, because they rely on relatively little fuel, are even more capital intensive than other generation facilities. As a result, federal tax incentives for investment tended to favor nuclear facilities, giving them an additional boost.

CHAPTER 6

1. The crisis itself originated in the weakening of the private international cartel in petroleum, a process that began in the 1950's and manifested

itself in an increase in the number of companies producing oil abroad—and, as might be expected, in a gradual but steady decline in prices. This weakening, more than anything else, explains the decision to establish OPEC in 1960. The goal of OPEC governments was to set up a public cartel that would take over from the private one. Though this eluded the organization for many years, it did promote a growing sophistication and self-assertiveness on the part of governments that were hosts to private companies. The market conditions involved are described in Adelman 1972; for the origins of OPEC, see Tugwell 1975.

2. For a description of the events and an analysis of the Arab goals, see Rustow 1982: chap. 5. See also Blair 1976: chap. 11. The burden of the embargo was distributed by the international oil companies, so that the "targeting" effort was frustrated. Also, there was some cheating by OAPEC members.

3. Rustow 1985: 173.

4. Schelling 1979: 14–15. Schelling based his estimate on the assumption that the doubling of oil prices would remain in place and that the costs of all fuels might double again in the next two decades. Imported oil accounted for 37 percent of U.S. petroleum consumption.

5. See Kalt 1981 and Verleger 1981.

6. See Blair 1976: chap. 10, for details on these conflicts.

7. The voluntary program was announced by Nixon in May 1973, and was replaced by mandatory controls in October, just before the embargo. The control system was institutionalized the next month when Congress passed the Emergency Petroleum Allocation Act (EPAA), granting the President broad authority to set prices and allocate supplies. For details on these actions and laws, see the excellent studies by Verleger (1981) and Pelham (1981).

8. *Caught Unawares* is the title of Greenberger et al. 1983, an insightful study of the role of policy analysis in shaping the way we came to understand the energy problem.

9. As Dankwart Rustow put it: "The American reaction, from the political leaders and technical experts to the mass media and the common citizenry, was a babble of conflicting voices that was not to subside for some years. Diagnoses of the problem ranged from near-fatal disease to mild indisposition to rampant hypochondria; prescription ranged from drastic surgery through a number of patent medicines to nothing more than conscientious dieting or fresh air and regular exercise." Rustow 1982: 174.

10. Greenberger et al. 1983 and Goodwin 1981. The goal of energy self-sufficiency, postponed by President Ford to 1985 and then quietly set aside by Carter, was finally formally abandoned as a plausible objective for this century in the *1983 Energy Policy Plan* of the Reagan Administration.

11. United States [33]: 23.

12. These were the short-term problems. As the energy crisis unfolded, it became clear that the international policy challenges were also more far-

reaching. Among other things, the United States had to (1) address the problem of supply security and the transfer of control of prices of world oil from Western multinational corporations to producer governments; (2) handle the associated international financial crisis; and (3) face up to the nuclear proliferation problem, one made more urgent because the crisis promoted a rapid increase in the growth of nuclear energy worldwide. For a statement of these problems and an assessment of the early response of the Western countries, see Sawhill et al. 1978. See also Lieber 1976.

13. For more details on these events, see Lieber 1976 and 1979. The latter is partially summarized in the chapter "Cohesion and Disruption in the Western Alliance," in Yergin and Hillenbrand 1982.

14. For the best detailed description of this program, see Willrich and Conant 1977.

15. France, jealous of its independence and fearful of provoking Arab retaliation, refused to join, but set up a relationship with the IEA through the Commission of the European Economic Community.

16. For further details of this complex agreement, see Willrich and Conant 1977.

17. For the legislative background to these bills, see the very helpful chronology in Pelham 1981: 131–36. Nixon signed the Alaska Pipeline Act immediately. It was he who had requested the bill, to clear legal obstacles to the construction of the pipeline, raised chiefly by environmentalists. The OAPEC embargo provided the momentum needed to overcome Congressional opposition to the measure.

18. For the best analysis of the economic consequences of these controls, see Kalt 1981.

19. For further details, see Pelham 1981: 136–38.

20. *Ibid.*: 138.

21. See National Research Council 1984. PL 93–239 is described in Pelham 1981: 138, 140. Congress also passed, in 1974, the Energy Supply and Environmental Coordination Act, which embodied the first regulatory effort to force users of gas and oil to switch to coal. The act was riddled with exemptions, and passed with little difficulty.

22. The personal and bureaucratic struggles that marked the early stages of energy decisionmaking are discussed at length by de Marchi in his chapter on the Nixon Administration in the administrative history edited by Goodwin (1981). The conflicts centered on tension between the Council of Economic Advisers and the Treasury Department on the one hand, both of which lost influence, and the Federal Energy Office (later the Federal Energy Administration) on the other. The conflicts had an ideological dimension as well, centering on the degree to which market forces should be allowed an immediate role in the setting of prices and the allocating of costs and benefits. In the event, the FEA, the agency with the most direct, day-to-day responsibility in managing Congressionally mandated controls and responding to the political demands for equity, won most of the battles.

23. See the chapter by de Marchi in Goodwin 1981 for an excellent historical analysis of this period.

24. As de Marchi put it (in Goodwin 1981: 455): "The decision for any sort of allocation scheme virtually guaranteed that Simon and his staff would spend much time dealing with hardship cases channeled through congressmen. . . . The effect of the decision and the significance of the allocation program for gasoline, therefore, was that they diverted the FEO from addressing medium- and long-term problems. Once again, crisis management was the order of the day."

25. See Kalt 1981: 9–13, for details.

26. As might be expected, this arrangement for allocation ran into many problems. See MacAvoy ed. 1977. See also de Marchi in Goodwin 1981: 454–58.

27. Kalt 1981: 14.

28. This was the idea, originally, of Vice President Rockefeller. Congress paid no attention to it, but it is mentioned here because it was the forerunner of Carter's synthetic fuels proposals.

29. United States [34]. Like so many other energy-policy alternatives, the windfall profits proposal was a carryover from early discussions in the Nixon Administration. Later on, Carter would adopt it. Note that there were many other proposals in this plan, as was the case with all the presidential energy pronouncements. The overall focus was on increasing production by allowing prices to rise and by removing obstacles (pollution regulations), subsidizing (especially nuclear energy and synfuels), and regulating (coal switching). There were also some modest conservation proposals.

30. See the de Marchi chapter on Ford in Goodwin 1981 for a favorable assessment of the Ford design and an analysis of the politics of energy policy within the Ford Administration.

31. A poll taken in late 1973 and early 1974 by Gallup revealed that 25 percent of the respondents believed energy problems were caused by "oil companies," while another 23 percent blamed the "federal government." Only 7 percent identified "Arab nations" as the cause. A poll taken in the spring of 1977 revealed that only 52 percent of the respondents were aware that the United States had to import oil from abroad. Gallup 1978, vols. 1 (p. 226) and 2 (p. 1106).

32. Although Ford did indicate a willingness to go along with mechanisms aimed at preventing unwarranted enrichment, such as the windfall profits levy and redistributive tax adjustments, it was also clear that these were not the administration's first priority; price decontrol and promotion of production came first.

33. For an account of this conflict, see de Marchi's chapter on the Ford Administration in Goodwin 1981: 503–8. As de Marchi notes, the EPCA had many other provisions, some of which did respond to Ford's energy proposals.

34. For details see, Kalt 1981: 14–17.

35. This, of course, made it necessary to complicate further the entitlements system. See Kalt 1981: 17.

36. Kalt 1981: 19. In 1979 Carter exempted jet fuel and, when the deadline passed, began a phased decontrol of domestic crude oil as well.

37. For this and other energy legislation, see United States [7].

38. See chap. 6 by de Marchi in Goodwin 1981.

CHAPTER 7

1. For his thoughts about this, see Carter 1982: 91–124.

2. Tugwell 1980: 57.

3. United States [1].

4. New sources of production, chiefly from Alaska and the outer continental shelf, were expected to provide an interlude of only a few years. The most widely cited expert on this problem is M. King Hubbert, whose projections of depletion have proved surprisingly accurate.

5. The plan was explicit with respect to the quantitative standard by which it measured success: the contribution of measures to the displacement of imported oil. The goal, in part, was to avoid the criticisms aimed at the Project Independence plans, in which the connection between "independence" (variously defined) and specific measures had not been clear enough. In the event, the Carter plan suffered criticism on the grounds that its more precise estimates were mistaken.

6. For details on the special group of advisers who formulated the *Plan*, see Goodwin 1981: 554.

7. Ford had also praised conservation, but the rhetorical emphasis on this source of energy by Carter went along with a somewhat greater willingness to target specific conservation opportunities for policy action.

8. All in all, the consolidation involved more than 18,000 government employees and a budget in excess of ten billion dollars (in 1978).

9. Carter 1982: 91. As the legislature proceeded to tear Carter's program to pieces, the acronym for this phrase, MEOW, became an irresistible characterization of the Administration's efforts.

10. Pelham 1981: 183. By February 1977, industries and schools in eleven states were closed because of shortages of natural gas supplies.

11. Among the changes in the DOE plan insisted upon by Congress, perhaps the most important was that the Federal Energy Regulatory Commission, successor to the Federal Power Commission, retain its autonomy from the DOE as an independent regulatory body.

12. Especially important, in this respect, was the fact that the Senate Finance Committee (in charge of tax legislation) was chaired by Sen. Russell Long of Louisiana, a lifelong defender of the oil and gas industry. Carter sought to cultivate Long's friendship, inviting him to the White House for private dinners, but with little practical result.

13. Pelham 1981: 195.

14. Sanders 1981: 138–41. Note here that the Senate voted for deregulation in 1975, passing a bill sponsored by James Pearson (R-Kan.) and Lloyd

Bentsen (R-Tex.), and did so again in 1977, despite a filibuster by two senators from consuming states.

15. Despite Carter's opposition, Congress continued to fund construction of the breeder-reactor program at Clinch River, Tennessee.

16. For an explanation of why this was the case, see Chapter 8.

17. Goodwin 1981: 601–3.

18. *Ibid.*: 603. See also Rustow 1982: 183 and chap. 6, for details on the crisis.

19. See Verleger 1981. As Rustow (1982: 184) put it: "Thus in the spring and summer of 1979, the world oil market bustled with unwonted activity. Anxious buyers and hopeful speculators, expecting that the shortage would send prices soaring, bought whatever oil they could get their hands on and paid whatever price was asked. The effect was that of a self-fulfilling prophecy."

20. Appropriately, the Washington, D.C., area suffered some of the worst effects of the shortage. For details on this, and criticism of the role of the government, see Verleger 1981.

21. Joseph Yager (in Goodwin 1981: 604) points out that some countries might have reached the 7 percent level, but that the oil companies evened out the impact of the shortfall. It was fortunate that emergency arrangements were not called into effect, since the United States was unprepared.

22. Goodwin 1981: 605.

23. Energy was a principal topic of discussion at the Bonn meeting in the summer of 1978 and at the Tokyo summit in the summer of 1979.

24. See the text of the speech in Pelham 1981: 257.

25. To veteran observers of the energy-policy process, the formula Carter proposed sounded hauntingly familiar: it was, in fact, a replay of the basic ingredients of Ford's approach in 1975. The speech, however, with its stress on fairness and its attack on the oil companies, differed greatly in emphasis.

26. Late in the fall Congress did pass some broad guidelines by which the Executive might formulate a gasoline-rationing plan, but this provided little comfort during the crisis itself, when it appeared that such a plan might actually be needed. Carter's observation on legislative behavior at this time: "The Congress is disgusting on this particular subject." Carter 1982: 111.

27. United States [30].

28. The meeting left OPEC divided between price "hawks" and "moderates," the latter led by Saudi Arabia. Since no consensus could be achieved on a single price, a two-tier system came into existence, with the lower tier at approximately $18 per barrel and the higher tier at approximately $24. Members would later agree to reunify the price-setting arrangements. See Rustow 1982 for background.

29. The decision to avoid another "energy" speech was taken on the advice of his pollster, Patrick Caddell. Carter 1982: 114.

30. Pelham 1981: 208. In imposing quotas, Carter acted on the basis of authority given him in the Trade Expansion Act (as amended), just as Eisen-

hower had when he imposed a quota system on imports in 1959. As it turned out, of course, imports were already on the decline, and the management of the import quotas—to which considerable analytical effort was subsequently devoted—would not pose the same political and administrative challenge that it did in the years between 1959 and 1973.

31. The industry itself was divided over whether independents should receive special treatment.

32. Independents thus did win special treatment in the legislation.

33. Pelham 1981: 221–25.

34. Only as a last resort was the SFC authorized to actually produce synfuels. Congress made clear its intention that the corporation was to provide incentives to the private sector, not substitute for it.

35. The $20 billion figure included funds already authorized in previous energy legislation, so that only approximately $17 billion was a new allocation for the first four years of SFC operation.

36. Carter 1982: 123–24.

37. Reagan's public statements on energy are peppered with so many factual errors that it is obvious he did not grasp many of the essentials of the energy-policy problems facing the country, but relied instead on appealing generalizations provided by trusted advisers. In formulating his approach, Reagan apparently drew on the advice of a small group of independent oilmen whose optimistic estimates of the amount of recoverable oil remaining in U.S. territory bore no resemblance to the evidence assembled by specialists on the subject (then or now). In this respect he differed from Carter, who had a good command of energy matters.

38. United States [20].

39. Edwards was replaced by Donald P. Hodel, who quickly adopted a more conciliatory approach to issues ranging from the dismantling of the Department to the possible benefits to be gained from tax credits for conservation.

40. Reagan ended price controls by executive order under authority granted in the EPCA. He also eliminated mandatory building-temperature controls.

41. *New York Times*, Jan. 29, 1981.

42. The administration introduced a similar bill in 1986, and it suffered a similar fate.

43. The Reagan proposal would have shifted about 70 percent of the Department's functions to the Department of Commerce and most of the rest to the Department of the Interior. The latter would have managed the Strategic Petroleum Reserve. Bits and pieces of work in other areas would have been scattered among the Departments of Agriculture, Housing and Urban Development, and Justice. *New York Times*, Feb. 14, 1982.

44. The most widely criticized cuts were in the budgets for solar energy and conservation, which were reduced more than 60 percent in the first round.

45. In August 1985 the House voted to strip $6.6 billion from the SFC budget. This left the corporation with no funds for new projects.

46. *The National Journal*, Feb. 18, 1984, p. 320.

47. Kash and Rycroft 1984: chap. 11.

48. The Reagan experience with offshore leasing is reviewed in an article in the *Washington Post*, Mar. 22, 1985.

49. *New York Times*, July 30, 1985. The areawide program was also heavily criticized for earning less: a report on the program by the General Accounting Office noted that average bids per acre declined from $2,624 under the old system to $628 under the areawide program. Critics of this report have noted that it did not present an accurate picture of the benefits that resulted from the program. For both points of view, see the *New York Times* report cited above.

50. See, for example, Lichtblau 1984.

51. *Ibid*. By mid-1986, the SPR contained 503 million barrels of oil. With prices very low, in August of that year Reagan urged an increase in the fill rate to take advantage of low prices.

52. See, among others, Yergin 1982 and Lichtblau 1984.

53. See *National Journal*, Jan. 29, 1983. The Congressional Office of Technology Assessment in 1984 published the results of its own study of the consequences of an oil shortfall crisis and concluded that, should the United States experience a shortfall of approximately 3 million barrels per day of indefinite duration, prices could be expected to rise rapidly to between $50 and $70 dollars per barrel. This estimate assumed that the SPR, as well as private oil stocks, would be immediately used to cushion the effects of the shortfall. Past experience suggests, however, that the latter expectation is unrealistic, especially with respect to private stocks, lending credence to higher price estimates. See United States [12].

54. For a report on this agreement, see U.S. Department of State, *Current Policy* no. 612, "International Energy Security: The Continuing Challenge," Sept. 12, 1984.

CHAPTER 8

1. Hirst et al. 1983: 240, estimated that about half of the general reduction in energy use can be attributed to the general slowdown in economic growth in the first years after the embargo.

2. Hirst et al. 1983: 241, estimated that of the 16 quads per year reduction in energy demand, about 11 could be attributed directly to price increases.

3. United States [12]: 41. Although the quantitative impact of renewable energy forms was far inferior to that of increased coal use, it represented a much larger absolute increase for those sources of energy.

4. End-use energy decreased more rapidly than total energy as a result of the shift to electricity (coal and nuclear).

5. United States [26]: 4. The analysis of energy use is divided, by convention, into five sectors: industrial, commercial, residential, transportation,

and utility. "End-use" is often distinguished from "total use" according to whether energy used to produce electricity is accounted for or not. The industrial sector includes mining, agriculture, manufacture, and construction. Over the time analyzed here, electricity as a percentage of total end-use energy increased significantly. Because of the losses involved in conversion of primary fuels to electricity, this transformation of the economy resulted in a growing gap between total energy consumption (i.e. including fuel for utilities) and end-use consumption.

6. United States [26]: 45.

7. *Ibid.*: 15.

8. *Ibid.*: 18.

9. *Ibid.*: 34.

10. United States [27], Oct 30, 1984: 1.

11. United States [26]: 60.

12. An obvious question raised by these changes is whether, given the right price incentives, the fuel mix could shift to further reliance on oil. The answer revolves around the degree to which the shift to coal and nuclear is structurally irreversible. In many instances, coal-burning power plants have the capacity to switch to oil.

13. See, in particular, Kalt 1981; Verleger 1981 and 1982; and MacAvoy 1983.

14. See United States [26], and National Research Council, National Transportation Board, 1984.

15. United States [23]: 121. Data are for 1977.

16. The most detailed and balanced study of the lowered speed limit is that which was prepared by the Transportation Research Board of the National Research Council in 1984. According to this (p. 3): "The speed limit was reduced in 1974 as an energy conservation measure, and currently [1984] some 167,000 barrels of petroleum per day are saved because of reduced speeds." Since, as the study notes, speeds have actually crept up in the years since, it is reasonable to estimate that fuel savings averaged about 200,000 barrels per day over the years between 1974 and 1983.

17. The reduction was just under 3 percent, assuming an average annual import level of 7 million barrels per day.

18. According to the study of the Transportation Research Board of the National Research Council (1984: 2–3): "these findings indicate that the slower speed and more uniform pace of travel due to the 55 mph speed limit accounted for 3,000 to 5,000 fewer highway fatalities in 1974. . . . Adjusting for the reduction in the fatality rate during the last decade as well as the increase in travel and average speeds during that period, about 2,000 to 4,000 lives were saved in 1983 as a result of the 55 mph speed limit. In addition, about 2,500 to 4,500 fewer serious, severe, and critical injuries and 34,000 to 61,000 fewer minor and moderate injuries occurred in 1983 because of the slower speeds and more uniform pace of travel brought about by the 55 mph speed limit." For present purposes, I have assumed an average of 3,000 lives saved per year and 2,500 serious plus 34,000 minor injuries for the ten

years involved. At the time of writing, 31 states had raised the speed limit beyond 55 mph on rural interstate highways in response to a new law allowing them to do so without loss of federal highway construction funds.

19. Calculated from data presented in United States [26]: 122.

20. Gimlin 1982: 15.

21. Yergin and Hillenbrand 1983: 128. To carry this argument a step further, it seems fair to conclude that if CAFE standards did force a change in the behavior of American automakers, it acted to save them from further loss to Japanese imports.

22. See *The New York Times*, Sept. 30, 1983. In October of 1984, Reagan cut back CAFE standards for light trucks, reducing them from 21 mpg to 19.5 for 1985 and from 21.5 to 20 mpg in 1986. The Administration also reduced standards for cars twice, in 1985 reducing the 1986 target to 26 mpg from 27.5, and in 1986 extending the 1986 figure through 1988. At the time of writing further cuts in auto standards were under consideration. In practice, the standards represent an extraordinarily cumbersome and intrusive form of regulation, and are likely to come under increasing assault to the degree to which they become seriously binding. See Kworka 1983.

23. United States [22]: 30.

24. Both EPCA (1975) and ECPA (1978) contained "demand-management" provisions. The most important are to be found in the second of these two bills. In a number of cases, the provisions took the form of grants to states.

25. United States [26]: 25.

26. Gimlin 1982: 15.

27. I have chosen half on the basis of the ratio of conservers to takers-of-tax-credits. Data from United States [23], 1985: 123.

28. Federal policies also affected production, the "supply" side of the energy equation. Among these, of course, more liberal leasing policies were especially notable. Here too, however, these were less important than pricing policy, which, until 1981, had the reverse effect.

29. The EPAA, then the EPAA plus EPCA, were to do this job. When legislators finally acknowledged that the price controls were not working, the WPT was to collect some of the unjust profits.

30. These profits were possible because, as one analyst has put it, price controls on refined products were "rarely and haphazardly binding." See Kalt 1981: 65.

31. Kalt 1981: 65.

32. *Ibid.*: 201, 203, 287. See also the similar estimates for import increases from price controls reported in MacAvoy 1983: 71–72.

33. *The Los Angeles Times*, Aug. 1, 1986, p. 1.

34. This point is stressed, quite appropriately, by Alvin Alm and others in Deese and Nye eds. 1981.

35. On the changing oil market, see Neff in Deese and Nye eds. 1981.

36. Verleger 1981: 512.

37. Among the best studies reporting this work are Alm and Weiner eds.

1983; Deese and Nye eds. 1981; Krapels 1980; Yergin and Hillenbrand 1982; and Verleger 1981 and 1982.

38. For a review of these and the problems associated with implementation, see Alm and Weiner eds. 1983, esp. chap. 1, by Alm.

39. United States [12].

40. Costs and benefits, as the terms are used in this section, refer mainly to direct payments made and received, not to the desirability of those payments with reference to important public goals. The latter are addressed primarily in other sections of this and the next chapter.

41. In constant dollars. United States [23] 1985: 91, 135.

42. The disagreements on these consequences between MacAvoy, Joseph Kalt, and Paul Joskow are described in MacAvoy 1983.

43. One of the less obvious consequences of demand-reduction policies, such as the CAFE standards, is that they can increase this disparity between the rich and the poor. Poor people buy the gas-guzzlers that middle- and upper-income people replace, creating a kind of energy cost-shift that lasts until the old vehicles are more efficient as well.

44. The impact of energy price increases on Americans of different income levels has been examined carefully by a number of analysts. For a range of approaches, see Landsberg 1982. Also useful are Herendeen and Tanaka 1976, United States [2], and United States [21].

45. The most dramatic example, of course, is Alaska, where proceeds permitted a negative tax.

46. The rationale for this approach is familiar: the owners of domestic oil had made their investments before the crisis and presumably were in a position to make an acceptable return by selling their products at precrisis prices. They had no "right" to the windfall profits created by the illegal actions of foreign governments. Owners of petroleum, of course, disagreed, arguing that free enterprise investment often involves unexpected windfalls, and that these in fact form an important incentive in the American system and are hardly illegal. However, Congress did not accept this answer, and by its action implied that very large companies must meet different standards with respect to the nature of their gains—especially when those gains involve sudden and massive transfers of wealth throughout the economy.

47. The best analysis of this is found in Kalt 1981: chap. 3.

48. Product price controls were in effect for portions of the period under consideration, but for a variety of reasons they were ineffective.

49. An excellent discussion of the various positions on this issue, and the analytical approaches involved, is presented in Kalt 1981: chap. 4. For further discussion, see MacAvoy 1983: 66–77. A critical issue in the debate concerns the degree to which domestic product prices tended to rise to meet world product price levels.

50. Phelps and Smith 1977.

51. Hall and Pindyck 1977.

52. Kalt 1981: 288. The total was not equal to the losses suffered by the

owners of oil, however; the difference, lost in economic inefficiency, was a gain to no one.

53. Criticism of Kalt's work by MacAvoy 1983, chap. 2, suggests that, if anything, Kalt has overestimated the benefit to consumers. MacAvoy's analysis indicates (pp. 74–75) that consumers may have garnered little or none of the benefit. With this caveat, I will continue to accept Kalt's conclusions as the most detailed and comprehensive.

54. Kalt 1981: 184.

55. MacAvoy 1983: 68, notes, for example, that while in 1976 more than half of domestic oil came from fully controlled "old" fields, by 1980 only one-fifth came from this source.

56. As noted above, the remainder, some $5 to $6 billion, was dissipated in deadweight losses to the economy, a result of allocative distortions caused by the system of controls and entitlements. Kalt 1981: 187. These are discussed below.

57. Tetreault 1986: 18.

58. Assistance for low-income households was passed at the same time as the Windfall Profits Tax, but the tax income was not specifically earmarked.

59. On the other hand, insofar as the nature of the regulations was responsible for the severity of the shortages experienced in 1973–74 and, especially, 1979–80, these regulations benefited those with a stake in other forms of energy to the extent that consumers subsequently turned away from oil.

60. As, of course, there were losses associated with private and public regulation of energy markets before the crisis. I will return to this point in Chapter 11.

61. These observations highlight the problem of judging economic efficiency without reference to the possible "external" benefits as well as costs.

62. Kalt 1981: 289.

63. MacAvoy 1983: 67.

64. *Ibid.*: 66.

65. Kalt 1981: 234.

CHAPTER 9

1. These factors coupled with the technical complexity of energy affairs help to explain why so little work has been done in this field by political scientists. For some of the best work, see Davis 1982, Rosenbaum 1981, and Chubb 1983.

2. Some energy interests and their representatives found themselves caught in the middle. An example is the United Mine Workers and representatives of coal-producing areas. Aware that increases in the price of natural gas and petroleum products would hurt their constituents, they for a while struck a compromise, allying with consumers on price control in return for support for forced conversion to coal.

3. Republican and Democratic presidents differed on the relative impor-

tance of efficiency and equity in the design of alternative programs. The degree of anxiety about supply interruption decreased as the last "shock" faded into memory, whereas the degree of anxiety about equity and economic impacts increased with the proximity of elections. But the point remains: presidents and their advisers saw it as their responsibility to address the broad problem of energy vulnerability by proposing a coherent program that took into account effects on the society as a whole.

4. All presidents agreed on this point; they differed on the importance of capturing the resulting rents and returning them to consumers.

5. There have been surprisingly few detailed, empirical studies of energy voting patterns in the Congress. Two that are of particular interest are those of Mitchell (1979) and Sanders (1981). Mitchell concluded that ideology, rather than constituent interests, dominated voting. Sanders, however, in a much more contextual analysis of positions taken on gas issues, was able to discern a complex variety of incentives, in which constituent interests continued to dominate. Kalt (1981), in his analysis of Senate voting patterns on petroleum regulation, concluded also that self-interest was a clear primary motivation, with ideology secondary but important. The voting-analysis approach to explanation has several problems. One is that there was so much confusion that many voters found it difficult to discern what their constituent interest really was. Another is that many states had combined concerns. For example, coal-producing states were also heavy consumers of interstate natural gas. Finally, there was the problem of trade-offs and second-best positions. Most key energy bills were composites, with elements that representatives and senators both favored and opposed. Under these circumstances, there were many opportunities to trade votes, and many instances in which second-best solutions—e.g. windfall profits as a means to deregulation—were chosen.

6. The inability to act on petroleum price regulation, of course, meant that the entitlements program had to be continued, since price controls on domestic crude created the need for a distributive mechanism within the refining industry.

7. Once this had been accomplished, Congress found it possible to tax away some of the rents (WPT) and, when prices weakened owing to world oversupply, to take advantage of consumer expectations to increase the gasoline tax.

8. The term "spectators" is from Sanders 1981.

9. The great disappointment to oil interests, of course, was the failure to convince Ford not to sign the EPCA and thereby let deregulation proceed immediately.

10. The key "loss" in this bargain was the failure by oil interests to assure that the WPT would not apply to newly discovered oil. Small independents, of course, fared better, winning an exemption for their first 1,000 barrels.

11. Sanders 1981: chaps. 6–7.

12. Recent studies of the role of the energy regulatory bureaucracy in

promoting or opposing industry interests come to conflicting conclusions. De Marchi, in his chapter in Goodwin 1981, feels that the bureaucracy acquired an interest in the continuation of regulation, and he blames the FEA for giving poor advice to President Ford regarding the signing of the EPCA. The gist of his analysis, based on an examination (from an economist's perspective) of the administrative history involved, is that the regulatory bureaucrats promoted a continuation of price regulation. The political scientist John Chubb, on the other hand, after collecting evidence concerning the degree to which regulators interacted with industry representatives (compared to consumers), concluded that the energy regulators opposed the regulations that they had to administer and can be classified as "captives" of the industry. See Chubb 1983: 161. Nuclear energy received its own, separate, Nuclear Regulatory Commission, charged with regulation (but not promotion) of that energy form.

13. On the tendency of Congress to disaggregate policymaking power when handling major, "crosscutting" events such as the energy crisis, and on the impact of this disaggregation on "subgovernments" such as the energy regimes, see Jones and Strahan 1985.

14. For details on these changes, see Pelham 1981: chap. 7; and Chubb 1983: 73.

15. Put differently, neither the Senate Energy Committee nor the House Commerce Committee was as likely to become a partner in behind-the-scenes decisionmaking with interests representing primarily the producers of single energy resources. On the emergence of a more integrated perspective, see Chubb 1983: 73.

16. Chubb 1983: 77.

17. For information on the early roles of some of these groups, including the Nader Organization, the Sierra Club, and the Consumer Federation of America, see McFarland 1976.

18. According to Chubb (1983: 77): "The petroleum and natural gas industries added three groups . . . and the Washington staffs of Chevron, Gulf, Shell, and Sun oil companies increased two- to threefold."

19. The defeat of Al Ulman in Oregon and Robert Eckhardt in Texas are two of the best-known cases. For more on the political role of oil and gas interests in the 1970's, see Engler 1977; Sherrill 1983; Chapman 1983: chap. 15; and Pelham 1981.

20. As Duane Chapman notes, not only were executives of four companies implicated in illegal cash contributions to the campaign committee that financed Watergate, but at least eight major companies had executives who were convicted, resigned, or signed consent agreements relating to illegal political activities during the 1970's. Chapman 1983: 328–29.

21. Greenberger et al. 1983 reviews a number of the most influential of these studies.

22. See Heclo 1978.

23. For example, the DOE decided in 1985 to create a Coal Council to serve the same purpose as the National Petroleum Council.

24. Chubb 1983: 43.

25. The distinction among "material," "solidary," and "purposive" benefits is found in Clark and Wilson 1961.

26. Note that this trend does not seem to have afflicted the community of environmentalists, possibly because the Reagan Administration, with its attacks on environmental regulation, created new incentives for mobilization. Because of their association with environmental issues, a number of energy problems—for example, those involved in matters such as the greenhouse effect or acid rain—have thus continued to receive attention.

27. Lovins 1977.

28. In another essay (Tugwell 1980) I have addressed these issues more directly. In brief, it seems clear that the adoption of renewable energy technologies will almost certainly require more rather than less regulation and political control of behavior.

29. The ugliest episode in this struggle was the murder of reform leader Joseph Yablonski and his family by union thugs sent by UMW head W. A. "Tony" Boyle in 1969. Boyle was eventually convicted and jailed.

30. For an analysis of these issues, see Rosenbaum 1981: chap. 4.

31. Gimlin ed. 1982: 187.

32. Pelham 1981: 66.

33. United States [24], 1983: 227.

34. As Chapman (1983: 195) put it: "Unlike the oil and gas industries, the coal industry cannot be considered to be independent. All the major petroleum companies have had oil and gas as their major economic activities. In contrast, most leading coal companies are subsidiaries or affiliates of oil, utility, or steel companies."

35. This change was accompanied by a marked reduction in the role played by various industry advisory bodies. Direct collaboration with industry representatives was now too risky politically. Goodwin 1981: 513–15.

36. The Reagan Administration abandoned two major inquiries into the conduct of the companies, one by the Justice Department against four companies operating in Saudi Arabia and another by the FTC that alleged "collusive action" by eight major firms. See the *New York Times*, Dec. 8, 1983.

37. According to the *New York Times*, Oct. 3, 1983: "By 1981, after years of investigation and charges by the Justice Department, hundreds of oil companies had agreed to out-of-court settlements and paid penalties totaling more than $3 billion for violations of the price controls."

38. *Washington Post*, July 2, 1985.

39. For a discussion of the significance of these changes, see Neff in Deese and Nye eds. 1981, and, more recently, Morse 1986.

40. Gimlin ed. 1982: 15; Chapman 1983: 213.

41. Chapman 1983: 309.

42. Interestingly enough, the new importance of Alaskan reserves and Sohio's extensive holdings there led to a situation in which the British Government controlled the largest single portion of domestic American reserves. This is because Sohio held a controlling interest in BP, which in turn

was controlled by the British Government through its holding of 39 percent of BP. See Chapman 1983: 99, 113. The purchase of Getty by Texaco was, at the time of writing, the subject of a suit by Penzoil. The acquisition by BP of the remaining shares of Sohio, and the sale by the British Government of its interest in BP to private interests, had been announced but not yet consummated.

43. Chapman (1983: 125), referring to concentration levels in U.S. crude oil production, notes: "The majors controlled 56 percent in 1955, and this has risen regularly in the succeeding 26 years to 79 percent in 1981. This increase will inevitably continue."

44. Reviewing basic changes in the petroleum industry, Duane Chapman (1983: 111) notes that, when changes of name and mergers are accounted for, "The basic structure is unchanged. The seven largest sellers of petroleum in 1981 were also the largest seven gasoline marketers in 1974, 1954, 1935, and 1926."

45. The price *decreases* in the years after 1983, I should add, took their toll of smaller, weaker companies—the ones most vulnerable to competitive market conditions.

46. The nuclear industry, especially, has tended to blame regulatory obstacles for the slowdown in plant construction, but evidence assembled by the Congressional Office of Technology Assessment and others reveals that this was not the primary problem. Rather, management failures, engineering problems, delays in equipment delivery, and deliberate slowdowns due to demand reductions and financial constraints were the main culprits. United States [11]: 157.

47. No final estimate of these costs is currently available, but it will surely exceed $4–5 billion. The costs of electricity purchases to replace lost capacity alone are nearing $1 billion. This does not include cleanup costs. It is significant that the Price-Anderson liability protection did not help, since the damage was within the plant. The 1986 Chernobyl disaster, of course, had an even greater effect on public attitudes.

48. United States [24], 1983: 124.

49. For a forceful characterization of this crisis as "the greatest collapse of any enterprise in industrial history," see Lovins and Lovins 1982b: 153–66. For comments on the more recent steps to recovery, see United States [10] and [4].

50. Although the structural complexity of the utility industry makes aggregate data difficult to collect, one careful study confirms that "public advocates" were able to become active participants in public utility commission proceedings in nearly three-fourths of the states. See Gormley 1983: 64.

51. On this point see Berry 1979 and Gormley 1979.

52. Mason Willrich, Vice President of Pacific Gas and Electric Company, speaking before the League of California Cities, Feb. 2, 1983.

53. United States [23], 1985: 184.

54. Two that have led the way in this are Pacific Gas and Electric, head-

quartered in San Francisco, and Southern California Edison Company of Los Angeles.

55. Environmental and safety regulations, it now seems clear, had a political life of their own. Many of the key laws, such as the Clean Air and Clean Water Acts, the National Environmental Policy Act, and the Surface Mining Control and Reclamation Act, were in place before the embargo, and they proved surprisingly resilient in the face of repeated attacks by critics who charged they were key obstacles to expanded domestic energy production, especially from coal and nuclear power. The political decision by Congress, in effect, was to continue to pay a price for environmental safeguards and worker safety, to deny energy industries a privileged place with respect to this price, and to forgo any increased domestic production that might have resulted. Efforts by officials of the first Reagan Administration to reverse this commitment by means of administrative neglect were largely unsuccessful.

56. As noted earlier, the oil market management arrangements at the state level had also lapsed into disuse, although they remained, for the most part, on the books. Local authorities, of course, continued to regulate gas and electricity.

CHAPTER 10

1. Yanarella and Yanarella 1982 contains a helpful bibliography. See also Viola et al. eds. 1983.

2. Examples of these are Greenberger et al. 1983, Pelham 1981, and Goodwin 1981.

3. In keeping with the growing importance of technical sophistication in political advocacy, most groups with a stake in energy decisions found it necessary to fund and publish research results supporting their positions.

4. As Walter Mead (1978:17) put it: "There is widespread agreement among academic economists that government interference is the primary cause of the energy crisis." Note that in blaming the government, Mead includes the regulatory interventions and subsidies that distorted the market before OPEC came along.

5. For the most recent of these studies, see Glasner 1985.

6. An exception is the thoughtful essay by Harvey Brooks in Zinberg ed. 1983. See also Davis 1982, Rosenbaum 1981, and Lindberg ed. 1977.

7. This estimate is based on the work of Kalt (1981) and others. See Chapter 8.

8. The sacrifices associated with national security or the attainment of other great national economic objectives are somewhat paradoxical in their political consequences. If they are based on broad national consensus about the nature of the threat and the appropriateness of the response, they can actually serve to unify society and increase the legitimacy of the government; but if they are not, they can be divisive and destructive to the body politic, especially if there is a widespread perception that the burden is not fairly distributed. The energy problem, clearly, was an example of the latter.

This suggests still another benefit associated with the way in which the American system handled it: the avoidance of unnecessary destabilizing domestic political conflict. Like the avoidance of unnecessary economic sacrifice in behalf of energy independence, it is both difficult to measure and easy to ignore in favor of technical criticisms of the conduct of policy.

9. For a different interpretation, to the effect that a stable and effective national energy policy system had emerged, see Kash and Rycroft 1984.

10. For discussions of this theme, see Lindblom 1965 and Dahl 1982.

11. It is perhaps too easy to conclude that nothing else could have been done. Surely a careful scrutiny of the administrative history would turn up a key "moment of decision" that might have led to a different outcome. But as we have seen, there was a kind of inexorable quality to the events after 1973 by which the temporary expedients embodied in the EPAA became the "permanent" solution to the crisis.

12. Once price controls became "permanent" and entitlements were in place, the arrangements they embodied became the yardsticks against which new proposals were measured by the stakeholders involved. And in each case important groups made it clear that new proposals did not contain assurances enough to justify breaking the stalemate. Pressures on Ford to sign the EPCA and the rejection of Carter's *Plan* were an outgrowth of this process. And the "formula" that governed petroleum in turn affected the other energy regimes.

13. As befits the breadth of the subject matter, the standards used here to evaluate the performance of the political economy are several. They include a concern for the ways in which actions affect: (a) conflict management, especially the avoidance of political violence associated with resource redistribution; (b) national security, especially the reduction of unwanted costs imposed by unilateral decisions taken by other governments; (c) economic efficiency; (d) equity in the distribution of costs and benefits; (e) the legitimacy of governing institutions; and (f) the capacity of our country to handle future problems. Needless to say, the assessment in the following pages is subjective: it represents my own best judgments about costs and benefits based on a careful weighing of the evidence and an estimation of what might have been accomplished under plausible, but politically and institutionally different, circumstances.

14. Among the most insightful of these observers is Charles Lindblom (1977).

15. Rowberg 1985: 17.

16. The prospect of the collapse of the OPEC monopoly prices caused serious consternation in Western financial circles. High prices, to a surprising degree, had become a premise of business. Oil producers had borrowed on expected earnings, thus linking the welfare of many large banks to high petroleum prices, and the price erosion raised fears of an international banking crisis. In addition, a significant stream of petroleum exploration and production decisions, in places like the North Sea and Alaska, had been made on the assumption of higher prices.

17. For a convincing analysis of the implications of this instability, see Morse 1986.

18. *New York Times*, Apr. 3, 1986: 1.

19. *The Energy Daily*, Mar. 10, 1986: 1.

20. *Ibid.*, May 9, 1986: 1.

21. Major forecasters differ on the rates of increase in imports but concur on the general trend. One of the best studies of the problem warns that imports are likely once again to reach historic levels—perhaps approaching 10 mmb/d—presenting serious dangers of vulnerability. See Rowberg 1985: 16. Confirming the seriousness of this problem, the Interior Department in 1985 quietly revised downward its estimates of recoverable oil and gas in U.S. offshore areas. Oil estimates were revised downward by 55 percent and gas by 44 percent.

22. As noted in Rowberg 1985: 17.

23. For examples of recent criticism of the Reagan position, see Hughes 1986 and Morse 1986. For a discussion of this problem, see Deese and Nye eds. 1981.

24. See United States [12]. In that study, after computer simulation of a long-term supply interruption assuming an active program of defensive technical development, the OTA reported that "The investment needed to replace 3 mmb/d of oil and, if necessary, to increase the efficiency of natural gas use would be about $150 billion to $200 billion over a 5-year period, or about $30 billion to $40 billion per year, on average (not including the cost of new cars, which is an ongoing activity). This level of investment is about 7 to 9 percent of recent annual investments in producer durables and residential and nonresidential structures. By comparison, [the] OTA estimates that crude oil prices would rise by $23 to $40 per barrel (above a pre-disruption level of $30 per barrel), increasing domestic oil and natural gas liquids production revenues by $84 billion to $146 billion per year (with domestic production at 10 mmb/d). Consequently, even in the extreme case, where Federal subsidies would pay a large part of these investment costs (and perhaps new cars received subsidies of $1,000 each, on average, or $6 billion to $10 billion per year), these costs could probably be financed through a windfall profits tax, if it were increased to collect 50 to 70 percent of the increased domestic oil production profits." United States [12]: 29.

25. The Reagan Administration also insisted that it would not consider economywide monetary and fiscal policies, either. For comments on the benefits and costs of such policies, see United States [5].

26. The coal market emerged from the crisis epoch with improved prospects for demand growth despite the breakdown of the union-management coalition that stabilized the market in that industry for nearly two decades prior to 1973. The demise of nuclear power and the prohibition (in the 1978 Fuel Use Act) of the use of oil or natural gas in new, large-scale facilities meant that coal would remain dominant in its principal market. Fluctuations in the price of its substitutes were thus less likely to affect it. The fact that an increasing percentage of coal was produced by utilities (and some

steel companies) in "captive" mines meant that more and more production was not being sold on the market in the conventional sense anyway. On the other hand, assurance of domination of a sector of end-use was not the same as control of supply or stabilized prices, and with continuing excess capacity the possibility of mounting price competition among producers remained very real. Coal also remained vulnerable to the same problems that afflicted the utilities industry: fluctuations in economic growth, in overall energy prices, and in interest rates could all be expected to influence demand patterns. In addition, the severe obstacles facing the construction of any new large-scale facilities, and the associated turn to dispersed, small-scale sources and co-generation, could be expected to constrain the expansion of coal demand as well. Finally, the industry remained vulnerable to union troubles, especially if competition for markets should bring harsher price competition among producers.

27. Electricity, of course, as a secondary energy form, enjoyed a stability derived from that of the fuels upon which utilities depended.

28. No one who is familiar with the behavior of large, integrated oligopolies in the U.S. economy really believes that the more integrated energy companies that emerged from the turmoil of the 1970's will suffer significant market instability without seeking, and winning, stabilizing remedies. The larger and more "essential" the industry, the greater its power to assure that this occurs. Early in 1985, a story in the *Washington Post* revealed that "The oil industry, which for years fought against government controls on its operations, has begun quietly lobbying for government sanctions on imports of refined petroleum products to the United States" (Feb. 21). In August a group of 43 senators announced in a letter to the Secretary of Commerce that they were requesting a government study of the impact on "national security" of imports of gasoline. To those familiar with the history of oil regulation, this had a very familiar ring.

29. Note that I refer here to market regulation, not to all forms of regulation. Market regulation is often analyzed along with regulation to assure safety or prevent degradation of the environment, since they all involve efforts to interfere with private, profit-seeking behavior in behalf of common objectives. Market regulation is the broad effort to control supply or price, and thereby influence the stability and distributional impact of the operation of an entire market. The distinction is significant, since, theoretically at least, health, safety, and environmental regulation can be conducted in a manner that does not impede the clearing action of the marketplace or the entry and departure of participants therein.

30. Peltzman 1976.

31. By "successful" I refer to control of competition, not the distribution of costs and benefits involved. As noted below, it is likely that the economic costs of "successful" proprietary regulation were as high as, or higher than, those associated with later, compensatory regulation.

32. It is this more than anything else, it would appear, that explains the tendency of academic economists to pay far less attention to the inefficien-

cies associated with proprietary supply regulation. Price regulation involves the government in setting price, and if consumers are successful in keeping this low, the government will have to intervene to manage the resulting shortage. The economic costs of the two systems may be equal, or supply prorationing may be the costlier of the two, but the extent of government involvement in market allocation will be greater.

33. For an analysis of this process in the electric utility industry, see Berry 1979.

34. Wilson ed. 1980 and Anderson 1981.

35. As this paragraph is written, two campaigns have just been launched by energy lobbies in Washington: the refinery industry has begun to pressure the government to restrict the entry to the United States of petroleum products refined abroad, and the alcohol fuels industry, supported by farm interests, has mounted an effort to block the entry of alcohol from Brazil and other sugar-producing countries.

CHAPTER 11

1. This discussion draws on material first presented in Tugwell 1980: 103–18.

2. Lowi 1979: chap. 20. The importance of security as a motivation in modern economic life and of compensation as a political obligation is stressed in Thurow 1980.

3. For a recent example in the energy field, see Glasner 1985.

4. On the concept of a "facilitative" state orientation toward the private economy, see Miller 1968: 87; and Means 1964: 88.

5. See Galbraith 1973, Heilbroner 1976, Commoner 1980, Engler 1966 and 1977.

6. Engler 1977: 214.

7. Chapman 1983 makes this point several times. This is likely to change as a result of the decision by the British Government to sell its ownership of BP.

8. Berle and Means 1932; see also Berle 1959 and Burnham 1942.

9. This insight I owe to Peter Drucker. The irony, of course, is that this represents an indirect accomplishment of the Marxist objective of worker ownership of the means of production.

10. On the contrast between corporatist and other forms of interest representation, see Schmitter 1974 and Schmitter and Lehmbruch eds. 1982.

11. See Hall 1986, Wilson 1985, and Katzenstein 1985 for more on the attributes of corporatist systems.

12. Katzenstein 1983 and Schmitter 1981 make this argument most persuasively.

13. Katzenstein 1985: 32.

14. Johnson 1982; Katzenstein 1985: 36. Still another variant, closer to the developmental state model, is the configuration called "state capitalism," which has been identified with Brazil and several of the other more industrialized developing countries.

15. Thurow 1980: 192. See also Lodge 1975. A number of American economists in the 1920's and 1930's advocated a form of corporatist arrangement in the United States. They included, among others, John R. Commons, Thorstein Veblen, and Rexford G. Tugwell, all associated with what came to be known as the "institutionalist" school of economics.

16. Peter Hall, in his study of state intervention patterns in Britain and France, argues convincingly that even "liberal" systems such as that of Great Britain contain significant elements of corporatism. He concludes that, to be useful, the analysis of corporatism must be based on a more complex range of attributes or yardsticks against which systems of political economy can be measured. See Hall 1986: 269–70.

17. Katzenstein 1983, 1984, 1985.

18. Johnson 1982: 12.

19. See Tussing 1985 for a rosy picture of the "old" days by an admirer of the accomplishments of proprietary regulation.

20. Katzenstein 1985: 209.

21. For a trenchant criticism from the right of industrial policy advocates and corporatist decisionmaking, see Melvyn Krauss, "'Europeanizing' the U.S. Economy: The Enduring Appeal of the Corporatist State," in Johnson ed. 1984.

22. This problem will be especially severe if private interests tend to dominate decisionmaking, or are perceived to do so, and if their goal is to circumvent the rigors of market competition. This was the case with America's experiment with formal corporatism in energy regimes during the New Deal, discussed in Part One, when it was widely charged that the sectoral boards which made up the decisionmaking bodies of the NRA had been "captured" by industry to the detriment of the consuming public. The other American historical episode of corporatist decisionmaking, the industry boards set up to handle the interests of separate industries during the two World Wars, were viewed as temporary.

23. The most persistent critic of the military political economy is Seymour Melman. See Melman 1974.

24. The most articulate general criticism of corporatist tendencies in the United States is found in Gross 1980.

25. An interesting parallel in a non-energy sector is the development of the Concorde supersonic airplane, known in the United States as the SST. A bitter political struggle led to an American decision to abandon subsidy of this craft, chiefly on the grounds that it was not going to be economical, and if it were, private companies would be willing to invest in it. France and Great Britain chose a massive public subsidy, ignoring domestic political opposition. The plane turned out to be too expensive (as well as noisy, for many locations), and production was halted.

26. Theodore Lowi has suggested the term "neo–laissez faire" for an arrangement with some similarities to the one suggested here. See Lowi 1979: 292.

27. Lindblom 1977: chap. 19.

28. *Ibid.*

29. This said, I should add that a lot of innovation does come from the smaller firms, especially if the technology involved does not demand large doses of capital and an enormous managerial superstructure.

30. Note that militant unions, themselves in part a product of the harsh competitive market, were one of the causes of the difficulty in introducing technical improvements.

31. The "institutionalists" in the 1930's and 1940's were convinced that a growing predominance of large, integrated firms is the trend of history, and this belief continues to inform many diagnoses of the problems of the modern political economy. See Galbraith 1973 for an example.

32. See Lindblom 1977; Galbraith 1973; Dahl 1982; Engler 1961, 1977; and Blair 1976.

33. See Lovins and Lovins 1982b. There has been a great deal of interest recently in the possibility of electric utility deregulation. The matter, however, is a complex one, as Brownell 1984 points out.

34. Lovins and Lovins 1982a addresses this problem.

35. Choosing the best means of managing the inevitable conflict in compensatory regulation is a critically important practical and analytical problem. Although the appropriate solution almost certainly depends on the character of the market and the regulated district, broad guidelines would be of great help. For example, are elected commissions more or less desirable than appointed ones on these grounds?

36. This problem was described by Mans Lonnroth in his essay "Swedish Energy Policy: Technology in the Political Process," in Lindberg ed. 1977: 265.

37. United States [12].

38. This, of course, requires some important decisions about the value of such things as security and the promotion of alternative technologies, as well as some guesses about future costs, but stabilization of any set of market arrangements will require such choices—this is what the "planned" part of planned markets implies. During 1986 a debate raged in Washington about an import fee of some kind, characterized by its conservative opponents as a "user fee," but no legislation came of it.

39. Such an arrangement was proposed by S. Fred Singer in 1986 following a public call for stabilized prices by Vice President Bush. See "Bush Was Right—Stabilize Oil Prices," *New York Times*, Apr. 13, 1986, Section III, p. 2. The idea of a major import fee—as much as $10 per barrel—was also endorsed, largely on security grounds, by a group of energy analysts at Harvard's JFK School of Government. See *Los Angeles Times*, Nov. 23, 1986, for a lengthy debate on the subject. Among the complications that this policy would encounter is the matter of its compatibility with American obligations under GATT. Since the world petroleum market is already seriously encumbered with political interventions of many kinds, this complication could be overcome.

40. Morse 1986.

41. It would also create domestic distributional problems since some consumers (e.g. users of home heating oil) would be hurt and some businesses would lose international competitiveness at times of low prices. These secondary effects might create pressure to introduce cumbersome regulatory interventions that could easily make the entire scheme counterproductive. These negative consequences would have to be weighed carefully against the possible gains of such a scheme. It is clear that the best time to impose such a program is when prices are at or close to the target level.

42. A recent version is found in Adelman and Davidson 1979.

43. My estimate is that the best way to do this is to give the money to the Treasury, but this might not be politically popular. Note that this does not respond to the problem of windfall gains in other energy sectors, such as natural gas. Still more difficult are problems that arise not from crises, but from more subtle foreign technical or political interference with markets. If, for example, Saudi Arabia subsidizes its burgeoning refining and petrochemical industries directly by agreeing to lose money on them to employ its workers, or indirectly by undercharging for feedstocks of natural gas and crude oil, and if the import of these subsidized products begins to damage American refiners, should the federal government intervene? As the many ongoing conflicts over trade policy reveal, the trade-offs are difficult, the more so because "proving" the existence of subsidies of this kind is so difficult. There is little question, however, that some measure of protection from international actions whose domestic consequences do not promote either efficiency or sensible adjustments at home must be granted. The kinds of import management arrangements described here would provide a means of accomplishing this.

44. As editorialist Charles Krauthammer put it, speaking of capitalism more generally: "It is the first system in human history to lift the mass of men out of economic misery. But to keep the engine going, it randomly visits misery on selected groups. Instead of searching for villains, it might be more humane for the rest of society, which benefits from that mighty engine, to devote some of its vast surplus to cushioning the fall of its victims." *Washington Post*, Mar. 22, 1985.

45. Lowi 1979: 279–81.

46. For the most forthright and articulate statement of this approach, see Thurow 1980.

47. This inadequacy has been the subject of a growing body of diagnostic studies, premier among them, of course, being Lowi 1979.

48. Blair 1976: 394.

49. The closest to such decisive action that occurred during the 1970's, as noted in Chapter 9, was the serious consideration of divestiture in the Senate.

50. In his revised edition of *The End of Liberalism*, Theodore Lowi presents a brief proposal for what he calls "neo-liberalism," a return to a more limited government accomplished chiefly by a reduction in the degree to

which the Congress grants discretionary authority to regulatory and administrative agencies. As the following paragraphs make clear, my view is that planned markets require a much more assertive government role as well as a much more fundamental transformation of constitutional and political processes.

51. The most famous piece on this, of course is Madison's essay in the *Federalist Papers*, Number 10.

52. These American attitudes contrast sharply with those obtaining in many other developed countries, a fact that many admirers of Euro-Japanese practice often seem to ignore. As Andrew Schonfield, one of the most perceptive observers of trends in advanced industrial economies has noted (1965: 298): ". . . there is something more than a semantic eccentricity dividing the common ideology of the United States from that of the rest of the world. Among the Americans there is a general commitment to the view, shared by both political parties, of the natural predominance of private enterprise in the economic sphere and of the subordinate role of public initiative in any situation other than a manifest national emergency. The West Europeans, who have no such assumptions . . . have in consequence been spared the awful doctrinal wrestling in which Americans tend to engage whenever any bit of the economic field has to be divided afresh between the public and the private sectors."

53. On this theme, see Lowi 1979.

54. These ideas about government and the economy have frequently been bundled together in American thinking in what is often called the "Jeffersonian" tradition, a tradition originating in the conflict between Alexander Hamilton and Thomas Jefferson over the degree to which government-promoted industrial and commercial development should be allowed to flourish at the expense of a more decentralized, pastoral vision of the country's future. As noted in Chapter 9, in the conflicts over energy policy that took shape in the late 1970's and early 1980's, promoters of dispersed, small-scale renewable energy found in the "neo-Jeffersonian" vision a highly attractive alternative to the values they saw being promoted in industrial society. There are contradictions here, of course, principally the result of holding together elements of libertarian capitalism and a version of what might be called ecological communalism, but this vision helped justify an attack on big government, centralization, nuclear energy, subsidies, and regulation. Though uncomfortable to private-sector managers inclined toward corporatist relations with the government, these ideas resonated well with the two key elements of (1) distrust of government, especially strong federal government, and (2) a belief in the liberating efficiency of markets freed of any government involvement.

55. Samuel P. Huntington's book *American Politics: The Promise of Disharmony* addresses the conflict between ideals and reality in American politics and helps clarify the persistence of this tension.

56. Mendelson 1960: 127.

57. Mancur Olson comes to a similar conclusion (1982: 177–78): "As I read it, the ark and covenant of the laissez faire ideology is that the government that governs least governs best; markets will solve the problem if the government only leaves them alone. There is in the most popular presentations of this ideology a monodiabolism, and the government is the devil. If this devil is kept in chains, there is an almost utopian lack of concern about other problems. If the less optimistic theory in this book is right, there often will *not* be competitive markets even if the government does not intervene. . . . There will be cartelization of many markets even if the government does not help. Eliminating certain types of government intervention and freeing trade and factor mobility will weaken cartels but will not eliminate many of them. Moreover, the absence of government intervention (even if it were invariably desirable) may not be possible anyway, because of the lobbying of special-interest groups, unless we fly to the still greater evil of continuous instability."

58. We saw clearly the consequences of this kind of effort in the coal industry under the Guffey Act.

59. In the U.S. context, this would almost certainly require an entirely new set of institutions accountable in new ways to both the executive and the legislature. In an incremental way, this has already been gradually occurring, most notably in the new role of the Office of Management and Budget since the Nixon Presidency and in the provisions of the Gramm-Rudman-Hollings legislation. National planning is by necessity a quasi-legislative activity, and must be both independent enough to allow coherent plans to emerge and politically accountable enough to allow political control of their directions.

60. A particularly interesting historical review of this problem is contained in Huntington 1968: chap. 3.

61. See Tugwell 1974.

62. Lowi 1979; Olson 1982; see also Gross 1980.

Bibliography

Abrams, Robert. 1979. *Foundations of Political Analysis: An Introduction to the Theory of Collective Choice.* New York: Columbia Univ. Press.

Adams, Walter, ed. 1961. *The Structure of American Industry.* 3d ed. New York: Macmillan.

———. 1971. *The Structure of American Industry.* 4th ed. New York: Macmillan.

———. 1977. *The Structure of American Industry.* 5th ed. New York: Macmillan.

Adams, Walter, and Horace Gray. 1955. *Monopoly in America: The Government as Promoter.* New York: Macmillan.

Adelman, M. A. 1962. *The Supply and Price of Natural Gas.* Special Supplement to the *Journal of Business Economics.* London, Eng.: Blackwell.

———. 1972. *The World Petroleum Market.* Baltimore: Johns Hopkins Univ. Press.

Adelman, M. A., and Paul Davidson. 1979. "Plans for Oil Import Purchasing," *Challenge,* July/Aug.

Alm, Alvin, and Robert Weiner, eds. 1983. *Oil Shock: Policy Response and Implementation.* Cambridge, Mass.: Ballinger.

Anderson, Douglas. 1981. *Regulatory Politics and Electric Utilities: A Case Study in Political Economy.* Boston: Auburn House.

Aronson, Jonathan D., and Peter F. Cowhey, eds. 1983. *Profit and the Pursuit of Energy: Markets and Regulation.* Boulder, Colo.: Westview.

Bain, Joe S. 1968. *Industrial Organization.* 2d ed. New York: Wiley.

Baratz, M. 1955. *The Union and the Coal Industry.* New Haven, Conn.: Yale Univ. Press.

Bardach, Eugene, and Robert Kagan, eds. 1982. *Social Regulation: Strategies for Reform.* San Francisco: Institute for Contemporary Studies.

Barkenbus, Jack N. 1982. "Federal Energy Policy Paradigms and State Energy Roles," *Public Administration Review,* Sept./Oct.

Battelle Memorial Institute. 1978. *An Analysis of Federal Incentives Used to Stimulate Energy Production.* Richland, Wash.: Pacific Northwest Laboratory.

Bell, Daniel. 1976. *The Cultural Contradictions of Capitalism.* New York: Basic.

Bellush, Bernard. 1975. *The Failure of the NRA*. New York: Norton.

Benjamin, Roger. 1980. *The Limits of Politics: Collective Goods and Political Change in Post-Industrial Societies*. Chicago: Univ. of Chicago Press.

Berle, Adolf. 1959. *Power Without Property: A New Development in American Political Economy*. New York: Harcourt, Brace and World.

Berle, Adolf, and G. C. Means. 1932. *The Modern Corporation and Private Property*. New York: Macmillan.

Berry, Brian. 1977. "Justice Between Generations," in P. M. S. Hacker and J. Raz, eds., *Law, Morality and Society: Essays in Honour of H. L. A. Hart*. Oxford: Clarendon Press.

Berry, Jeffrey. 1977. *Lobbying for the People*. Princeton, N.J.: Princeton Univ. Press.

Berry, William D. 1979. "Utility Regulation in the States: The Policy Effects of Professionalism and Salience to the Consumer," *American Journal of Political Science*, May.

Binder, Leonard, ed. 1971. *Crises and Sequences of Political Development*. Princeton, N.J.: Princeton Univ. Press.

Blair, John. 1976. *The Control of Oil*. New York: Random House.

Bohi, Douglas, and Milton Russell. 1978. *Limiting Oil Imports*. Baltimore: Johns Hopkins Univ. Press.

Brand, Donald R. 1983. "Corporatism, the NRA, and the Oil Industry," *Political Science Quarterly*, Spring.

Brown, Keith, ed. 1972. *Regulation of the Natural Gas Producing Industry*. Baltimore: Johns Hopkins Univ. Press.

Brownell, William A. 1984. "Electric Utility Deregulation: Analyzing Prospects for Competitive Generation," *Annual Review of Energy*. Palo Alto, Calif.: Annual Reviews.

Bupp, Irvin C., and Jean-Claude Derian. 1978. *Light Water: How the Nuclear Dream Dissolved*. New York: Basic.

Burnham, James. 1942. *The Managerial Revolution*. New York: Putnam.

Carman, Harry J., Harold C. Syrett, and Bernard W. Wishy. 1961. *A History of the American People*. Vol. 2. New York: Knopf.

Carter, Jimmy. 1982. *Keeping Faith: Memoirs of a President*. New York: Bantam.

Chapman, Duane. 1983. *Energy Resources and Energy Corporations*. Ithaca, N.Y.: Cornell Univ. Press.

Chester, Edward. 1983. *United States Oil Policy and Diplomacy*. Westport, Conn.: Greenwood.

Chubb, John E. 1983. *Interest Groups and the Bureaucracy: The Politics of Energy*. Stanford, Calif.: Stanford Univ. Press.

Cigler, Allan J., and Burdett A. Loomis, eds. 1983. *Interest Group Politics*. Washington, D.C.: Congressional Quarterly Press.

Clark, Peter, and James Q. Wilson. 1961. "Incentive Systems: A Theory of Organizations," *Administrative Science Quarterly*, Sept.

Commoner, Barry. 1979. *The Politics of Energy*. New York: Knopf.

Cook, James. 1985. "Nuclear Follies," *Forbes*, Feb. 11.

Cottrell, Fred. 1955. *Energy and Society*. New York: McGraw-Hill.

Curry, R. L., and L. L. Wade. 1968. *A Theory of Political Exchange: Economic Reasoning in Political Analysis*. Englewood Cliffs, N.J.: Prentice-Hall.

Dahl, Robert A. 1982. *Dilemmas of Pluralist Democracy: Autonomy Versus Control*. New Haven, Conn.: Yale Univ. Press.

Darmstadter, Joel, et al. 1983. *Energy, Today and Tomorrow: Living With Uncertainty*. Englewood Cliffs, N.J.: Prentice-Hall.

Davis, David H. 1978. *Energy Politics*. 2d ed. New York: St. Martins.

———. 1982. *Energy Politics*. 3d ed. New York: St. Martins.

DeChazeau, Melvin, and Alfred E. Kahn. 1959. *Integration and Competition in the Petroleum Industry*. New Haven, Conn.: Yale Univ. Press.

Deese, David, and Joseph Nye, eds. 1981. *Energy and Security*. Cambridge, Mass.: Ballinger.

Deudney, Daniel, and Christopher Flavin. 1983. *Renewable Energy: The Power to Choose*. New York: Norton.

DeYoung, Tim, and T. Michael Lechner. 1983. "Privately-Owned Public Utilities: A New Political Economy." Paper presented at the Western Political Science Association annual meeting, Seattle, Mar. 25.

Dirlam, Joel. 1958. "Natural Gas: Cost, Conservation and Pricing," *American Economic Review*, May.

Downs, Anthony. 1972. "Up and Down With Ecology: The Issue-Attention Cycle," *The Public Interest*, Summer.

Duchesneau, Thomas D. 1975. *Competition in the U.S. Energy Industry*. Cambridge, Mass.: Ballinger.

Edmunds, Jae, and John M. Reilly. 1985. *Global Energy: Assessing the Future*. New York: Oxford Univ. Press.

Elliott, John, and John Cownie. 1975. *Competing Philosophies in American Political Economics*. Pacific Palisades, Calif.: Goodyear.

Engler, Robert. 1961. *The Politics of Oil: A Study of Private Power and the Public Interest*. Chicago: Univ. of Chicago Press.

———. 1977. *The Brotherhood of Oil: Energy Policy and the Public Interest*. Chicago: Univ. of Chicago Press.

Fainsod, Merle, Lincoln Gordon, and Joseph C. Palamountain, Jr. 1959. *Government and the American Economy*. 3d ed. New York: Norton.

Field, G. L. 1938. *The Syndical and Corporative Institutions of Italian Fascism*. New York: Columbia Univ. Press.

Fisher, Waldo. 1948. *Collective Bargaining in the Bituminous Coal Industry*. Philadelphia: Univ. of Pennsylvania Press.

Fisher, Waldo, and Charles James. 1955. *Minimum Price Fixing in the Bituminous Coal Industry*. Princeton, N.J.: Princeton Univ. Press.

Frey, John, and Chandler Ide. 1946. *A History of the Petroleum Administration for War: 1941–5*. Washington, D.C.: Gov't Printing Office.

Frohlich, Norman, and Joe A. Oppenheimer. 1978. *Modern Political Economy*. Englewood Cliffs, N.J.: Prentice-Hall.

Funigiello, Philip J. 1973. *Toward a National Power Policy: The New Deal and the Electric Utility Industry.* Pittsburgh: Univ. of Pittsburgh Press.

Galbraith, John Kenneth. 1973. *Economics and the Public Purpose.* Boston: Houghton Mifflin.

Gallup, George H. 1978. *The Gallup Poll: Public Opinion 1972–77.* Wilmington, Del.: Scholarly Resources.

Georgescu-Roegen, Nicholas. 1972. "Economics and Entropy," *The Ecologist,* July.

Gimlin, Hoyt, ed. 1982. *Energy Issues: New Directions and Goals.* Washington, D.C.: Congressional Quarterly Press.

Glasner, David. 1985. *Politics, Prices and Petroleum: The Political Economy of Energy.* Cambridge, Mass.: Ballinger.

Goodwin, Craufurd. 1981. *Energy Policy in Perspective: Today's Problems, Yesterday's Solutions.* Washington, D.C.: Brookings.

Gormley, William T., Jr. 1979. "Consumer Representation Before State Public Utility Commissions." Paper prepared for delivery at the American Political Science Association annual meeting, Washington, D.C., Aug.

———. 1983. *The Politics of Public Utility Regulation.* Pittsburgh: Univ. of Pittsburgh Press.

Graham, Otis L., Jr. 1976. *Toward a Planned Society: From Roosevelt to Nixon.* New York: Oxford Univ. Press.

Greenberger, Martin, et al. 1983. *Caught Unawares: The Energy Decade in Retrospect.* Cambridge, Mass.: Ballinger.

Gross, Bertram. 1980. *Friendly Fascism: The New Face of Power in America.* New York: M. Evans.

Hall, Peter. 1986. *Governing the Economy: The Politics of State Intervention in Britain and France.* New York: Oxford Univ. Press.

Hall, Robert, and Robert Pindyck. 1977. "The Conflicting Goals of National Energy Policy," *The Public Interest,* Spring.

Hawley, Ellis. 1966. *The New Deal and the Problem of Monopoly.* Princeton, N.J.: Princeton Univ. Press.

Hayes, Michael. 1983. "Interest Groups: Pluralism or Mass Society?," in Allan J. Cigler and Burdett A. Loomis, eds., *Interest Group Politics.* Washington, D.C.: Congressional Quarterly Press.

Heclo, Hugh. 1978. "Issue Networks and the Executive Establishment," in Anthony King, ed., *The New American Political System.* Washington, D.C.: American Enterprise Institute.

Heilbroner, Robert L. 1976. *Business Civilization in Decline.* New York: Norton.

Hellman, Richard. 1972. *Government Competition in the Electric Utility Industry.* New York: Praeger.

Herendeen, Robert, and Jerry Tanaka. 1976. "Energy Cost of Living," *Energy,* June.

Himmelberg, Robert. 1976. *The Origins of the NRA.* New York: Fordham Univ. Press.

Hirsch, Fred. 1976. *The Social Limits to Growth*. Cambridge, Mass.: Harvard Univ. Press.

Hirst, Eric, et al. 1983. "Recent Changes in U.S. Energy Consumption: What Happened and Why," *Annual Review of Energy*. Palo Alto, Calif.: Annual Reviews.

Hoberg, George, Jr. 1980. "Electricity, Decentralization and Society: The Socio-Political Aspects of Dispersed Electric Generating Technologies" (working paper). Washington, D.C.: Office of Technology Assessment.

Hollander, Jack, and Harvey Brooks, eds. 1984. *Annual Review of Energy*. Palo Alto, Calif.: Annual Reviews.

Hughes, Barry B. 1986. "The First Two Oil Shocks: Policy Response and Effectiveness," *Policy Studies Review*, May.

Huitt, Ralph K. 1952. "Federal Regulation of the Uses of Natural Gas," *American Political Science Review*, June.

Huntington, Samuel P. 1968. *Political Order in Changing Societies*. New Haven, Conn.: Yale Univ. Press.

———. 1981. *American Politics: The Promise of Disharmony*. Cambridge, Mass.: Harvard Univ. Press.

Jacoby, Neil. 1974. *Multinational Oil: A Study in Industrial Dynamics*. New York: Macmillan.

Johnson, Chalmers. 1982. *MITI and the Japanese Miracle: The Growth of Industrial Policy, 1925–1975*. Stanford, Calif.: Stanford Univ. Press.

Johnson, Chalmers, ed. 1984. *The Industrial Policy Debate*. San Francisco, Calif.: ICS Press.

Johnson, James P. 1979. *The Politics of Soft Coal: The Bituminous Industry from World War I Through the New Deal*. Urbana: Univ. of Illinois Press.

Jones, Charles O., and Randall Strahan. 1985. "The Effect of Energy Politics on Congressional and Executive Organization in the 1970's," *Legislative Studies Quarterly*, May.

Kalt, Joseph P. 1981. *The Economics and Politics of Oil Price Regulation: Federal Policy in the Post-Embargo Era*. Cambridge, Mass.: MIT Press.

Kalter, Robert J., and William A. Vogeley. 1976. *Energy Supply and Government Policy*. Ithaca, N.Y.: Cornell Univ. Press.

Kash, Don E., and Robert W. Rycroft. 1984. *U.S. Energy Policy: Crisis and Complacency*. Norman, Okla.: Univ. of Oklahoma Press.

Katz, James E. 1984. *Congress and National Energy Policy*. New Brunswick, N.J.: Transaction Books.

Katzenstein, Peter. 1983. "The Small European States in the International Economy: Economic Dependence and Corporatist Politics," in John G. Ruggie, ed., *The Antinomies of Interdependence: National Welfare and the International Division of Labor*. New York: Columbia Univ. Press.

———. 1984. *Corporatism and Change*. Ithaca, N.Y.: Cornell Univ. Press.

———. 1985. *Small States in World Markets*. Ithaca, N.Y.: Cornell Univ. Press.

Kavass, Igor I. 1980. *Energy and Congress: An Annotated Bibliography of*

Congressional Hearings and Reports, 1974–78. Buffalo, N.Y.: William S. Hein, Inc.

Kohl, Wilfred, ed. 1982. *After the Second Oil Crisis: Energy Policies in Europe, America and Japan.* Lexington, Mass.: D.C. Heath.

Kohlmeier, Louis. 1969. *The Regulators.* New York: Harper and Row.

Krapels, Edward N. 1980. *Oil Crisis Management.* Baltimore: Johns Hopkins Univ. Press.

Kwoka, J. E., Jr. 1983. "Limits of Market-Oriented Regulatory Techniques: The Case of Automotive Fuel Economy," *Quarterly Journal of Economics,* Nov.

Landsberg, Hans. 1982. *High Energy Costs: Assessing the Burden.* Washington, D.C.: Resources for the Future.

Levy, Walter J. 1982. *Oil Strategy and Politics: 1941–1981,* ed. Melvin A. Conant. Boulder, Colo.: Westview.

Lichtblau, John. 1984. "Fill up the Strategic Reserve—Fast," *New York Times,* Mar. 1.

Lieber, Robert. 1976. *Oil and the Middle East War: Europe in the Energy Crisis.* Cambridge, Mass.: Harvard Center for International Affairs.

——. 1979. "America and Europe in the World Energy Crisis," *International Affairs* (London), Oct.

Lindahl, M. L. 1956. "Federal Regulation of Natural Gas Producers and Gatherers," *American Economic Review,* May.

Lindberg, Leon, ed. 1977. *The Energy Syndrome: Comparing National Responses to the Energy Crisis.* Lexington, Mass.: D.C. Heath.

Lindblom, Charles. 1965. *The Intelligence of Democracy.* New York: The Free Press.

——. 1977. *Politics and Markets: The World's Political-Economic Systems.* New York: Basic.

Lodge, George C. 1975. *A New American Ideology.* New York: Knopf.

Lovins, Amory. 1977. *Soft Energy Paths: Toward a Durable Peace.* Cambridge, Mass.: Ballinger.

Lovins, Amory B., and L. Hunter Lovins. 1982a. *Brittle Power: Energy Strategy for National Security.* Andover, Mass.: Brick House.

——. 1982b. "Electric Utilities: Key to Capitalizing the Energy Transition," *Technological Forecasting and Social Change,* Oct.

Lowi, Theodore J. 1979. *The End of Liberalism: The Second Republic of the United States.* 2d ed. New York: Norton.

MacAvoy, Paul. 1962. *Price Formation in Natural Gas Fields: A Study of Competition, Monopoly, and Regulation.* New Haven, Conn.: Yale Univ. Press.

——. 1983. *Energy Policy: An Economic Analysis.* New York: Norton.

MacAvoy, Paul, ed. 1977. *Federal Energy Administration Regulation: Report of the Presidential Task Force.* Washington, D.C.: American Enterprise Institute.

MacAvoy, Paul, and Stephen Breyer. 1974. *Energy Regulation by the Federal Power Commission.* Washington, D.C.: Brookings.

MacAvoy, Paul, and R. S. Pindyck. 1975. *The Economics of the Natural Gas Shortage*. New York: Elsevier.

McFarland, Andrew. 1976. *Public Interest Lobbies: Decision Making on Energy*. Washington, D.C.: American Enterprise Institute.

Mead, Walter. 1967. "The Competitive Significance of Joint Ventures," *Anti-Trust Bulletin*, Fall.

———. 1976. "Petroleum: An Unregulated Industry?," in Robert J. Kalter and William A. Vogeley, eds., *Energy Supply and Government Policy*. Ithaca, N.Y.: Cornell Univ. Press.

———. 1978. *Energy and the Environment: Conflict in Public Policy*. Washington, D.C.: American Enterprise Institute.

Means, Gardiner C. 1964. "Collective Capitalism and Economic Theory," in A. Hacker, ed., *The Corporation Takeover*. New York: Harper and Row.

Measday, Walter S. 1977. "The Petroleum Industry," in Walter Adams, ed., *The Structure of American Industry*, 5th ed. New York: Macmillan.

Melman, Seymour. 1974. *The Permanent War Economy: American Capitalism in Decline*. New York: Simon and Schuster.

Mendelson, Wallace. 1960. *Capitalism, Democracy and the Supreme Court*. New York: Appleton-Century-Crofts.

Messing, Mark, et al. 1979. *Centralized Power*. Cambridge, Mass.: Oelgeschlager, Gunn, and Hain.

Mill, John Stuart. 1899. *Principles of Political Economy with Some of Their Applications to Social Philosophy*, rev. ed. Vol. 1. New York: Colonial Press.

Miller, Arthur Selwyn. 1968. *The Supreme Court and American Capitalism*. New York: The Free Press.

———. 1976. *The Modern Corporate State: Private Governments and the American Constitution*. Westport, Conn.: Greenwood.

Mitchell, Edward J. 1979. *Energy and Ideology*. Washington, D.C.: American Enterprise Institute.

Mitnick, Barry M. 1980. *The Political Economy of Regulation: Creating, Designing and Removing Regulatory Forms*. New York: Columbia Univ. Press.

Moe, Terry. 1980a. *The Organization of Interests*. Chicago: Univ. of Chicago Press.

———. 1980b. "A Calculus of Group Membership," *American Journal of Political Science*, Nov.

Morse, Edward L. 1986. "After the Fall: The Politics of Oil," *Foreign Affairs*, Spring.

Nash, Gerald D. 1968. *United States Oil Policy: 1890–1964*. Pittsburgh: Univ. of Pittsburgh Press.

National Research Council, Transportation Research Board. 1984. *55: A Decade of Experience*. Special Report 204. Washington, D.C.

Nearing, Scott. 1915. *Anthracite: An Instance of Natural Resource Monopoly*. Philadelphia: Winston.

Nelkin, Dorothy, and Michael Pollak. 1979. "Public Participation in Technological Decisions: Reality or Grand Illusion?," *Technology Review*, Aug./Sept.

Noll, Roger. 1983. *The Political Economy of Deregulation*. Washington, D.C.: American Enterprise Institute.

Nye, Joseph, and Robert Keohane. 1977. *Power and Interdependence*. Boston: Little, Brown.

Olson, Mancur. 1965. *The Logic of Collective Action*. Cambridge, Mass.: Harvard Univ. Press.

————. 1982. *The Rise and Decline of Nations: Economic Growth, Stagflation and Social Rigidities*. New Haven, Conn.: Yale Univ. Press.

Oppenheimer, Bruce I. 1974. *Oil and the Congressional Process*. Lexington, Mass.: D.C. Heath.

Pelham, Ann. 1981. *Energy Policy*. 2d ed. Washington, D.C.: Congressional Quarterly Press.

Peltzman, Sam. 1976. "Toward a More General Theory of Regulation," *Journal of Law and Economics*, Aug.

Perelman, Lewis J. 1980. "Speculations on the Transition to Sustainable Energy," *Ethics*, Apr.

Perelman, Lewis J., and A. W. Giebelhaus. 1981. *Energy Transitions: Long-Term Perspectives*. Boulder, Colo.: Westview.

Phelps, Charles E., and Rodney F. Smith. 1977. *Petroleum Regulation: The False Dilemma of Decontrol*. Santa Monica, Calif.: The Rand Corporation.

Phillips, Almarin, ed. 1975. *Promoting Competition in Regulated Markets*. Washington, D.C.: Brookings.

Posner, Richard A. 1974. "Theories of Economic Regulation," *The Bell Journal of Economics and Management Science*, Autumn.

Pratt, Joseph A. 1980. "The Petroleum Industry in Transition: Anti-Trust and the Decline of Monopoly Control in Oil," *Journal of Economic History*, Dec.

————. 1981. "The Ascent of Oil: The Transition from Coal to Oil in Early Twentieth-Century America," in Lewis J. Perelman et al., *Energy Transitions: Long-Term Perspectives*. Boulder, Colo.: Westview.

Pringle, David F. 1981. *Petroleum Politics and the Texas Railroad Commission*. Austin: Univ. of Texas Press.

Redford, Emmette S., ed. 1956. *Public Administration and Policy Formation*. Austin: Univ. of Texas Press.

Riddick, Winston. 1973. "The Nature of the Petroleum Industry," *Proceedings of the Academy of Political Science*, Dec.

Rowberg, Richard E. 1985. "The Role of Offshore Petroleum in Meeting Future Energy Needs," in United States [13].

Rosenbaum, Walter A. 1981. *Energy, Politics and Public Policy*. Washington, D.C.: Congressional Quarterly Press.

Rothwell, Geoffrey. 1980. "Market Coordination in the Uranium Oxide Industry," *The Anti-trust Bulletin*, Spring.

Rudolph, Richard, and Scott Ridley. 1986. *Power Struggle: The Hundred Years War over Electricity*. New York: Harper and Row.

Ruggie, John G., ed. 1983. *The Antinomies of Interdependence: National Welfare and the International Division of Labor.* New York: Columbia Univ. Press.

Rustow, Dankwart. 1982. *Oil and Turmoil: America Faces OPEC and the Middle East.* New York: Norton.

Salisbury, Robert. 1969. "An Exchange Theory of Interest Groups," *Mid-West Journal of Political Science,* Feb.

———. 1983. "Interest Groups: Toward a New Understanding," in Allan J. Cigler and Burdett A. Loomis, eds., *Interest Group Politics.* Washington, D.C.: Congressional Quarterly Press.

Sampson, Anthony. 1975. *The Seven Sisters: The Great Oil Companies and the World They Made.* New York: Viking.

Sanders, M. Elizabeth. 1981. *The Regulation of Natural Gas: Policy and Politics, 1938–1978.* Philadelphia: Temple Univ. Press.

Sawhill, John C., et al. 1978. *Energy: Managing the Transition.* New York: Trilateral Commission.

Schattschneider, E. E. 1960. *The Semi-Sovereign People.* New York: Holt, Rinehart and Winston.

Schelling, Thomas C. 1979. *Thinking Through the Energy Problem.* Washington, D.C.: Committee for Economic Development.

Schmitter, Philippe C. 1974. "Still the Century of Corporatism?," *Review of Politics,* Jan.

———. 1981. "Interest Intermediation and Regime Governability in Western Europe and North America," in Suzanne Berger, ed., *Organizing Interests in Western Europe: Pluralism and the Transformation of Politics.* New York: Cambridge Univ. Press.

Schmitter, Philippe, and Gerhard Lehmbruch, eds. 1982. *Patterns of Corporatist Policy-Making.* Beverly Hills, Calif.: Sage.

Schneider, William. 1980. "Public Opinion and the Energy Crisis," in Daniel Yergin, ed., *The Dependence Dilemma.* Cambridge, Mass.: Harvard Center for International Affairs.

Schonfield, Andrew. 1965. *Modern Capitalism: The Changing Balance of Public and Private Power.* New York: Oxford Univ. Press.

Schurr, Sam H., et al. 1960. *Energy in the American Economy: 1850–1975.* Baltimore: Johns Hopkins Univ. Press.

———. 1979. *Energy in America's Future: The Choices Before Us.* Baltimore: Johns Hopkins Univ. Press.

Seltzer, Curtis. 1970. "The United Mine Workers of America and the Coal Operators: The Political Economy of Coal in Appalachia." Ph.D. diss., Columbia Univ.

Selznick, Phillip. 1966. *TVA and the Grass Roots.* New York: Harper and Row.

Sherrill, Robert. 1983. *The Oil Follies of 1970–1980: How the Petroleum Industry Stole the Show (and Much More Besides).* Garden City, N.Y.: Anchor.

Simpson, David. 1983. *The Political Economy of Growth.* New York: St. Martins.

Stigler, George. 1971. "The Theory of Economic Regulation," *Bell Journal of Economics and Management Science*, Spring.

Stobaugh, Robert, and Daniel Yergin, eds. 1979. *Energy Future: Report of the Energy Project at the Harvard Business School*. New York: Random House.

Stocking, George. 1925. *The Oil Industry and the Competitive System: A Study of Waste*. New York: Houghton Mifflin.

Stone, Alan, and E. J. Harpham, eds. 1982. *The Political Economy of Public Policy*. Beverly Hills: Sage.

Tetreault, Mary Ann. 1985. *Revolution in the World Petroleum Market*. Westport, Conn.: Quorum Books.

———. 1986. "The Response of the United States to Oil Price Fluctuations." Paper presented at Scripps College, Dec.

Thurow, Lester. 1980. *The Zero-Sum Society*. New York: Basic.

Troxel, Emergy. 1937. "Corporate Control in the Natural Gas Industry," *Journal of Business*, Apr.

Truman, David. 1951. *The Governmental Process*. New York: Knopf.

Tugwell, Franklin. 1975. *The Politics of Oil in Venezuela*. Stanford, Calif.: Stanford Univ. Press.

———. 1980. "Energy and Political Economy: A Review Essay," *Comparative Politics*, Oct.

Tugwell, Rexford G. 1974. *The Emerging Constitution*. New York: Harper's Magazine Press.

Tussing, Arlon. 1985. "Oil Prices Are Still Too High," *The Energy Journal*, Jan.

Twentieth Century Fund. 1948. *Electric Power and Government Policy*. New York.

United States Government Publications

[1] Central Intelligence Agency. 1977. "The International Energy Situation: Outlook to 1985," Report, April.

[2] Congress. Congressional Budget Office. 1981. *Low Income Energy Assistance*. Washington, D.C.

[3] ———. ———. 1982. *Promoting Efficiency in the Electric Utility Sector*. Washington, D.C.

[4] ———. General Accounting Office. 1984. *Analysis of the Financial Health of the Electric Utility Industry*. Washington, D.C.

[5] ———. ———. 1985. *Benefits and Limitations of Economic Policy Responses to an Oil Supply Disruption*. Washington, D.C.

[6] ———. ———. 1986. *Petroleum Products: Effects of Imports on U.S. Oil Refineries and U.S. Energy Security*. Washington, D.C.

[7] ———. House of Representatives. Committee on Interstate and Foreign Commerce. 1979. *Compilation of Energy-Related Legislation*. Vols. 1–4. Washington, D.C.

[8] ———. ———. Select Committee on Small Business. 1972. *Anticompetitive Impact of Oil Company Ownership of Petroleum Product Pipelines*. Washington, D.C.

[9] ———. Office of Technology Assessment. 1979. *The Direct Use of Coal*. Washington, D.C.

[10] ———. ———. 1983. *Industrial and Commercial Cogeneration*. Washington, D.C.

[11] ———. ———. 1984. *Nuclear Power in an Age of Uncertainty*. Washington, D.C.

[12] ———. ———. 1984. *U.S. Vulnerability to an Oil Import Curtailment: The Oil Replacement Capability*. Washington, D.C.

[13] ———. ———. 1985. *Oil and Gas Technologies for the Arctic and Deep Water*. Washington, D.C.

[14] ———. Senate. Committee on Foreign Relations, Subcommittee on Multinational Corporations. 1975. *Multinational Oil Corporations and U.S. Foreign Policy*. Washington, D.C.

[15] ———. ———. Committee on Governmental Affairs, Subcommittee on Reports, Accounting, and Management. 1978. *Interlocking Directorates Among the Major U.S. Corporations*. Washington, D.C.

[16] ———. ———. Committee on Governmental Operations, Permanent Subcommittee on Investigations. 1973. *Investigation of the Petroleum Industry*. Washington, D.C.

[17] ———. ———. Committee on the Judiciary, Subcommittee on Antitrust and Monopoly. 1969. *Governmental Intervention in the Market Mechanism*. Washington, D.C.

[18] ———. ———. ———. 1969–1970. *Hearings on Governmental Intervention in the Market Mechanism: Petroleum*. Parts 1–5. Washington, D.C.

[19] ———. ———. Select Committee on Small Business. 1952. *The International Petroleum Cartel*. Washington, D.C.

[20] Department of Energy. 1981. *National Energy Policy Plan*. Washington, D.C.

[21] ———. Fuel Oil Marketing Advisory Committee. 1981. *Low Income Energy Assistance Program: A Profile on Need and Policy Options*. Washington, D.C.

[22] ———. Energy Information Administration. 1980. *Energy Programs/Energy Markets: Overview*. Washington, D.C.

[23] ———. ———. 1982–85. *Annual Energy Review*. Washington, D.C.

[24] ———. ———. 1982–85. *Annual Energy Outlook*. Washington, D.C.

[25] ———. ———. 1983. *Annual Report to Congress*. Washington, D.C.

[26] ———. ———. 1984. *Energy Conservation Indicators: 1983 Annual Report*. Washington, D.C.

[27] ———. ———. 1984. *Energy Information Administration Reports*. Washington, D.C.

[28] ———. ———. 1984. *Performance Profiles of Major Energy Producers: 1982*. Washington, D.C.

[29] Executive Office of the President. N.d. *Energy Planning and Policy*. Washington, D.C.

[30] ———. 1979. *Domestic Policy Review of Solar Energy*. Washington, D.C.

[31] Federal Trade Commission. 1974. *Concentration Levels and Trends in the Energy Sector of the U.S. Economy.* Washington, D.C.

[32] Library of Congress, Congressional Research Service. 1979. *Centralized Versus Decentralized Energy Systems: Diverging or Parallel Roads?* Washington, D.C.

[33] National Archives. 1975. *Public Papers of the Presidents of the United States, Richard Nixon, Jan. 1-Aug. 9, 1974.* Washington, D.C.

[34] Office of the Federal Register. 1975. *Weekly Compilation of Presidential Documents.* Vol. 2, no. 3, Jan. 20. Washington, D.C.

Verleger, Philip K., Jr. 1981. "The Role of Petroleum Price and Allocation Regulations in Managing Energy Shortages," in Jack Hollander et al., eds., *Annual Review of Energy.* Palo Alto, Calif.: Annual Reviews.

———. 1982. *Oil Markets in Turmoil.* Cambridge, Mass: Ballinger.

Vietor, Richard K. 1980. *Environmental Politics and the Coal Coalition.* College Station: Texas A & M Univ. Press.

Viola, John, et al., eds. 1983. *Energy Research Guide: Journals, Indexes, and Abstracts.* Cambridge, Mass.: Ballinger.

Walker, Jack L. 1983. "Origins and Maintenance of Interest Groups in America," *American Political Science Review,* June.

Weidenbaum, Murray. 1982. *Business, Government, and the Public.* 2d ed. Englewood Cliffs, N.J.: Prentice-Hall.

Wildavsky, Aaron. 1962. *Dixon Yates: A Study in Power Politics.* New Haven, Conn.: Yale Univ. Press.

Williamson, Harold F., et al. 1963. *The American Petroleum Industry: The Age of Energy: 1899–1959.* Evanston, Ill.: Northwestern Univ. Press.

Willrich, Mason, and Melvin Conant. 1977. "The International Energy Agency: An Interpretation and Assessment," *American Journal of International Law,* Apr.

Wilson, Graham K. 1985. *Business and Politics: A Comparative Introduction.* Chatham, N.J.: Chatham House.

Wilson, James Q., ed. 1980. *The Politics of Regulation.* New York: Basic.

Winner, Langdon. 1977. *Autonomous Technology.* Cambridge, Mass.: MIT Press.

———. 1980. "Do Artifacts Have Politics?," *Daedalus,* Winter.

Yanarella, Ernest J., and Ann-Marie Yanarella. 1982. *Energy and The Social Sciences.* Boulder, Colo.: Westview.

Yergin, Daniel. 1982. "America in the Strait of Stringency," in Daniel Yergin and Martin Hillenbrand, eds., *Global Insecurity.* Boston: Houghton Mifflin.

Yergin, Daniel, and Martin Hillenbrand. 1982. *Global Insecurity.* Boston: Houghton Mifflin.

Zinberg, Dorothy, ed. 1983. *Uncertain Power: The Struggle for a National Energy Policy.* New York: Pergamon.

Index

Library of Congress Cataloging-in-Publication Data

Tugwell, Franklin, 1942–
The energy crisis and the American political economy : politics
and markets in the management of natural resources / Franklin
Tugwell.
p. cm.
Bibliography: p.
Includes index.
ISBN 0-8047-1500-9 (alk. paper) :
1. Petroleum industry and trade—Government policy—United States.
2. Energy policy—United States. I. Title.
HD9566.T85 1988
333.79'0973—dc 19

88-12175
CIP